Letters from the CBI

"While serving as an orderly in a Civil War army hospital, Walt Whitman discovered what he called the 'real war.' This was the war experience by ordinary soldiers, whose struggles, conditions, and heroic actions constituted what he regarded as the 'interior history' of the war, which, he predicted, would 'never get into the books.' Until recently, that has been true, as was so for virtually all wars, thereby leaving us with little understanding of the most personal dimensions of warfare. Fortunately, Robert Forster's very well-crafted book, featuring his father's letters sent home to small-town Wisconsin from World War II Burma, takes us down into the details of the GIs' 'real war.' It's a fascinating read that responds to Whitman's lament by fully humanizing, with admiration and affection, that war experienced by the boys who fought the good fight for us all."

—**Kerry A. Trask, author of** *Fire Within: A Civil War Narrative from Wisconsin* **and** *Black Hawk: The Battle for the Heart of America*

"This moving, richly detailed, and well-written book explores the powerful sense of linkage between generations of families—that amazing sense of someone long gone who still comes to life in your mind and heart and is with you decades later, hugging or holding you. You can feel it.

"More than seventy years after WWII, the author read hundreds of letters his father sent . . . during the war. [Forster] reflects on the war world his father lived in versus the one he wished he was in. He comes to realize that reflection is the key to understanding many things in life; you can philosophize about things and put them in perspective, even though it's sometimes painful. I highly recommend this book, especially if you are struggling to understand and make sense of something important in your life happening now or in the past. It's a must-read."

—Bruce K. Berger, PhD, author of *Brothers Bound*

"Hauntingly nostalgic. The lost art of letters sets a stage of history, romance, and longing, not just for home and true love but for clarity as well. A must-read for anyone with questions of the same."

—Nathan Aguinaga, master sergeant, US Army (Retired), and six-book author at Koehler Books

Letters from the CBI:
A Soldier's Journey Through the
Forgotten Theater of World War II
by Lt. Louis J. Forster
and Robert L. Forster

ISBN 979-8-88824-466-1

Published by

köehlerbooks™

3705 Shore Drive
Virginia Beach, VA 23455
800-435-4811
www.koehlerbooks.com

Letters from the CBI

A Soldier's Journey Through the Forgotten Theater of World War II

LT. LOUIS J. FORSTER
and Robert L. Forster

VIRGINIA BEACH
CAPE CHARLES

Table of Contents

Preface

There aren't many of us left who remember the early days of World War II, a scary time that had our country on the ropes. Having been born in 1947, it was before my time, and even many of those who are older than me have no memory of how frightening it was. Most of us living now remember only that the United States and its allies were victorious in that war, our enemies were humiliated, and their leaders were purged. With World War I as a prelude, and after a year and a half of bloody fighting in 1917 and 1918, America's belly was already full of war; when Hitler began to reclaim the Rhineland in 1936, and with the Austrian "Anschluss" and takeover of the Sudetenland in 1938, it was as if it was all starting over again. As a result, the country's mood was decidedly isolationist. Unfortunately, the "War to End All Wars" hadn't lived up to its name, and our country was not prepared for World War II. Our defenses deteriorated after the armistice of 1918, and we had merely 139,000 troops in arms in 1939. The country was in no mood for another costly European affair. We were just emerging from the Great Depression, and most Americans felt that if Europe wanted to "fight it out," we should let them. We, however, would stay home. Many prominent Americans, including Charles Lindbergh and Henry Ford, joined the America First Committee, an isolationist and anti-Semitic group founded in 1940 that advocated for appeasing Hitler's Germany. It was wrong then, and it's just as wrong now. The United States is a world leader, and isolationism is an abdication of that responsibility. In 1940, the United States avoided war even as Hitler overran Europe and Japan took large sections of China, leaving death and destruction in their wake. Had Britain fallen to Hitler, who knows what the outcome of that war might have been.

President Franklin D. Roosevelt understood the national mood and knew he would not be able to get his country onto a wartime footing anytime soon. During the 1940 election cycle, when he ran for an unprecedented third term, he publicly declared that he would not send our boys to fight in another European conflict. However, those declarations were only for public consumption. He could see the handwriting on the wall. He knew the winds of war were blowing and his country would eventually be drawn into an even more destructive worldwide conflict.

Despite his public declarations, Roosevelt did everything he could to prepare his country for the inevitable conflict, eventually instituting the Lend-Lease program. Under this program, the United States sent large amounts of military equipment and supplies to Britain and China. This helped Britain defend itself from a Nazi invasion, supported China's resistance against Japan, and ramped up military production in the United States. Roosevelt also instituted a draft, increasing the size of our grossly undermanned armed forces to meet the challenges that he knew would eventually come. In addition, he engaged with British Prime Minister Winston Churchill, with whom he found mutual understanding and even developed a friendship. They met in secret on a warship off the coast of Canada on August 9, 1941, to discuss strategy for the inevitable conflict. On August 12, 1941, they agreed on the Atlantic Charter, a declaration that formulated wartime strategies and established goals for the postwar world. Meanwhile, in opposition to Japan's military actions in Manchuria and China, the United States froze all Japanese assets in the US in July 1941 and eventually instituted a series of embargoes that imposed restrictions on the Japanese economy.

On December 7, 1941, the Japanese bombed Pearl Harbor, devastating America's Pacific fleet. A declaration of war with Japan was now inevitable, and after Roosevelt addressed Congress on

December 8, Congress indeed authorized such a declaration. Even so, Roosevelt worried that public support for joining the war in Europe may still be lacking since opposition had previously been so strong. But due to the Tripartite Pact between Germany, Italy, and Japan, Hitler and Mussolini made it easy for Roosevelt by declaring war on the United States on December 11, 1941, four days after the Japanese attack. Within hours of the Pearl Harbor attack, the Japanese invaded the Philippines and moved to take many of the Pacific islands. Despite Roosevelt's efforts to prepare us, we were not yet ready for war.

Historically, military leaders have always prepared themselves for the last war they fought in, designing tactics and strategies that disregard advances in technology in favor of what had been tried and proven. World War II was no different. The Japanese air force quickly wiped away inadequately prepared British and American air forces in their Pacific and Asian holdings and used seasoned troops to attack them on the ground. The Japanese took the Philippines within a couple of months, as well as the British colonies of Malaya, Hong Kong, and Burma. They even threatened India. Much of 1942 was an unmitigated disaster for the United States, the British Commonwealth, and their allies. Meanwhile, recruiting offices in the United States were swamped with new enlistees following the Pearl Harbor bombing. War production also increased exponentially as America put everything it had into preparing for the war to come.

This book is about my father's participation in the war effort as a soldier. Although it tells his unique story, his experience was similar to that of many other soldiers during that time. Much of this story will be told in my father's own words, as he expressed it while he was living it, via letters he sent to his family and fiancée—my mother—while he was deployed.

I have made as few changes to his wording and punctuation as possible, and these minimal changes have been made to enhance clarity and readability while retaining his intended meaning and tone. Occasionally, I have added clarifying information to the letters through the use of brackets. Some comments made in his letters are disparaging to people of color or of different ethnicity. I'm not proud of that aspect of this type of speech, but neither do I believe him to have been of ill will toward these people. My father lived in a time before political correctness became the norm, and he grew up where people of color or certain ethnicities were rare. Being unaccustomed to life in a cultural context that was foreign to him, it was easy for him to judge things that he did not fully understand. I also experienced this in my early days as a Peace Corps Volunteer until I became more adapted to the customs and conditions of life in a different country. I learned that it takes a while to build that bridge and see the humanity in people of different backgrounds who live in environments that are so different from ours. But with time, we understand their adaptations to those environments.

The remainder of the book consists of my commentary, including historical notes and information that Mom and Dad told me later in life as I became old enough to understand. Millions of soldiers lived dangerous and eventful lives during that war. Some of their stories are fascinating, many are dangerous, and some are tragic. Before reading Dad's letters, I thought I knew his story. However, I wasn't fully aware of the part he played in significant world events or how he weathered the dangers he confronted in the jungles of Burma. Dad would never have called himself a hero, but in a way, all those men and women were heroes. What they did then, as many had done before and many have done since, was part of the price to preserve our freedom. This is a story about how Lt. Louis J. Forster and his future wife, Gloria I. Galloro, weathered those times and came together to become my mom and dad. It is an emotional story for me—one that has increased my respect for my parents, members of America's Greatest Generation.

1

The Shoebox

In early 2017, my brother, sisters, and I were cleaning out the house we grew up in to prepare for selling it. No one from our family was going to live there anymore. I had retired not too long before and had considered moving back to Durand, Wisconsin, but that would take my wife and me far away from our kids and grandkids. We had made a life for ourselves on the other side of the state. My sister Mary Sue, who had lovingly taken care of Mom in her final years, had her own house about a mile away, my sister Diane lived in La Crosse, and my brother Steve lived in New Jersey. Each of us took what we wanted from the house—mementos from our lives and childhoods, mementos of Mom and Dad. On the kitchen table were tons of pictures, and we split them up according to who was in them. There was also a small cardboard box, inside of which was a shoebox. Inside the shoebox were bundles of hundreds of letters, each in its own envelope. There was a layer of dust over all of them. I immediately knew what this was, and a quick look at the date and addresses on one of the letters confirmed my impression. They were letters Dad had sent to Mom while he was deployed to the Far East during World War II. Mom had kept them all these years. My parents had remained unmarried during his deployment, which lasted one year, ten months, and twenty-nine days. But it was clear that they intended to marry immediately upon Dad's return. The letters began with Dad embarking on his travels in Greenville, Pennsylvania, continued by describing his train trip to Miami, and resumed upon his arrival in

Karachi, which, at that time (1944), was part of India.

At first, I didn't know what to do with the box of letters. So many things from that house were going into the thirty-yard dumpster parked in the driveway—an electric organ, old magazines, a rickety old kitchen table and chairs. I couldn't bring myself to dump this box full of letters, but I wasn't sure what I wanted to do with it, either. So I took it home and stored it for a few years.

I initially retired in 2013, but I didn't adjust well to being away from work; it became clear that, for me, retirement didn't mean "retirement." I thought, "We spend our lives progressing, sometimes from job to job, and raising our families, but when we're done with all that, we do nothing? Who are we then?" My dad used to say, "When that old farmer leaves the farm and moves into town, he has about one year left in his life." In other words, after our careers are over, we still need a purpose—a reason for being.

After briefly returning to work in 2015, I again retired in 2017. That time, I knew what I wanted to do with the rest of my life. I had honed my writing skills during my career, so I dedicated myself to writing in retirement. In late 2021, I published a memoir of my Peace Corps experiences, *Mariantonia: The Lifetime Journey of a Peace Corps Volunteer.* Once that project was complete, I finally pulled that old shoebox of letters from under the bed and began digging into its contents. It soon became clear to me that there was a significant story within that dusty old box. It was about one young man's journey through wartime danger in the jungle, boredom, frustration, and dedication at a time when all he wanted was to come home and marry his sweetheart. But he knew a happy ending was never guaranteed.

As I organized Dad's letters and wrote my commentary for this book, I was conscious of the fact that I was reaching back through time—almost eighty years—to the period when my own parents were beginning to plan their young lives amidst the dangers and uncertainties of World War II. They made these plans while being separated for a very long time, unable to communicate through any means other than cryptic telegram messages or letters, which were often delayed by over a month. Of course, I knew my parents well as I grew up, but when I knew them, the war was over, and they could finally settle down. The letters in the shoebox were from a time when they were young and single, before they started a family. The letters gave me a look into their lives before I knew them—and the letters also gave me a glimpse of the origins of my own life.

I am grateful beyond words for this old shoebox. The letters within were not artfully crafted, and the penmanship was often difficult to decipher. Some of them originated from under a tarp in the Burmese jungle while Dad wrote by flashlight during the monsoons. After growing up in my parents' household, there wasn't much I didn't know about them, and the raw information I gathered from the letters added little to my existing knowledge of who they were. But somehow, the letters increased my respect and admiration for my parents. Throughout my life, I was always proud of Mom and Dad, but I am even more so now because of what they revealed about themselves in that dusty old box of letters.

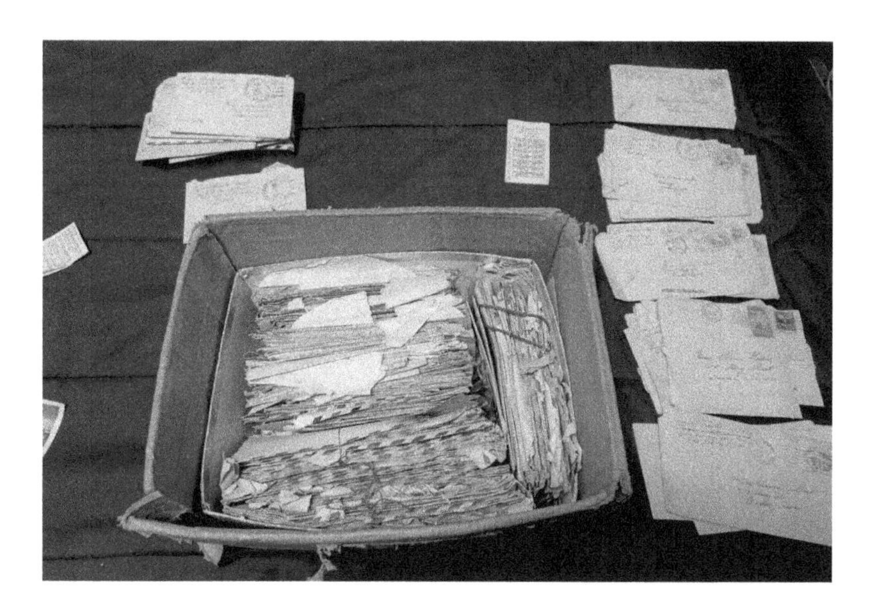

2

A Job to Do

My father, Louis J. Forster, a native of rural West Central Wisconsin, was born in June 1917 and was raised on his father's farm. Dad's great-grandfather, Anton Forster, had emigrated from Austria in 1856 and, after working for several years near Mazomanie, Wisconsin, he buried his first wife there. Finally, in 1868, he and his six children drove eight head of cattle, carried all their earthly possessions, and walked almost two hundred miles from Mazomanie to a rural township called Lima, near Durand, Wisconsin. There they established a homestead on land that's still in the family. There is a story that my great-great-grandfather Anton married three women in his life and is quoted to have said, "The Lord took my first wife, and the devil took the second. The third, neither one of them wanted, so I had to keep her."

Through at least three generations, the family continued to speak German, or as they called it, "Austrian." That was my father's first language, so he had to spend some time living with the nuns at Lima before he could attend school there. In those days, farmers raised their crops, but they also raised their own workforce, so Dad learned to work at a young age. He was the youngest of the surviving boys. All but one of his older brothers bought farms of their own, but Dad had other ideas. He liked electronics and decided to learn radio repair through correspondence courses. As war approached in 1940, he decided to enlist. Unfortunately, he was only five foot two, so the army told him he was too short. Thus, the army almost missed out on my dad and his talents. He often told me, in a somewhat irritated manner, "I was too short when I tried to enlist in 1940, but I wasn't a damn bit too short when they drafted me nine months later."

Dad entered the service of his country on January 16, 1941. He took his basic training at Camp McCoy in Wisconsin and was initially designated as US Army Infantry. However, he felt that he was better suited for the US Army Signal Corps because of his radio background. The army finally agreed. After he completed basic training, Dad was sent to various places in the country during his first year in service and was on maneuvers in places like Wartrace, Tennessee and Fort Leonard Wood, Missouri. Since the army was growing rapidly after so many years of downsizing, it needed to develop men to lead. As a result, Dad advanced rapidly and ended up as a Technician Fourth Grade (T/4). Being older than most draftees and recruits, he was eventually sent to Signal Corps training and Officer Candidate School (OCS) at Fort Monmouth, New Jersey. He was in New York on the day Pearl Harbor was bombed and heard about it as he emerged from a matinee at a movie theater there. On October 15, 1942, he graduated from OCS as Second Lieutenant.

My Mother, Gloria Isabel Galloro, was from an Italian immigrant family that settled in Central Iowa. My grandma, Edvidge Valentina Trevisol Galloro, whom my siblings and I called Nonna, was a loving soul who lived to be two weeks shy of 102 years old. My grandpa, Tony Galloro, had the thickest Italian accent you could imagine. It was beautiful, almost musical. Although he was occasionally mocked for his thick accent, he was able to make friends and a living in Ogden, Iowa. He was barely five feet tall, but he was tough and held his own as a coal miner and railroad worker in Boone County. He was a minor league bootlegger during Prohibition, making wine and beer in his basement. My mom often told me about the time she unintentionally drained one of his wine vats when she was little after taking a sip from the siphon and forgetting to stop it. She also told me about one horrible day when her father and oldest brother went to work in the coal mines. Her brother, Tony, had good-naturedly asked her to bake him a pie to eat when he came home from work. But on that fateful day, both her father and her brother were caught by a huge piece of coal that fell on them in the mine. The younger Tony died that day—without ever getting to taste that pie, which I think always haunted my mom.

In the early days of World War II, Mom and one of her girlfriends went to Banning, California, and joined the Girls Service Organization, which was related to the USO and sponsored by the YMCA. She also managed to get a job at a local establishment. It was my great fortune that this was where my father was sent after Officers Candidate School to refine his radio skills during the early days of the war. Banning was located in part of what was called the Desert Training Center in those days. It included areas in the desert where General George Patton trained his troops to help liberate Africa and Europe. Maneuvers were held in many places within the vast training area that spanned Southern California and Arizona, but Dad spent much of his time in Banning and San Bernardino. He was there for many months in 1943. Dad had said he wasn't looking to find his soulmate in that environment, but that's where he met Mom. After meeting her it didn't take long. Dad knew right away that she was the one, and they dated from then on. When Dad was sent on maneuvers and other assignments that took him away from her, they still corresponded. Those were happy times in California, but more difficult and frightening times were still ahead.

Late in 1943, almost three years after being drafted, Dad received notification that he was about to be assigned. He didn't know where he was going, but he hadn't been training all this time to sit on his skills in some backwater of the war. He was pretty sure that he was about to be sent overseas—somewhere. He wanted to introduce his fiancée to his family before he left. They had thought of getting married before he was assigned to a place thousands of miles away, but there wasn't much time. Their plans would have to wait, much like the plans of many other young people during that time. First, there was a job to do, and it was an urgent job that required many to make sacrifices. My dad was one of those men whose lives and plans were on hold—for the duration of the war.

3

Assignment Overseas

Dad didn't know where he was going, but it was obvious he was probably about to be assigned overseas. It was late 1943 and he had been in the Army for more than two and a half years, training and burnishing his skills as a Signal Corps officer. It was time to put them to use. Back then, soldiers didn't know where they were being sent when they were deployed, and they sometimes didn't find out until they arrived. Most often, they got on a ship somewhere and could vaguely sense which direction they were sailing in. But since the United States was fighting all over the world, the final destination was often still in doubt. Dad confirmed in a letter that he didn't know where he was going or even where he was until after he arrived. He had left his sweetheart near his hometown of Durand, Wisconsin, where she visited him and his family in anticipation of his new assignment, and he said goodbye to her at the train station in Eau Claire, twenty-five miles away. He was initially sent to Greenville, Pennsylvania, but that was just for a few days, only one stop along the way.

Dec 13, 1943

Dearest Gloria

Still haven't received my mail but I guess you'd like to get some from me. I wrote a letter to the folks so I'll just write a note.

I imagine you're still [in Durand] but I suppose you will take off before long. I don't believe there is any chance of me coming home before Christmas so you can leave there as soon as you like. I'm afraid I won't see you until I get back & I hope it won't be too long. I miss you terribly already. It's funny when I said goodbye to you at the station it seemed so easy. I guess I was excited about the new assignment & everything. I hope you didn't have any trouble, you certainly looked very calm when I left you. Frankly I was afraid you'd go to pieces & make a fuss but I was proud of you the way you stood up under it, so calm & sweet.

I don't know any more than I did when I wrote you last night. I might have to take off in a hurry & I might not be able to let you know when I've left so if you don't hear from me for a while don't worry. I'll be O.K. Just take good care of yourself, I don't want to come home to find a wreck. I'm sure I won't.

I guess I'd better close I write more tomorrow.

With love

Shorty

As promised, he wrote again the next day. He teased her, as he often did, knowing that the possibility of receiving any mail from Gloria was remote so soon after he had left her.

Dec 14, 1943

Dearest

No letter as yet. Your breaking my heart little girl. If I don't get a letter pretty quick I'll come home & see what's wrong. Then you'll be sorry. I guess there is still time for letters from you but it seems like a terrible long time since I left. It is almost a week ago since I kissed you goodbye. How am I going to be able to stay away a year or so, I'll go batty.

Still no more news but rumors are that we won't leave until about Christmas. We probably will spend the holidays enroute to our new station. What a way to spend them. I hope by a year from now I'll be able to be with you for good.

Tomorrow I'm going out to do a little firing on the range. Rifle & carbine are on the list. I hope to do O.K. but I'm afraid I'll get mighty cold out there. I still am not used to this cold climate.

I'm getting over my shot that I got yesterday but my shoulder is still a little sore.

Got my check today for travel $174.21 was the amount. I expected a little more but even so I cleared about 100 bucks.

I don't know whether you're still [in Durand] or not but will send the letters there till I hear different.

Don't forget I love you & give my regards to everyone.

Love

Shorty

Louis J. Forster was called a lot of different names in his life, and he didn't seem to mind as long as they didn't call him late for supper. Later on, in civilian life, many people called him Louie. Shorty was probably a name that soldiers gave him in the army since he was only five feet two inches tall. But much earlier, he had acquired the name Jack. Although his middle name was John, that wasn't the origin of his nickname. It came from his older brother, Fritz, who called him Little Jackass, and Jack was shorthand for that. From then on, family members and even friends called him Jack. However, Gloria met him in Banning, California, where fellow soldiers probably called him Shorty, so at first, Gloria knew him by that name.

Dec 16, 1943

Dearest Gloria

I finally got your letters today and was I glad to get them. I was beginning to wonder whether you loved me or not but I guess I've nothing to worry about, or do I. Such a pretty little thing certainly wouldn't have any trouble picking up something pretty desirable without any trouble.

I see you are doing O.K. with my family. I told you they couldn't help liking you when they got to know you. I know it will always be that way. I can't see how you can keep from being the favorite sister-in-law. I hope it won't be long before you will be that. If we only had had more time you would be Mrs. now instead of Miss. Sounds pretty good I'd say. Coming down to earth though, I guess it's better this way. Things are not quite as complicated for you this way. Your family can still accept you as their own but if you were my wife you'd be more or less on your own. I'm sure you could have lived with my family O.K. but things could possibly happen that might not be too pleasant. I don't speak from past experience in my family but I've seen it in others & I guess we're not different than others. I guess that's enough of that for a while.

I went out on the range at 8:30 this morning & didn't get back until about 1:30 this afternoon. Got pretty cold out there. I was shivering all over & couldn't hit anything. I guess I did as well as anyone else but I usually did do better than most of them. My ears are still ringing from the shooting & my right shoulder got jarred a little. I usually get a nice black & blue mark where the butt hits me, I love to shoot but not on a day like this.

I see you're running around a little already. Of all things & I thought you would be true to me. Just goes to show you that you can never trust a woman. I'm not worried. Frankly, I trust you for years anywhere. You just let your conscience be your guide as far as going out is concerned & I won't mind. The only thing I wouldn't like is going out with enlisted men that I know. Officers don't like that or are to allow that. Of course I don't ask you to go out in fact if you even look at another guy I'll feel hurt. I guess I'm too jealous to have you pulling any cute stuff. You have nothing to worry about as far as I'm concerned. I've made my choice & I intend to stick by it. I never did fool around much anyway. You can ask my family about that. Of course I might kid & joke a little but in any case you're still "it."

I could continue but there is another day so I'll close. I'll always love you.

Sincerely
Shorty (Jack)
(PS) I would like to have you call me Jack.

As Dad began his voyage from Greenville, Pennsylvania, his first stop was in Chicago. There, he got his reservation for the train trip south on the streamliner City of Miami and prepared to go on his long journey—to somewhere.

Dec 23, 1943

Dearest

Just got into Chicago & hit it lucky all the way. I've got my reservation on the "City of Miami" without any trouble & also got a good room at the Y.M.C.A. without trouble. I was rather worried about both but everything went so smooth that I [was] surprised [to] no end. I guess someone must be doing a good job praying for me. I know you do. I suggest that every time you get lonely or down to say a prayer or so & I'm sure it will do you a lot of good. I don't mean to preach but I believe it helps. I'm a fine one to talk after the way I behaved while I was home. I guess I just love you too much & can't control myself.

I hope you make it O.K. before Christmas. I imagine this will sound a little funny. After all you will be home when you read this.

How did mother take my leaving? Was she very much upset? I do worry about her a lot. That's one reason I haven't quite resigned myself to rushing into marriage. I want her complete consent & make it easy on her as possible. She always has been so wonderful to me that it almost makes me feel like a heel even to get married. I can't understand why she feels about it as she does but I guess she can't help it.

How was Christmas? Was your mother glad to see you? What a question; I know darn well she was. Give her my regards & tell her I'm sorry we haven't met. I wanted to but you know how it is.

I'll try my darndest next time I get around.

I guess I'll go to bed now, it's 10:30. Remember I love you & don't worry about me.

As always

Jack

Dad had always been conscious of his mother and her feelings. He was the youngest of her boys and held a special place in her heart. That had been especially true ever since he left home to join the army—and now he was being deployed to somewhere so far away. He was also concerned about her health since she had exhibited cardiovascular symptoms in the years before his deployment.

That year, Dad spent Christmas on the train to Miami. This was the first Christmas he would spend away from home and family. There would be another, and almost a third. Soldiers during that time were gone for a very long time, often "for the duration," as the United States was fighting tenacious and obstinate enemies all over the world. As he wrote to his girl in the following letter, he was preparing her for the possibility that she wouldn't hear from him for a while due to his travels, trying to put her mind at ease as he prepared for his long journey.

Dec 26, 1943

Dearest Gloria

I've arrived at Miami without any trouble & am comfortably settled for the time being. We live in a hotel & get about everything we want. Another thing, it's nice & warm here. I'm sitting near an open window without a shirt or shoes on & I'm plenty warm. It's about 7 PM. Pretty soft I'd say. There is one thing about it though & that is it's sort of sticky. Not uncomfortable but you can notice it. I do like Florida, in fact I think it's better than California. I guess it's because we are in about the nicest part of it. We are right in the tourist center & if we were civilians during peacetimes we'd pay plenty for this.

I feel terrible tonight. I had a couple more shots today & they really got me down. Nothing to worry about though. I'll snap out of it in a day or so. My cold is a lot better but I do cough a little yet.

I don't know how long I'll be here but I don't believe it will be long. It could be a matter of hours but more than likely it will be a couple of days. In any case I'm all set. I'll write every day until I leave so you'll know when I'm gone. It probably will be a couple of weeks or a month before you will hear from me, so don't worry if you don't get mail right away. I'll be O.K. & will write as soon as I can. Just think of me, I won't get any mail either & will miss it every bit as much as you. I don't know if mail addressed as you got it will reach me for sure or not. There is no unit designation on it but just the APO. It might get through but I wouldn't send anything of value until you hear from me. You can send letters, if they don't deliver them they'll return to you so don't be alarmed if you get some back.

I hope you had a nice Christmas & let me know how you made out on your trips. Are you getting used to the cold climate? By the way, give my regards to your folks & to any of our mutual friends you write to & let them know about my trip, etc.

I guess I'll cut this short & say good night. I miss you very much & love you more every day.

As always

Jack

P.S. I just found out that it's better to use this address:

Lt. Louis J. Forster 01627436

Station #10 Caribbean Wing ATC

APO 4136 c/o Postmaster

Miami Beach, Florida

I don't know how much Dad knew about his upcoming trip, where he was going, or how he would travel. He wasn't at liberty to say even if he did know. Most soldiers didn't, and most soldiers traveled by boat. But on December 28, 1943, Lt. Forster boarded a C-87 aircraft—the transport version of the Consolidated B-24 bomber—and flew southeast. He wrote years later, in a description of his service to the *Ex-CBI Roundup*, "Left Miami with a plane load of staff officers." This route, regularly used by the US Army during World War II, was described in *Life* magazine's June 5, 1944, pictorial "To India and Back in 10 days"[1] as a trip that took soldiers to San Juan, Puerto Rico, then Belem, Brazil and across to Ascension Island. (On Dad's trip, the plane had an engine replaced there.) Next, they crossed Africa and the Mideast, finally landing in Karachi. Upon his arrival, he sent a telegram to Gloria—which, unfortunately, didn't arrive until two weeks later: *"All well and safe writing all our love."* On January 4, he wrote short letters to everyone back home. This one was to Gloria.

Jan 4, [1944]

Dearest Gloria.

I guess I'd better start getting a letter on its way. I could have written a couple of days ago but I guess I don't have a real good excuse. I sent you a cable gram the other day. I wonder if you received it.

I don't know exactly what I can or cannot say but here goes.

So far I've found my trip very comfortable, far more so than I expected. The only thing that really bothers me is being away from you. The food is good, can get beer, see a movie, go to church, got good bed & all the things that you could ask for. I went fishing this afternoon but didn't catch anything so I went swimming. Also washed some clothes. I got pretty good at it but don't let that give you any ideas. That's something I'll stop doing just as soon as [I] can get someone else to do it for me.

I guess I [will] cut this short & write more later. I've got to write home too. Give my regards to everyone & remember I love you.

As always,

Jack

---

1 Tom McAvoy, "To India and Back in 10 Days," *Life* 16, no. 23 (June 5, 1944): 91-100.

From Karachi, he embarked on a two-day train trip to New Delhi, where he was assigned to the China, Burma, India (CBI) Signal Office. He and other Signal Corps officers were initially assigned to live in different apartment buildings in New Delhi, but later, the commanding officer wanted them all in one place. The new living quarters were near some hotels and the CBI Signal Office. Dad learned he was originally supposed to go to China, but he was taken off that assignment because he had arrived in theater later than expected. On January 11, he wrote:

> *. . . I'll continue to send these messages just to let you know I'm OK. Of course I can't tell you where I am or what I'm doing at the present but I am somewhere in India & I might be able to let you know more about what I'm doing later on. The main thing is that I love you very much & with God's help I'll be allowed to come home safe to marry you . . .*
>
> *. . . I want to remind you again that I'm O.K. & that I'm being taken care of very well, I guess I'm more comfortable than I've been sometimes in the States. Maneuvers were sometimes much rougher than anything I've seen so far . . .*

Jack felt the need to constantly remind Gloria that he was okay and living well. He didn't want her to lose hope that he would come home and marry her, and he didn't want her to worry about his welfare.

I'm not sure what Dad knew about the situation in India at that time, much less the situation in Burma, India's neighbor to the east. However, soldiers received booklets about the places they were sent—the army knew it was important for them to have at least some understanding of the people and cultures of the places where they were stationed. *A Pocket Guide to India* was one of those booklets[2], and it contained a basic overview of the different cultures

2 Special Service Division, "A Pocket Guide to India" – Service of Supply, United States Army. Washington, D. C., War and Navy Departments, August 12, 1942.

and religions within India, as well as the status of the Indian armed forces, which were under the command of the British. It also gave the soldiers a basic guide for remaining healthy.

But there was much more about India that couldn't be covered in a tiny booklet. Many soldiers were surprised that India's population was triple that of the United States at the time, and those people lived on half the land area. Additionally, the caste system made India one of the world's most strictly stratified societies, if not the most.[3] This system was primarily a Hindu construct, but it was later institutionalized by the British and practiced by other religions. It kept people "in their place"—social mobility was almost non-existent in the Indian Hindu world. What was left unsaid was that cracks were forming in the old British Empire all around the world, and India was no exception. By the time World War II began, Indians were already showing signs of wanting to throw off their colonial chains. The complicating factor was religion. India's two main religions were Hinduism and Islam, with the Sikhs and Christians comprising only small percentages each. Already there was a movement toward independence, with Mahatma Gandhi becoming a principal character in the independence movement. It was apparent that the Hindus (who comprised the largest segment of the population) and the Muslims would not get along. There would eventually be two Indias—the second being called Pakistan.

In 1941, with the onset of war in Asia and the Pacific, both the United States and Britain had lost possessions to the invading Japanese. Britain had also withdrawn many of its military resources to defend its home island against Hitler. The Japanese landed at the British colony of Hong Kong on December 18, 1941, and by December 25, the British had surrendered. Malaya was second with the fall of Singapore, the worst defeat the British had ever suffered in their military history. Burma was next, and in early 1942, the Japanese quickly took the capital of Rangoon. This meant that

---

3 Rayburn, M.P. *I'll Never Forget: The Forgotten Theater of World War II, China, Burma, India.* 3rd ed. City: Charles Fuller, Editor and Publisher of the Connecticut Beacon, 1996: 124-143

the Burma Road, which was the Allies' logistical lifeline to China to bolster Chinese resistance to the Japanese, was closed. It soon became apparent that British General Harold Alexander's army was no longer able to hold a defensive line in Burma. The British retreated up the Irrawaddy and Chindwin valleys and out of Burma altogether. It turned out to be the longest retreat in British military history.

Meanwhile, in order to maintain his lifeline in Burma, Chinese Generalissimo Chiang Kai-shek sent three Chinese armies to Burma to help stabilize the situation. American General Joseph "Vinegar Joe" Stilwell was put in charge of this Chinese Expeditionary Force, and he contemplated a counteroffensive against the Japanese. But Stilwell had command and control problems with his Chinese troops from the beginning. Although he loved the Chinese people, considered China a second home, and spoke fluent Mandarin, he felt his assignment was "the worst command of the war" due to the many problems with Chinese leadership. He was reluctant to take the assignment and had to be goaded into it by his superiors, including Army Chief of Staff, General George C. Marshall. Once Stilwell was assigned leadership of the Chinese Expeditionary Force in Burma, problems immediately arose—his Chinese subordinates often went over Stilwell's head to consult the Generalissimo, thereby receiving conflicting orders. While General Alexander failed to hold the line against the Japanese onslaught, Stilwell's Chinese troops were pushed aside in the east. As a result, the Japanese took Lashio, the city at the southern end of the Burma Road.

By the end of April 1942, many Chinese troops in Eastern Burma had escaped back to China any way they could. Stilwell was with a second group of Chinese troops in Shwebo, north of Mandalay, when Alexander ordered the wholesale evacuation of Burma in April 1942, which became a helter-skelter flight toward India with the Japs nipping at their heels. Stilwell decided not to evacuate himself by plane or other conveyance. Instead, he elected to retreat on foot to the north with 114 soldiers plus some refugees, including medical missionary Dr. Gordon Seagrave and his Burmese nurses. As they evacuated Burma, they retreated over the mountains and through the jungle, finally making it to Imphal after crossing the Chindwin River into India at Homalin. Stilwell's now-famous on-camera quote was, "I claim we got a hell of a beating. We got run out of Burma and it is humiliating as hell. I think we ought to find out what caused it, go back and retake the place." Of the original 100,000 troops of the Chinese Expeditionary Force sent to Burma, about 25,000 did not survive.

The retreat from Burma was another humiliation for the British, and they could barely withdraw fast enough to stay ahead of the rampaging Japanese, who were soon knocking at the door to India. The Japanese proved to be masters of the Jungle, and the British had no answer for them. But the Burmese jungle, mountains, and rivers, which run north to south, proved to be taxing to the Japanese supply line, which ran first through 3,000 miles of the American submarine-infested South China Sea, then Thailand, and finally through the mountains and jungles of Burma. This delayed their attack on India, which didn't occur until March 1944.

Even so, the Japanese took virtually all of Burma in 1942, and having set up an air base at Myitkyina (pronounced Mitch-in-AH) in Northeast Burma, they could control all of Northern Burma. The Allies were left to airlift supplies to China, having lost the land bridge through the Burma Road. American C-46s and C-47s couldn't fly the straight route from India to Kunming or Chongqing in China. Since the Japanese controlled the Myitkyina airfield, the Allies had to bend their route to the north over the "Hump," their name for the Himalayas, to avoid interception by the Japanese air force. This route was much more perilous than the direct route, and it was later called the Aluminum Highway due to the many aircraft that were lost over the Hump.

On the return trip to India, the planes were filled with Chinese troops of the former Expeditionary Force in Burma who had escaped the Japanese onslaught in Eastern Burma. These troops were reunited with General Stilwell and the rest of the Expeditionary Force that had escaped to India. Throughout 1943, Stilwell would train these troops at Ramgarh, India, and they eventually became a force of about 50,000.

One of the bright spots in the war in Burma proved to be the emergence of General Orde Charles Wingate, a brilliant if unconventional British commander. He had been involved in the North Africa campaign, after which he was offered to General Archibald Wavell in India. Wingate arrived in theater in March 1942. As unconventional as Wingate was, his attention to detail and his creativity were unsurpassed. He surveyed Northern Burma before it was completely overtaken by the Japanese in 1942 and began to promote his theories for long-range penetration units in the jungle. He had explored guerrilla tactics in Africa and commanded the Gideon Force, a force of only 1,700 men who caused chaos among Britain's Italian adversaries there. Once in India, Wavell gave Wingate the 77th Indian Infantry Brigade, which became known as the Chindits, and this brigade was trained as a long-range penetration unit.

Originally, the Chindits were meant to support a major planned British offensive into Burma, but that operation was canceled. However, General Wavell gave the go-ahead for the Chindits unit to enter the field anyway, and in February 1943, Wingate led his Chindits across the Chindwin River into Burma in the first Chindit operation. The force was split into eight columns totaling about 3,000 men and 800 mules. Resupply and transportation were huge problems in Northern Burma's jungles and mountainous terrain, and the mules themselves had problems navigating this treacherous topography.

As the columns advanced, they began to receive airdrops from C-47 aircraft, which proved to be the only effective way to support troops in most parts of Northern Burma. Resupply by air was continuously overhauled throughout the Burma campaign. It became the most common means of resupply in Burma and was effectively used throughout the campaign to retake Burma.

The first Chindit operation was undermanned at a time when the originally planned offensive had been canceled. Since the Allies hadn't undertaken any additional initiatives, the Japanese were able to concentrate their efforts on weeding out these columns. After these Chindit columns had some initial successes and cut one of Burma's main rail lines, they were recalled to India as a diseased and depleted force. However, they did learn some valuable lessons and did dispel the myth of the invincibility of the Japanese forces.

At the Quebec Conference (Quadrant) of August 1943, Allied leaders decided to form an American deep penetration unit that would attack Japanese troops in Burma. This force would find itself under the overall command of General Stilwell. Veterans of Guadalcanal and other Pacific Island jungle campaigns were recruited—just under 3,000 strong—to participate in the 5307th Composite Unit, known as the Galahad Force. This force was put under the command of Stilwell's subordinate, General Frank Dow Merrill. This force later became known as "Merrill's Marauders." This new group of American soldiers would employ lessons learned from the Chindit operations when they began engaging in operations starting from Northeast India. In late February 1944, the Galahad Force penetrated into Northern Burma behind Japanese lines.

Dad, meanwhile, was settling into his new role at the CBI Signal Office in New Delhi, far from the action in Northern Burma. He included his first impressions of India in his January 11, 1944, letter to Mom.

> *. . . As for the natives here, I can't say too much. They work well & look on you as some sort of a God. It's just hard to explain such things. The Cities are something I won't even try to describe in a letter. Something to talk about while our children grow up . . .*

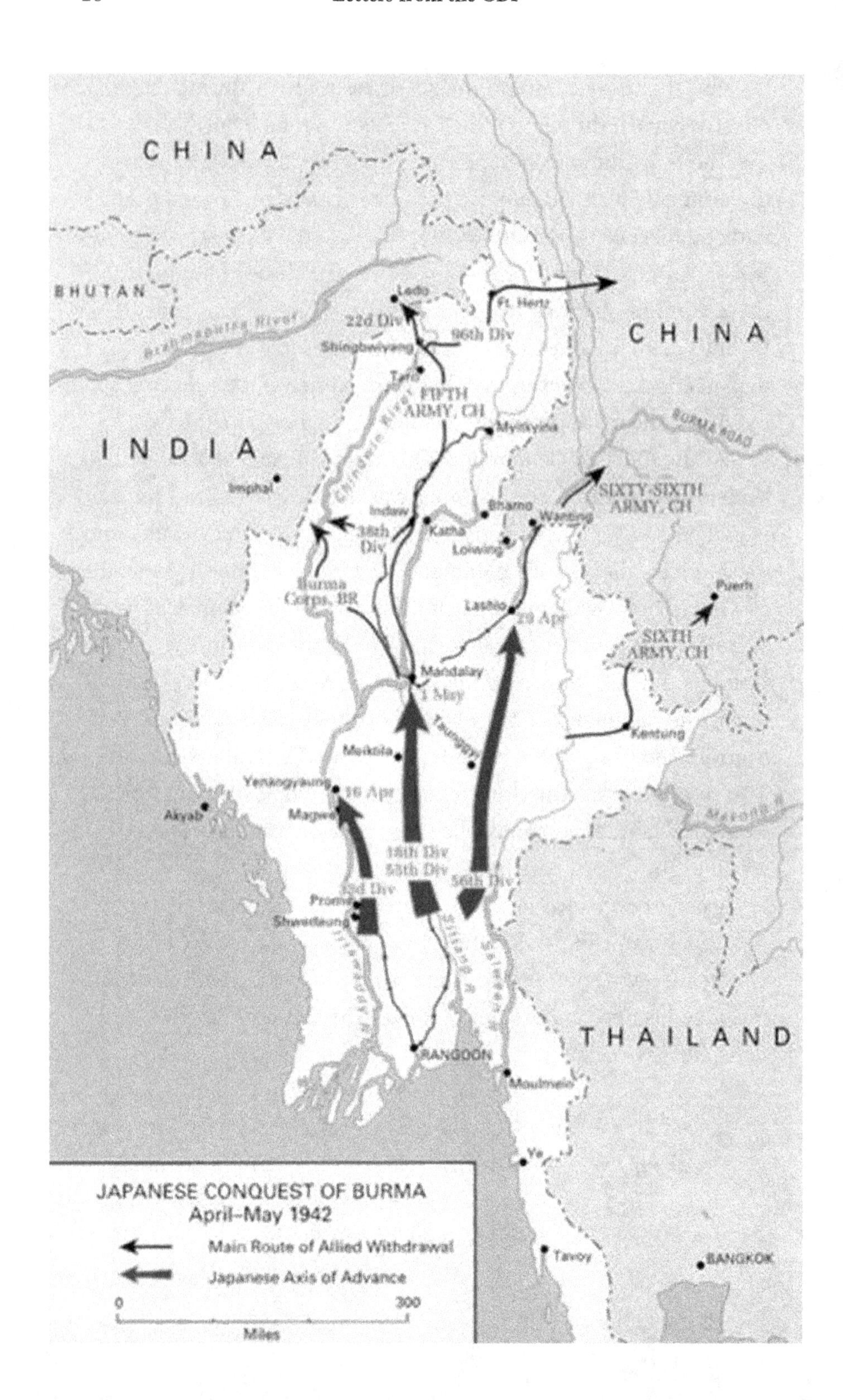
CHINA
BHUTAN
Brahmaputra River
Ledo
22d Div
96th Div
Ft. Hertz
CHINA
Shingbwiyang
FIFTH
ARMY, CH
Myitkyina
BURMA ROAD
INDIA
Imphal
Chindwin River
Indaw
Katha
Bhamo
Wanting
SIXTY-SIXTH
ARMY, CH
38th
Div
Loiwing
Burma
Corps, BR
Lashio
29 Apr
Puerh
SIXTH
ARMY, CH
Mandalay
1 May
Taunggyi
Kentung
Meiktila
Yenangyaung
16 Apr
Akyab
Magwe
18th Div
55th Div
56th Div
33d Div
Prome
Shwedaung
Sittang R
Salween R
THAILAND
RANGOON
Moulmein
Ye
Tavoy
BANGKOK
JAPANESE CONQUEST OF BURMA
April–May 1942
Main Route of Allied Withdrawal
Japanese Axis of Advance
0
300
Miles

One of the first things he had to get used to was military censorship—what he could say in a letter and what he couldn't. Many of the envelopes for his letters bore the mark of these censors in the form of a plastic seal with "Opened by US Army Examiner" printed on it. His next letter to Gloria was a prime example of that type of censorship. Someone had used scissors to cut away a large section, leaving only a couple narrow strands of text.

20 Jan 44

Dearest Gloria;

I guess I'd better get started writing again before I get disowned. It's rather hard writing every day when you don't receive any mail in return. I guess you've found that out by now. Some of my letters should have reached you by now.

(CENSORED)

I guess I'll close now & write more tomorrow. I can't tell you how much I miss you. How I'll be able to stand a couple of years away from you I can't say

With all my love

Jack

The censor's trail

Jan 25, [1943]

Dearest Gloria

Just a note before I go to bed.

I still haven't received any mail. I guess I'm looking for it a little too soon, but it's been so long since I've heard from you. The other fellows have received a letter or so, so I guess mine should be reaching me any day now.

In my last letter I enclosed a shoulder patch. Did you get it OK? If not, I [will] send another one.

I didn't feel so hot today so I laid off this afternoon. Most all the fellows have the same trouble getting used to the place. I guess the water is to blame for it. The British drink a lot of tea around here and I can see why. I was told to try it so I had the boy bring me some into the room this afternoon & it sort of fixed me up

Rented a bicycle today so I'll be able to get around a little better. I've been trying to get one ever since I got here but didn't have much luck so I sent the boy out & he came back with one.

This is turning out to be another dull letter so I'd better sign off. Just remember I love you & miss you very much.

As Always,
Jack

Dad rented a bicycle shortly after his arrival in India. As he learned, it was often difficult for soldiers and other foreigners in New Delhi to find the things they wanted or needed without consulting a native "bearer" or "boy," so they employed natives who seemed to mutually benefit from the arrangement. This was a tradition for foreigners in India.

The thing that bothered my dad the most during his first weeks in theater—even more than lacking transportation—was the fact that the mail didn't catch up to him for at least a month and a half. It led him to complain to his fiancée, his buddies, and even the US Army Post Office itself. He made recommendations to Gloria to try and speed up the mail, including his suggestion to use V-mail (short for "victory mail"). V-mail was a hybrid form of mail designed to eliminate the many tons of mail sent between the troops and the folks at home in favor of transporting more war matériel and supplies. A small sheet of mail would be photographed and printed to microfilm, sent overseas, and then reconstituted at its destination at 60 percent of its original size, printed on a 4 1/4-inch by 5 1/4-inch piece of paper, and delivered to the soldiers. Dad originally recommended that Gloria use V-mail while he used airmail. Later, he changed his mind and suggested that they both use airmail instead.

Jan 25, 1944

Dearest Gloria,

Another day & another letter. I still haven't received my mail, but I'm still hoping every time the mail comes in that at least one letter will be mine.

I'm writing a little early in the evening tonight because I expect to go to the movies tonight. I've seen the picture but it was a good one so I'll see it again.

By the way when you receive this, better look at the date & let me know how long it takes for mail to get there. I'll do the same when I get mail from you regularly. I mentioned it before but in case that letter got lost I'll mention it again. When you write to me use V-Mail. I'll answer by air mail because that's the fastest system. I can't explain why my mail should go air mail and yours v-mail but the fellows claim that's the best system . . .

Jan 27, 1944

Dearest Gloria

Time to pound out another letter. One of the more pleasant things of the day. It always makes me feel nearer to you. It's funny how one little girl can be missed so much. I've sort of made a special attempt to find out what makes foreign service seem tougher than US duty & I've come to the conclusion that there is, as a rule, some woman that [the] boys miss so much. You can usually pick out the ones that are really devoted to their wives or sweethearts. Lots of things are said that would not be said under different circumstances. A man really pours out with things he would be embarrassed to say at home. Things that show respect & devotion. I only hope they all (the women) deserve this trust placed in them. I'm sure you do. I also hope you don't mind my rambling like this but I get that once in a while as you should know by now.

No letters yet & baby I'm looking hard for them. I haven't heard from you for over a month. I know it's not your fault. If I know you, you've written every day since I left. I'll have to take a day off when they arrive. Say, I believe I put the wrong date on last night's letter, it should have been the 26th instead of the 25th so remember that when you tell me how long it took to reach you.

The show was pretty good last night but I didn't get home until about 12:30 so I guess I'll go to bed early tonight. You know how sleepy I get. Remember how I went to sleep one night at home & you let me sleep for a couple of hours while you were awake. Made me feel like a heel. Those were daffy days.

Got my quart of whisky today but haven't opened it yet. "Canadian Club," pretty good stuff and fairly cheap. I never bought much whisky in the States but it seems like a gift here when you can't go to a bar & buy a drink. We should be getting our twelve cans of beer pretty soon & I can get my cigarettes tomorrow, so you can see I'm pretty well taken care of as far as my vices are concerned.

Played a game of badminton tonight after work. By the way I work from 8:30 to 12:30 & from 2 to 5, pretty good I'd say. What a way to fight a war. I'll be WPA[4] *material when it's all over. There*

4 Dad was referring to the Works Progress Administration, an employment and infrastructure program created in response to the Great Depression.

are things that make up for it, I'd go back to [illegible] any time especially if you were near & I think that could be arranged.

We got another piece of furniture today one of these soft easy chairs. It's a strong affair, strong enough to hold you & me & not start going to pieces . . . One of these days I'll take a picture of our room to give you an idea of the "horrors" of war. That's a job for Sunday.

You know there is one thing I've never done that I should have done long before this & that is to write to your folks. I know I write to you but I'm sure they would appreciate a letter direct. I guess I'm too thoughtless for any use.

Well this thing is turning out to be a book so I'd better quit.

With all my love

Jack

It's evident from these letters that Dad had begun settling into his job with the CBI Signal Office in New Delhi. For all practical purposes, it was a lot like any job back in the US with its regular hours. Dad also had daily entertainment, new furniture, and liquor and cigarette allotments. In his words, "What a way to fight a war!" But his letters also show the feelings young soldiers were confronted with so far away from home—missing their sweethearts and their families. Although his living and working conditions seemed to be to his liking, he felt anxious over his lack of mail from home. His mother had a stroke some time before his deployment, so he worried about her condition going forward. But above all, he wanted to hear from his sweetheart.

31 Jan 1944

Dearest Gloria,

I guess I'm in the dog house about now. I haven't written for two days. I'm slipping. I'm sorry. I'll never do it again.

Got paid today. I got about 600 Rupees, that's roughly 200 bucks, not bad after sending 100 bucks home every month. It doesn't go too far around here though after you pay everybody. It costs us 6 rupees a day for meals, about 25 per month for our boy or bearer as they call him, 11 for laundry, about 20 for dry cleaning and all sorts of little things like that. Even so, if I don't buy too many trinkets, I'll be able to save money out of what I get here. It will come in handy one of these days if & when. Seems so far away though. This past month did fly by pretty rapidly for me. How about you. I wish I'd hear from you. One of the boys with me got about four letters today so I should get some very shortly, that is if you wrote any. You'd better have or you'll be sorry (I guess). I saw a WAC Lt. That was about your size & general dimensions so if—I'll throw my hat in the ring. I saw her walking out of church with some officer. I shouldn't tell you such things, you'll get ideas. You have nothing to worry about. I only looked the second time because she was so tiny. Besides that any white female can write her own ticket around here so I don't trouble any of them. I guess that's enough kidding for a while . . .

. . . I'm sending another picture tonight. This one is of the tongas [horse-drawn carts] I was telling you about. We took a ride in this one Sunday afternoon. The place is lousy with them & they are continually trying to overcharge. I usually ask what they want & then give them about half & walk away . . . I don't use them much now since I rented a bicycle. I intend to buy a bicycle one of these days. If I stay about six months I'll be able to pay for one with the rent I'll save & have the bicycle too.

I don't have your picture here tonight. I sent it to have a larger print made. I hope it turns out OK. I'll miss it while it's gone. I can't understand how such a little girl can be missed so much.

I've got to write home tonight and I'd better chisel a little on you. You know I love you & I hope you don't mind.

As always

Jack

Tongas

1 Feb, 1944

Dearest Gloria

Another day & another letter & still no news from you. I miss it so much.

I'm writing in another room tonight. One of the captains bought a puppy tonight & it was making a fuss while he was taking a shower so he asked me to stay in his room until he was finished. First time I've ever minded a puppy. That's worse than taking care of a baby.

I'm running out of things to talk about. I guess you have had that trouble but you should have heard from me more regularly, in fact you should have heard from me at least once a week since I left.

I watched some natives work on a building today & it's quite a sight. They are about as crude about the whole affair as you'd expected to have seen a thousand years ago.

I started this letter last night but didn't get it finished. I was watching the dog & when I got back to my room the fire was out. I spent about an hour getting it started again.

Tonight is one of those nights that I guess everyone has now occasionally. In other words I feel sort of low. Things didn't go to well today & I have a problem or two I just don't quite know how to attack. I've used all sorts of methods but don't seem to have the answer as yet. If & when I ever get to see you & explain the details you will be able to understand why I'm a little worried. I have a job to do that I know little or nothing about & I have to get it done within a certain time. First I have to learn the job & then do it. I know it doesn't make sense but that's about how puzzled I am with the assignment. I'm sure I can do it but [I'm not sure] how I'll do it.

(CENSORED)

I still haven't received any mail & believe me it's getting me down. I suppose I'll get it all at once & then I'll have to take a day off in order to read it all. I should have at least 30 in the mail from you by now or am I expecting too much? I can dream if I like it.

I'm running out of gas about now so I'll end this thing before I get into trouble. Tonight is one night I would really like to have you around. You would cheer me up like no one else could.

With all my love
Jack

3 Feb, 1944

Dearest Gloria,

Still no letters or am I repeating myself too often again. I'm about the only one left now that hasn't received any. I'll bet I get some tomorrow.

Well I feel a little happier tonight, I'm quite sure I'm going to be able to swing my job with not too much trouble. A lot of things won't work the way I'd like to have them but you can be sure I'll make the best of them. I can't see any particular reason for not telling you what I'm doing as long as I don't go into detail. I'm actually writing the historical record of the places & me never having any reporting experience in my life. This job is to record the things that have happened in the past. I guess that's enough said.

(CENSORED)

Getting back to the picture, it was taken in front of our quarters. The Lt. is my roommate & the captains have the room next to ours. We use the same bathroom. The Captains are both swell fellows & the Lt. is not so bad but he does have a lot of crazy ideas. Sajjab is the bearer for the four of us.

(CENSORED)

I've got a little work to do tonight so I guess I'll make this letter a little shorter. I was about to say I won't write till I get a letter but you're not to blame so I guess I'll write you again tomorrow. My writing is getting worse, the first thing you'll imagine I don't love you anymore but that's not true, I write so much during the day that I get sloppy & love you as much or more than ever.

As always

Jack

Captains Miller and Ostrom, Sajab (bearer), Lt. Filiak and Lt. Forster

Dad had been living in a suite with two captains in the adjoining room, Miller and Ostrom; Dad's roommate was a lieutenant by the name of William Filiak, who, on February 8, was replaced by Lt. Johnson. Dad would later find out that Filiak had gone to Camp Galahad to join the force that would soon be called Merrill's Marauders. Several months later, Dad would again meet up with Filiak while they were both on leave. By then, both of them had endured their baptism by fire.

Feb 4, 1944

Dearest Gloria

Only a note tonight. I've got to write my folks too so—

No letters yet, but I'm hoping more every day. It takes a little while for them to get here & they probably went by way of China or something. Something must be wrong . . .

Dad was supposed to have gone to China, but his arrival in theater had been delayed, so another officer was sent in his place. It's not out of the question that his mail may have been sent to China, causing a delay. In any case, it's clear that the mail situation caused him a lot of angst.

Feb 9, 1944

Dearest Gloria

I'm writing a little earlier tonight so I can get a little sleep. I usually get to bed about 10:30 but I seem to need a lot of sleep here. The same goes for eating. I seem to eat a lot more. I don't think I'll get any heavier than I was. For one thing I get a lot more exercise, I ride from 4 to 6 miles every day & play badminton a lot of evenings.

We fired our old bearer tonight. The old boy was getting pretty independent. He seemed to understand us very well when things went in his favor then [not so well] when we wanted something or if he had done something wrong. It happened we found another fellow much younger & who can speak English pretty well. This boy has been a bearer for a British Officer recently & I think he will turn out better. His father is bearer for another officer here & this officer is very well satisfied so maybe we'll do O.K. I hope so. The way the system is set up you almost have to have one & a good one does come pretty handy at times. I guess I'll be spoiled when I get home. You can imagine who will be my bearer when I do get home. I promise to treat you right though. Even so you had better enjoy your freedom while you can . . .

I don't know if Dad had a bearer because US soldiers adopted British colonial ways or if it was because the Indians were so accustomed to that employment option that any foreigner became a potential employer to pursue. Regardless of rationale, the arrangement was common. It was an attractive option to the soldiers since they didn't know the landscape and thus Indians could provide an invaluable service to them. Soldiers were not rich, so three or four would pool their funds and share one bearer who did errands and found things those soldiers would otherwise have difficulty finding (like Dad's bike). Apparently my dad and the others were not satisfied with the guy that they had so they hired a new one, Angus, who spoke more English and seemed to work out better.

Feb 10, 1944

. . . I mentioned earlier that I watched a construction job. Well, I've got a picture of the job I'm sending you. Notice the woman with the child. You see all ages in both men and women on the job. They all work even the children. Entire families follow the contractor from job to job. The men do the digging and put up the wall while the women & Children carry all the material. Besides that, it's all carried on their heads. How they do it I can't understand but they seem to get along O.K. Just try to balance about two blocks on your head & then imagine these people carrying ten or twelve without a slip. It looks

impossible but they do it.

. . . By the way I haven't received any mail yet. I sound pretty casual about it but I'm not. It is cutting down on my efficiency something terrible. I'd like to find the guy responsible for it. I'm afraid I'd give him a piece of my mind regardless of his rank. I'm convinced that a mistake has been made somewhere in the Postal Department because of the fact that the rest of the boys did get theirs. Seems funny, they were under identical orders, left & arrived the same time & all conditions were the same & still the condition exists. I don't get it. I went to see the Postal Officer here today & he said he'd check into it but I don't think he can do much. Well, anyway I don't get some mail and I'm getting very unhappy at the A.G. & when I get unhappy they had better get on the ball or someday when they want something from me I might find my thumb & my nose awful close together & then they will be unhappy. I guess I'm all done raving for a while . . .

Indian Construction Site

And as desperation set in:

Feb 12, 1944

Dearest Gloria

Didn't write last night as you probably noticed by the date. It happened I had a little work to do that took me longer than I expected so when I got finished I went straight to bed.

I'm getting more & more peeved with the Army Postal System. About now I think they are about the biggest jerks on earth. All the fellows that came with me are getting mail right along & I haven't got a letter yet. I simply can't understand it. I came on the same orders, orders were changed at the same time, we all signed in the same time & place, filled out the same cards where ever we went and all conditions were identical & still they receive mail. What in hell is wrong? First of all I want to hear from you so much & besides that I wonder how my mother is coming along. In her condition anything might happen so it's worrying me a lot. Every time a stack of mail arrives I expect to get some & every time I'm disappointed. About the most trying thing I've ever heard of. If the joker who is responsible knew what he was doing I believe he would have acted differently. You just can't imagine how I feel about it . . .

Feb 15. 1944

Dearest Gloria

I got some good news today. Received 4 letters this morning. 2 from you & 2 from mother. The ones from you were written Dec 27 & 30th. I have a terrible cold again & was feeling awful but that certainly cheered me up. I just dropped everything & read them all. So far I've only read them three times. I guess seeing the col. in the Postal dept. did some good after all.

Too bad you feel the way you do about your brother leaving. I guess I'd feel the same way. As for getting into a place where there is danger you never can tell for sure but I did a pretty good job of guessing. I feel as far away from the war here as I did in the states. In fact further when I got here I put my gun in the corner, threw my helmet and my gas mask on the shelf & it still is where I put it. I don't say that I might not visit some of the areas a little closer to where things are going on but not as a steady diet so I still insist there is nothing to worry about. A taxi ride such as I took on the 23 of December 1943 is much more hazardous. This was in Chicago. What I wouldn't give to be back in Chicago tonight.

You speak of New Years Eve. You'd never guess where I spent that day. I was right out in the middle of the Atlantic still wondering if my guess as to where I was going. I actually didn't know where I was to be stationed until the 16th of Jan & I didn't do so bad at guessing. I actually was to go to China but because I was a little late in getting here another Officer went in my place & I stayed here. I like it better this way . . .

Finally! I can't imagine the relief he felt when getting his first letters after a month and a half. It's obvious Dad was heartened to have received mail from home and his girl. His subsequent letters were much more relaxed; at times, Dad even said they were dry and boring. He had trouble finding things he could write about during this time in his mundane life in New Delhi. Nothing much changed on a day-to-day basis, and there wasn't much he could talk about other than the things he did for entertainment and what he did outside of his job. He couldn't mention his work, or anything associated with his work, as demonstrated by the fact that some of his early letters were cut up by censors. For the first couple of months, he couldn't even mention what city he was in. He constantly complained about not having anything to say. But Mom wanted him to write every day anyway. She wanted to know that he was safe and alive, even though in the early months of his deployment, he was about as safe as he would have been stateside. But he would eventually be proven wrong about not being close to "where things were going on, at least not as a steady diet."

Feb 24, 1944

Dearest Gloria

Did I get the mail today! Only six from you & one from my mother. Of course three of these were valentines. I got a big kick out of the one valentine from you. I didn't get to send any valentines this year. I didn't seem to be able to get any anywhere so—I guess I even failed to mention anything about it before this. I've slipped. Such an important day to miss, Shorty, you should be ashamed of yourself. I hang my head in shame. It's alright baby I love you just as much.

Getting back to the letters, today I received those written Jan 28, 30, 31 & Feb 3. Of course the two valentines. The other one was from my Mother so don't worry, that should be O.K. I think she's very much O.K.

As for Riordan [Dad's CO] having anything to do with my being here I guess you're barking up the wrong tree there gal. Nope I'm quite sure he had nothing to do with it. He didn't get here much sooner than I & I know that he has been trying to get other people over here that are not here yet. What if he did? I'm glad I got the opportunity although I'm ready to go back already . . .

. . . About our bearer, I'm afraid I won't be able to take him along. I guess the one you mention is our old one, well he wasn't so good. You should see our new one. He's O.K. If he was a little lighter complected he could pass for a college kid. He's O.K., on the ball or what have you, but I'll try to struggle along without you & leave him here.

As for the ivory, etc., I'll keep picking up little items here & there & send them, hoping you like them.

Yep I've got plenty of cigarettes & my brand, too. The only thing I can think of I could use are some rubbers for my Eversharp pencil. Don't seem to be able to get them here. You know the pencil that Fritz got for me? I'm wearing the one I've got pretty fast. I can get plenty of lead.

I found out that Florence Brunner is up at Ledo & hope to be able to get to see her one of these days. I don't know when but if I do get into the area I'll surely drop in to pay her a visit. I went to school with her for twelve years. One of the fellows, in fact he lives next door to me now, was in the same area & knew her.

I stopped writing for a while to see a magician perform. A private of the Air Force. Did pretty good, too. Also found out that Capt. Corrigan arrived & if I move around a little I might get to see him along with some of the other boys from Banning. It's getting to seem like home. The only thing lacking is Hal's group & a little pest behind the drug counter [Gloria]. Col. McNeal is around & I expect to see him. He was a pretty good old "Joe."

I know I haven't remarked about all the things you mention in the letters as yet but maybe I can polish them off tomorrow night, as I've got to shave & take a shower yet & it's getting late again. Seems like the evenings are just too short. I came home a little after 5 o'clock & spend about five or six hours & don't know where they've gone to. Now if you were here I suppose, or should I kid you again.

I almost forgot we took a few pictures this noon of the gang, the room & also a snake charmer who was out in front tooting away, so when I get them back I'll be sending some more of the trash I've been giving you. Hope you like it . . .

Snake Charmer in New Delhi

Once Dad started getting mail, he felt much more at ease. He had run into some old buddies from Banning, too. He had also heard of a high school classmate and a cousin from back home who was an army nurse stationed in Ledo, in Northeast India. Dad's high school was in a very rural setting next to a church and a cluster of only a few houses among farms and fields. His high school class had only sixteen graduates.

March 1, 1944

Dearest Gloria

. . . I've given some awful big hints lately as to where I am but today I can tell you exactly where I am. Yep, I guessed right I'm in New Delhi. Letter came out effective today the boys here are allowed to say where they are. This guess was absolutely a guess too because I was to go on to China but got transferred after I got into India. New Delhi is a modern city or at least it's supposed to be but it's still India & even Ogden Iowa would be better . . .

. . . Bill [Dad's roommate] isn't feeling good tonight. I guess he got what we call the Delhi Belly, in other words an upset stomach. Nothing serious but it can make you feel terrible at times. I had it shortly after I came here & I didn't do anything about it until I felt pretty tough. Finally I went to the Doc & he fixed me up in pretty short order . . .

For most of his time in theater, Dad was not allowed to say where he was or what he was doing. However, New Delhi was relatively far from the real action. Besides that, many different groups met there, and various functions took place in the city. The military finally determined that it was pointless to try to conceal the fact that soldiers were stationed there.

One of the things that always made life difficult in the tropical environment was the food and water, as Dad had mentioned. To some degree, locals tend to have acquired immunity to the food and water in their area while foreigners struggle. Quite often, it's simply the change in diet or ingredients in food that can cause upset, but on the more serious side, microbes can also be the culprit. Amoebas are a more serious cause, and in tropical areas around the world, amoebic dysentery is endemic. Locals develop a degree of resistance to this type of thing, but one never develops total immunity to it. Foreigners can become deathly ill.

March 4, 1944

Dearest Gloria . . .

. . . You again mention something about joining. I guess it's the Waves this time. Are you serious about this business? I don't think you are & I hope not. First of all I don't think you would like it & secondly I'm not too fond of the idea. Of course it's your life & as yet I have no right to tell you what to do. If you feel that you are missing something or have a great desire to join I guess I could forgive you, but I warn you, you'd be playing with fire & I'm afraid a little girl like you might get burned. If it's just for a job I'd say absolutely No. So use your own judgement. I'll love you no matter what you do & all I'm interested in is that you remain the same sweet good little girl I kissed Good Bye on Dec. 13. Something that would be twice as hard to do in the Service . . .

. . . Had an Indian get killed here yesterday when a British station wagon hit him. We wondered whether Angus had seen it & what he thought about it. He said he had seen it & when we asked him if the man was dead he broke out in a broad grin & said "Yes, he dead." Couldn't quite understand this but it seemed funny the way he expressed it, also his reaction to it. We thought he would be serious about it or blame the British because the Indians & the British don't get along so good if you remember the newspaper of about two years ago, but he just grinned. A good lad & I believe he likes working for us . . .

Dad's next letter, dated March 6, was an interesting one. Every year during the last week of December, a lot of news outlets come up with a "Year in Review" to go over the highlights of the year. In his March 6 letter, he did something similar by giving a two-month review of his trip and time in theater.

March 6, 1944

Dearest

Three v-mail from you today. Two dated the 18th of Feb (Remember the night you didn't write) & one dated sometime in Jan. I sorted all your letters according to date & read through all of them. I didn't read every word of it but I wanted to get a little clearer picture of what went on since I left. You stay at Fort Dodge until around the 16th of Jan & then went to work in Boone. Were sick the week of the 11& 12, 13 and then got into a fight with the family you were staying with & moved. Otherwise it mentioned a lot of people I don't know but as a general rule I could tell you who you were talking about. I sure didn't know anything about some of the people until I read all the letters. You see I missed some of the details you gave me in the letters I still haven't received. Maybe it would be a good idea if I sort of gave you a review of what went on since I left. First of all I can't tell you all about the trip but I can tell you that I saw South America, stayed there a couple of days on an island in the Atlantic, West Africa, Arabia & finally India. Landed in India on the 8th of Jan but didn't get to New Delhi until the 16th. Went by train all the way in India, what a ride. Took a couple of days to get around 700 miles. Went to work right away. Moved in with Lt. Filiak as my room mate with Capt. Miller & Ostrom next door. Capt Miller went on a trip & Filiak, at his request got reassigned & Capt Ostrom under protest got reassigned, Lt. Bill Johnson moved in with me & Lt. Petrie moved in where Capt Ostrom moved out. Capt Ostrom had a dog that gave me trouble & Petrie has a mongoose that doesn't bother me much but I don't like the nasty little devil, he spits & snaps at me. Bought a bicycle and some other little junk some of which I sent to you some time ago & I've told you I love you about every letter I wrote you. You are now probably pretty well mixed up after that little story so if you have any questions fire away. I'm ready. I forgot to mention we had Sajjab as a bearer at first but fired the old devil because he wasn't much good & got Angus, who is working out pretty good . . .

. . . Today I turned my first report over to the General (the result of 7 weeks work) and expected to get shipped out into the jungle as a result but instead he said he wants one every month. The next one will be a lot easier & I'll have as much time to get it out because it took me at least a couple of weeks to know a few people & where to find things. Besides that, things are a little bit complicated in this theater & it took me awhile before I got on to things.

Lt. Forster's new bike

I got this far when I was interrupted by a couple of telephone men raving about dial systems so it got late. Guess I'd better wind it up & say Good night.

As always
Jack

Dad had finally settled into his assignment in New Delhi. Aside from the fact that he was in a different country with different smells, different customs, and different ideas, he had a pretty mundane day-to-day existence. But life in the service of country seldom stays the same for long, and a soldier never knows what's on the horizon.

As of spring 1944, the war was going well for the Allies in Europe and the Pacific, and they were making progress on those fronts. By comparison, things had not been going well in the CBI. Other than the first Chindit expedition and the second Arakan offensive under British General Bill Slim's 14th Army, there hadn't been much offense from the Allies in Burma. The CBI was seemingly the backwater of the war effort worldwide, and it was treated as such. It was last on the priority list for resources from Britain and the US. In addition, the Allies were more diverse in the CBI than anywhere else in the world. Indian, British, Nepalese (Gurkha), Australian, Kachin tribal, Naga "headhunters," West African, East African, Burmese, Chinese, and American troops all fought there. They had different languages, different national priorities, and different levels of training. It was truly a polyglot army, and they dealt with an experienced, well-organized enemy.

Despite the challenges, it was important for the Allies to maintain this front and keep shipping supplies to the Chinese so China would stay in the war and fight the Japanese. This effort required lots of tenacity and creativity—and guts—and it was just getting started. Dad was destined to have a role in all of this, and it wouldn't be the easy life he had experienced so far. Lt. Forster was in for a change. In a way, he welcomed it—but it would eventually be harder to convince Gloria that he was in no danger.

4

Settling In

March 10, 1944

Dearest Gloria

Got two letters from you today. The letter dated Feb 24 and a V-mail dated the 23. Seems like air mail is faster than V-mail. You mentioned [a whole line of this letter was blurred by moisture on a fold] with the letter but I haven't got it yet. I received a letter about a week or more ago dated the 22nd & today the V-mail of the 23rd so I guess you might forget about V-mail being faster.

Wrote a big long letter to your folks tonight. Something I should have done long ago, but just didn't get at it until you mentioned it might be appreciated if I did. I'm sorry, I guess I [am] just a thoughtless dope or something. Anyway I've been writing to you pretty often & I suppose you've been keeping them up with the news of me. I'm going to write more often from now on, I can't be having you poison their minds against me or maybe you're building me up to something I'll never be able to live down. So just take it easy, I don't want any in-law trouble in years to come. Anyway I've broken them in, the rest should be easier. In this letter of Feb 24 you flatter me to death but I love it. There was a time when a burst something like that would have made me say the hell with her she's too anxious & forget about the girl but times have changed or I have. So I'm cute, I won't tell anyone around here about that, I'd get a horse laugh on that. You must be showing them the picture of me when I first graduated from Officers School. I look like a baby on that one. The photographer really touched that one up to make me look like a little kid. I wish I was as young as I look on that picture, I'd still be going to high school . . .

. . .This is getting to be pretty long so I'd better end it quick. I don't think I'll be writing one tomorrow night, I'm going out hunting so I'll leave early in the afternoon and won't get back until Sunday morning some time. Wish me luck in my hunting, I might bring a little piece of skin home to show you whatever we're hunting. It's time to say Good night. I love you, Baby.

As always

Jack

P. S. I not hunting Japs, this is purely recreation so don't worry. I'll probably never see a Jap soldier in my whole stay in CBI.

The postscript was wishful thinking, or perhaps another effort to soothe Gloria's nerves and keep her from worrying. It also showed the comparatively leisurely life Dad had in the backwaters of the Asian war. Still, the long separation from his sweetheart and the difficulties of carrying on a long-distance relationship exacted a price. Misunderstandings can arise from poorly worded letters and reading between the lines—both common pitfalls couples encountered in this type of relationship. I marvel at my parents for having suffered through this time and coming through strong in the end. Not all relationships survived these long deployments.

March 13, 1944

Dearest Gloria . . .

. . . I found two letters and five V-mails on my desk this morning. V-mails dated Feb 20, 21, 24, 25 & 29th, letters dated Feb 16 & 26.

I'm sorry I made a fuss about not getting any mail; I see it caused you to worry. I believe I even hinted in a joking way that you maybe were not writing. I hope you didn't take me seriously because even though I didn't get your letters I know you were writing . . . As for me not trusting you, I hope you know better than that. I feel that I can trust you as much as anyone, including my Mother & you know how I feel about her. No, Baby, don't ever think for a second that I don't believe you or trust you. I wouldn't have gone as far as I have with you if I didn't . . .

. . . I might tell you a little something about my hunting trip. We went out about 65 miles to a little village where there are some panthers & thought we might be able to come home with a skin for a rug, but no such luck. First of all you don't hunt the things but set a trap for them & wait to shoot them when they come around. We had little goats tied to a stake & then got into a tree above the goats & the idea was to shoot the panther when he came to kill the goat. The reason we didn't get any was because it rained & stormed both nights. We do expect to go out again in a few weeks. You have to wait for a full moon in order to be able to see to shoot. During the daytime we hunted deer but never got close enough to get a shot at them. I took a few pictures, so I'll tell you more about the trip when I get some prints.

I'm finishing this letter in the morning because I was interrupted last night. First of all I wrote to my mother, then the light went out & after that Capt. Miller came in from his trip & we stayed up late while he told us all about China. Capt. Miller is one of the officers on the picture. I was glad to see him again. He's a good Joe.

Well Baby I guess I'd better end this & get to work. Remember I love you very much & don't worry too much about me, I'll be O.K.

As Always

Jack

March 15, 1944

Dearest Gloria

Another day & another letter, but none from you today. I should be getting a couple tomorrow.

I'm going to send a couple of pictures tonight. One didn't turn out so hot in fact both are pretty bad. Sun was too sharp, which makes the eyes look like holes in a blanket. One is of myself, Angus & Bill Johnson & the other Myself, Lt. Petrie, Angus & Johnson. Notice the bicycles in the background. Mine is directly behind me & I believe the one behind Johnson belongs to him . . .

. . . By the way I believe I mentioned it before but Angus is our new bearer. Pretty good boy. Sunday night when we came in I was surprised to see our beds made up & mosquito bars up because we had our blankets sheets and mosquito bars with us. I asked him where he got the blankets & stuff so he told me he thought we'd be in late & would be too tired to make up our beds so he took Capt. Miller's blankets, etc., put them on our beds. That's the most initiative I've ever seen any Indian show. I think it would be pretty good for most Americans, let alone an Indian who usually has a one track mind. I've got him now where he darns my socks & mends my clothes, does a good job too. He used to be a tailor so he can sew on shoulder patches & I'll bet he does some of the alterations on our clothes. Besides that he's a mechanic so whenever anything goes wrong with a bicycle or something he digs up a wrench somewhere & fixes it up right quick like. He isn't quite as black as he looks on the pictures. He is pretty dark but I've seen some white men with a tan as dark as he is. Another thing he's always neat and clean . . .

Lt. Forster, Angus, Lt. Johnson

Lt. Forster, Lt. Petrie, Angus, Lt. Johnson

March 17, 1944

Dearest Gloria

Didn't write last night, was too busy & I mean busy. You'd never guess how many letters I had to read. Just exactly 40 in number. About 37 of them were old ones from December & January but I did get some of Feb & I believe two from you dated the 1st & 2nd of March. In addition to that I had to get ready to move out today. I'm on temporary duty out of New Delhi. Left all the letters in my room at New Delhi so I won't be able to answer any specific question in your letters until I get back. I guess I'll be able to write most every night while I'm here.

I believe this is St. Patrick's Day, not too sure about that but the orchestra downstairs is playing a lot of Irish tunes tonight & if my memory isn't too bad this is it.

I'm pretty tired tonight & don't know much news that I'm allowed to tell so I'll make it short. Remind me to tell you about this trip when I get back. Good night baby & love you a lot.

As Always

Jack

[Written in left margin] *Continue to write me at APO 885 because I'll be back soon.*

[Written in right margin] *I received those pictures you sent me at Reynolds & also those two candy hearts. Hearts were in perfect shape. Pictures were as good as when you sent them, some pretty good & some not.*

Dad was sent on a temporary assignment out of New Delhi. As always, he couldn't say where he was going or what he was going to do there, so I'm not sure where he was, exactly. In later letters, however, he mentioned that he'd been at another location in India. His trip was far enough that he went by plane.

British General William Slim had taken the British 14th army south to the Arakan peninsula in February 1944, in another attempt to push toward Rangoon, but had encountered some of the same difficulties as had been experienced by British troops in earlier months. Much of the energy for this offensive became diverted as the Japanese began their offensive on Kohima and Imphal in India, further north. Other Allied forces had entered Northern Burma in late February 1944 along the border in Northern India's Assam Province. These forces included Chinese troops commanded by American General Joseph Stilwell as well as the 5307th Composite Unit under General Frank Dow Merrill. These two forces acted in concert and were involved in fighting the Japs in Northern Burma at Walawbum and Shaduzup. Assam Province was to become the start of the Ledo Road, which would eventually connect to the Burma Road in Eastern Burma. Over time, the engineers building that road would comprise the largest force of American troops in the CBI. But that road did not yet exist in early 1944, and Assam Province was also the base from which the Allied air link to China over the Hump began. The Japanese still controlled most of Northern Burma, and there could be no land bridge to China without clearing the Japanese from the proposed route in places like Mogaung and Myitkyina. The offensive began at Ledo in Northern India, and the Ledo Road would follow American Generals Merrill and Stilwell across Northern Burma.

All indications are that Dad was sent to do some work in this area of Northern India, in Assam Province—possibly Ramgarh. Being a skilled Signal Corps officer, it's likely that he provided some sort of radio or other communications support to advance units that were already in Northern Burma.

March 18, 1944

Dearest Gloria

Three months ago today I was on my way home to visit you & my family for the last time. Remember when the telegram came saying I was on my way home. What a time that was . . .

. . . I'm staying in a Hotel now, that's like [the ones] you see in the movies, that is it's that type. Oriental Style, the kind you see in murder mysteries, etc. Haven't heard of anyone being murdered in bed, with a big long knife left in the body so I guess its safe enough. Besides that, there are five other officers in the same apt so I guess I'll live through it. Yep, India is a funny country & I'm seeing plenty every day. I've got a few shots left on a roll of film so I'll shoot it just to show you this place. I found out my locker & bed roll has arrived so if no one got into it I should have ten rolls of film in it. I hope it's not spoiled. I don't believe it was packed for tropical use so it might not be any good . . .

March 20, 1944

Dearest Gloria

Another day & I didn't sleep this afternoon. I was at it all day. This work wears you down especially when it's hot. Its cooling off pretty good now so it should be pretty nice sleeping.

I read a little this evening (a murder mystery, a very poor one at that) so I'm a little late in writing. I should write my letters in the morning while I'm rested & alert in order to write a better & more interesting letter. As it is, my mind is tired & can't think of a thing to write about. During the day I see hundreds of things I intend to tell you but by night I forget everything & then I just ramble on like this.

I do remember one thing & that is about a dead Indian I saw today. I don't know how he or she died but I saw four others carrying the body down the street. They had the body on a bed or Charpoy (an Indian bed with short legs about 2 1/2 feet wide & about 6 feet long. It's just a frame with a rope lattice work as a spring) Anyway they had the body on the bed covered with a sheet & were going down the street with it as though they had a dead pig on it. The body pitched around like [a side of] of pork or something. The head was bobbing from side to side & they just kept walking along as though there was nothing to it. At home everyone handles a body with a little care but here it's just another dead Indian. I don't know why I tell you all this but maybe it will give you some idea of the strange land I'm in. I honestly haven't breathed clean and fresh air since I left home. You can always detect the smell no matter where you are. You get used to it like you would a stable but it's always there. When I first got here I thought I couldn't stand it, I always felt itching and dirty but I guess I'm getting used to it. I still get into some sections where the smell is a little worse & it almost turns my stomach, something I've never had any trouble with before. I'll be glad to get back to get a good clean whiff of the barns at home. They should smell sweet compared to this.

As I said before it's getting late so I'd better get some rest. I miss you so very much, sometimes I wonder if I'll go raving mad before I get enough time in here to expect to get back. The mental strain is terrific. I love you very much.

As always

Jack

P.S. In reading this thing over I notice the wording toward last makes it look as though I didn't expect to get back but what I really mean is [I'm] actually realizing the time has come for me to be looking forward [to] seeing you sooner. I'm telling everything & I'm in no danger.

Again, Dad took great pains to convey to Mom that he was in no danger, as he did often during his deployment to the Far East. In the closing of his letter, Dad was beginning to show signs of the strain one can encounter when adapting to a new reality.

March 23, 1944

Dearest Gloria

. . . I'm still not at home [in New Dehli] but I suppose I'll be going back in a few days. It's up to me when I go back and I don't

expect to get done looking around for a few days yet. This might sound like quite a lot of fun but it's not. I see plenty & am glad to get the opportunity but moving around in India is a little different. First of all you get dirty as hell, then besides that transportation is pretty bad compared to the staff cars I used to get at Banning. Don't have Jackson to fix me up any more. By the way I wonder what happened to him, I haven't heard from him for a while.

[CENSORED]

I guess I'd better get some sleep so I guess I'd better say Good night. Remember I love you very much Baby & miss you terribly.

Jack

Clyde Jackson was a friend of Dad's from Banning. Jackson, or "Jake" as he was called, was a bit of a finagler, always able to make things a little more comfortable for himself and his friends. Since he liked my dad, my dad benefitted from that friendship.

Throughout his deployment, Dad had a problem finding things to write about. He was obviously occupied during the day, but he couldn't talk about much of what he did because of censorship. To this day, I don't know what his job was in New Delhi, but it must have consisted primarily of administrative duties that he couldn't be specific about in his letters. Even with nothing to write about, however, he understood that it was essential to maintain communication in order to reassure Gloria.

March 24, 1944

Dearest Gloria

Another day ended about the same as usual, lots of things happened but they are either uninteresting or I can't write about them.

Found out my foot locker is in the theater & was shipped to the wrong place so I had to notify the transportation office there to forward it to my address. Hope it gets there. I've got a quite a little stuff in it I want such as film, ink for my pen, pliers & screw drivers, extra clothes, Etc. I did get a chance to fill my pen with "Parker 51" last night . . .

. . . Got a storm coming up again, had one this afternoon & practically every night. A good hard rain helps this place a lot because it washes the streets. They certainly need it.

. . . Well, Baby it's 11:15 so I guess I'd better sign off so I can be fresh enough to meet a General I [am] supposed to meet tomorrow morning. Yep we have them here too.

One thing more & that's I love you.

As always

Jack

March 25, 1944

Dearest

Pretty tired tonight so maybe I won't write much. I don't know why I should be tired I didn't work hard today. Maybe I'm just lazy . . .

. . . We don't get any U.S. papers but the local paper here seems to bring it out that the U.S. papers are making quite a fuss about the Japs coming into India for the first time. Nobody seems to think much of it here. In other words I'm not much worried about it. They still seem as far away as ever & I'm not running yet. I know they won't get very far. The newspapers do a good job of confusing the public. For example one newspaper might come out with two facts that when the two come together it makes them look terrible, like "Roosevelt was elected in 1932 & in the following twelve years the national debt increased by billions." Two facts like that might make the President look like a horrible spendthrift. Nothing would be mentioned about the depression & the War to increase the debt but they are actually to blame for the National Debt. Anyway the Japs are not pounding on our back door as yet & if you did worry, stop it now . . .

. . . As I said before I'm tired tonight and believe I'll turn in

early, besides that the bugs are bad tonight. Good night, Baby. I still love you very much & think of you often during the day & always when I go to sleep.

As always

Jack

The GIs never seemed to get their news through official channels. Except for the military newsletter, *Stars & Stripes,* news was often dispersed on a need-to-know basis, and the folks back home often seemed to know more about what was happening in the war than the individual soldiers. Dad was somewhat better informed than other soldiers because, as an officer in the Signal Corps, he had access to the best radio receivers in the world, and some of the higher-level communication came through the office where he worked. However, Dad got this bit of news about the Japanese invading India from a local Indian newspaper.

The Japanese had felt the British might be vulnerable in India because there had been a large independence movement in India since well before the war; India had been trying to throw off the English colonial yoke for years. There was even an Indian army that had aligned itself with the Japanese. The thought within the Japanese hierarchy was that if they made a push on India, they may well set off an insurrection that could topple British rule in India. However, the Japanese didn't account for the infamy they had earned via their brutal conquests in China, Malaya, and Burma. The idea of trading the current imperial master (British) for a worse one (Japanese) was not an attractive option to Indians.

The invasion of India began a period during which a lot was happening at once in Eastern India and Northwest Burma. Both Allied and Japanese armies had their eyes on advancing during the pre-monsoonal period of 1944.

Japanese General Renya Mutaguchi admired the tactics of British General Wingate's Chindits and intended to use those same tactics on a much larger scale to make his push through the jungle into India. He confidently brought three Japanese divisions and one Indian National Army division through the Burmese jungle and mountains to attack Kohima and Imphal in India. If they had been successful, the Japanese would have been able to interdict the supply chain from India to China. They also would have had a base from which to launch air attacks against India. As it turned out, these two cities were the site of some of the bitterest close-quarter fighting of the entire war; the Japanese invaders initially outnumbered the defenders in Kohima and Imphal by at least three to one, causing British General Slim to divert some of his forces from his Arakan campaign to Kohima and Imphal.

At this same time, the Chindits were embarking on their second mission, part of which was to penetrate into Burma east of the Japanese drive on Kohima and Imphal. This second Chindit operation was launched by air from Lalaghat in India. Two airstrips, named Broadway and White City, were created in open areas behind enemy lines. Chindit troops were inserted into this relatively flat and sparsely populated area south of Mogaung by gliders and planes, threatening the rear areas of the Japanese drive on India. The net effect of these Allied incursions frustrated the Japanese supply line to both their invasion operations in India and threatened their rail line to Northern Burma. Chindit operations continued through most of April and into May 1944.

From extreme Northern Burma, at precisely the same time the Japanese were pushing further south into India under General Mutaguchi, the Allied armies were finally making their move to retake Northern Burma. Stilwell's Chinese army, in tandem with the Galahad Force, was pushing south through the Hukawng Valley, taking Walawbum and Shaduzup.

The battle of logistics was very important in Kohima and Imphal. Whereas the British were able to resupply both men and matériel by air, Mutaguchi's Japanese force needed to rely on captured supplies and a long and difficult supply trail through the jungles and mountains of Western Burma. In planning this operation, General Mutaguchi had failed to recognize the importance of air superiority at the far reaches of the Japanese supply line. The fighting on the ground was intense. British and Indian soldiers were aware that surrender was not an option—both sides would have to fight to the death. The fighting was so intense at close quarters that no quarter was given. One British soldier remarked, "They did not give us a chance, and we didn't give them a chance." The failed offensive broke the back of the Japanese army in India and weakened Japan's hold on Burma. At the end, citing the Japanese losses in their failed invasion of India, British General Slim remarked, "They will never come back."[5]

Although Dad was probably only about one hundred miles north of the Japanese invasion during his temporary assignment in Northern Assam Province, I don't know how much of this he was aware of. He certainly wouldn't have made any comments in his letters that would frighten Gloria. Based on what he wrote, it didn't appear that he was involved in any of the offensives that were being undertaken in Burma at that time other than in a temporary rear-echelon role.

March 26, 1944

Dearest Gloria

Sunday evening again & nothing to write about. I'll be glad to get back to Delhi so I get some mail again.

Worked most of the day so I'll get finished & get away from here. First of all I went to church, then I dashed out to a place & got a job finished that I've been trying to get most of the week & in the afternoon I got my notes in a little better order & typed them up. What a job I've had wished on me.

5 "It's a Lovely Day Tomorrow: Burma (1942 – 1944)," Director, David Elstein, The World At War; Thames Color Productions, Feb. 6, 1974.

One of the boys in the room got 64 letters today. He hadn't received any mail for about four or five months. He was a pretty happy Joe. I should have a dozen or so letters waiting for me when I get back. Lord knows when that will be, seems like I'll never get finished here. I expected to stay a week or ten days but I guess it will be two weeks or more. Just didn't anticipate some of the things that could & did happen. Of all the things that could go wrong I guess I got my share. Didn't cause me any trouble but it's taking me a lot longer than I expected. Why should I tell you all about this? I can't tell you everything & I suppose this half story sounds funny. My letters must be really something to read. I just don't take the effort to compose a letter, just ramble on . . .

[CENSORED]

. . . One thing I've noticed about all soldiers in India & that is every last one of them is just waiting and long for the day when he gets that certain paper in his hand shipping him home. Actually I don't know whether I'd want to go back right away or not. I'd almost feel like a coward if I did have a choice as to whether I'd stay or not & took the chance to go home. I guess I'd take it though. I miss you so darn much. This courtship by air is such a poor substitute for the real thing.

I've got to get to bed so Good night, Baby & remember I love you.

Jack

I don't know exactly what town Dad had been in, but I'm pretty sure that it was in northern Assam Province, somewhere near Ledo. There was a lot going on in Assam at that time. Stilwell had trained his Chinese troops in Ramgarh and had moved them into Northern Burma. At the same time, the Japanese offensive to take Kohima and Imphal was unfolding further south. Furthermore, flights to China over the Hump were happening several times daily to haul the supplies that kept China in the war. Although the air link wasn't totally adequate, it was helpful to the cause.

Supplies arrived at the Port of Calcutta and were taken to northern Assam Province, where they could then be air-lifted to China. But this supply chain from Calcutta northward was a mess. It involved boats pushing up the Brahmaputra River as well as trains that used different track gauges, which required transferring goods from one train to another, doubling the handling load. Then, upon reaching Assam, the goods—including heavy equipment and vehicles—piled up due to lack of adequate means for transporting them to China.

The Ledo Road was in its initial stages of construction during this time. The plan was to connect it with the Burma Road to increase the flow of matériel to China. But the road couldn't be built much further than the India-Burma border until the after offensive into Northern Burma was initiated. Planning for both the road and the offensive was happening in northern Assam.

Dad couldn't tell Mom what his role was in all of that, but it's safe to say he was part of it in some capacity, probably helping to set up communications for those efforts. But it was only a temporary assignment, and he returned to Delhi after completing his work in Assam.

April 1, 1944

Dearest Gloria

I guess you'll disown me when I tell you I didn't write last night & the night before. Last night I had a good excuse. I was sitting several thousand feet off the ground on my way back to Delhi. Only got a few hours sleep, but the night before I went to see "Hit the Ice" & then went to bed without writing, expecting to get up early enough the next morning to write. You've guessed it, I got up early enough to get my business finished & get to the field. I'm sorry, I really am.

Found a flock of letters here where I got here. After those forty I got a couple of weeks ago & now about twenty again I'll never get caught up. I was really glad to get them though. A couple of weeks without mail ain't good. I miss you so darn much. Even though letters can't come near taking the place of the real thing, it does help some.

Got a V-mail from Marcella [Dad's sister] today, or rather, I picked it up today & she gave you a little "plug." It's a little funny coming from her because she doesn't usually do much of that in letters. Here's what she had to say. "We've missed the 'small fry' a lot. Time passed all too quickly while she was here I'll bet you agree with me. She's a pretty nice kid." It's a funny thing they never did comment themselves too much while I was at home but since then every once in a while something like this comes out. Knowing them as I do it's a sure sign of approval. They wouldn't commit themselves if they didn't approve, just keep quiet about it & live it down. I just guess you're in . . .

. . . I've been sitting around most of the evening just trying to find out what happened while I was gone so I'm late at writing again, so I won't attempt to answer any of your questions until tomorrow (Sunday).

I've got to get some sleep so I'll close now. Good night "small fry" & remember I'll always love you.

All my love
Jack

April 2, 1944

Dearest Gloria

. . . Now answer a couple of questions. As for Echelon I could tell you to get a "Webster" to help you but I'll try to give you an idea what it means in the Army. It's one section of a headquarters, in other words in battle one part of the headquarters is up near the front while a big part of it is left behind to make detailed plans, keep records, etc. Usually the commanding General is up in the front giving direct orders while a good share of his staff remains behind to do the paperwork. The General & his party up in front would be the forward Echelon while the staff behind is the rear Echelon . . .

. . . About the Hindu gals picking cooties & undressing, they don't seem to be a bit ashamed to show anything above the belt & where was I when that went on, well what do you suppose I was doing—I watched them. What do you want me to do, stop them or help them? I assure you it wasn't very exciting, they hardly seem like humans to a white person . . .

. . . This is one of the dreamy Sunday afternoons like we have at home during May & June. Beautiful but it makes me terribly homesick. It's times like these that make me wonder whether I'll be able to stand being away from you more than another minute. It certainly will be a happy day when I'll be able to come back to stay. I often wonder what this meeting will be like. I try to picture it but I suppose I'd probably be surprised if I really knew how it will be or when & where. I hope, anyway it can't be too soon for me.

We've got a radio station (Broadcast) in New Delhi now. A Special Service station that puts on good old American broadcasts. They transcribe the regular programs in the States & ship them over & run them off. We get them late but they are exactly like those at home. Sounds pretty good but it has a tendency to make me miss you all the more . . .

. . . I guess I've written enough nonsense for one time besides I've got a raft of other letters to write. I haven't written to hardly anyone but you & my folks since I got here. Mostly to you. I believe I've written as many letters to you as I've written to anyone, including my folks since I've been in the Army. Well maybe not quite but I have written 60 or 70 to you. I must be in love with you . . .

As always
Jack

In the days before speech sensitivity or political correctness became the norm, speech could often seem insensitive. For example, General Stilwell was notorious for using language that today would be considered politically incorrect—although, paradoxically, he was also known to be empathetic toward different ethnicities and races. In early 1946 when Nisei[6] Sgt. Kazuo Masuda's family was presented with his distinguished service cross, Gen. Joseph Stilwell stated:

"The Nisei bought an awful big hunk of America with their blood. Those Nisei boys have a place in the American heart, now and forever. We cannot allow a single injustice to be done to the Nisei without defeating the purpose for which we fought . . . Who, after all, is the real American? The real American is the man who calls it a fair exchange to lay down his life in order that American ideals may go on living. And judging by such a test, Sergeant Masuda was a better American than any of us here today."

Stilwell commanded Chinese and Indian troops in the field and had few Americans directly under him other than specialists and officers. Furthermore, American armed forces were segregated until 1947. Schools in the US remained formally segregated for many years after that, and one might say they still are segregated to some degree. Much of the US civil rights legislation didn't take place until the '60s. My dad was a product of his time and grew up in an area of the country where there were few, if any, black or brown people or people of ethnicities other than his own. Without having that type of contact, it can be hard to relate to people of different backgrounds.

April 7, 1944

Dearest Gloria

I was selfish last night & went hunting instead of writing to you, even after getting two letters from you. One dated 19th of March & one dated 21st (Both were postmarked March 22) & one contained 43 cent stamps. Is that a reminder to write more letters or longer ones. You didn't mention anything about them in your letters.

As I mentioned before I went hunting last night. No real luck

6 The Nisei were Japanese American troops, often from Japanese families interned at the beginning of the war as a precautionary measure.

but know for sure now that there are some big cats around & they can be had. I & first Sgt. were up in one tree above a little goat tied to a stake near a well with two paths leading to it. We were waiting there for a little while when I notice the Sgt. raise up, take aim didn't think anything of it because we had been doing that to get used to the sights in the dark, but all of a sudden he tore loose with about five rounds before I knew what went on. I had been covering one path while he covered the other. It happened he seen this big tiger come up the path, hesitate & then slowly turn around & at that instant he opened up on him. I thought he was kidding & didn't bother to look in the direction he was shooting. Both he and the bearer we had with us saw the tiger & were plenty excited. He just got into a little bit too big a hurry & missed him completely. We were using Tommy guns last night & I'm darn sorry I didn't get a shot. The Sgt. had his gun on single fire (just fires one round each time you pull the trigger) but I had mine on full automatic. If I'd have seen the beast I'd have really sprayed the bushes for awhile. Tough luck but we're going out again Sunday & maybe we'll get a pelt. I did see a cub tiger along the road on our way to the spot . I should have shot him. On the way back I carried my pistol in a shoulder holster & popped away at jackals along the road. Really made them run. Didn't kill any but kicked dirt up all around them. Couldn't hit them driving forty miles per, shooting out the side of a truck at a running jackal but I did get closer than I expected to. I guess that's plenty of hunting for now.

So old Hank Ford thinks the war will be over in 60 days. You send Hank over & I'll show him why it won't be over by then. I wish it would be but about the only way that would be possible would be if they gave up, they most certainly would not be licked. I'm afraid he could add 300 days to that & maybe then some. Of course any guess might be worse than his first but I'd take odds or any kind of a be that it won't be over after the 60 day period or twice 60. We'll just have to wait & see what works. Did Hank give any reason for making such a statement? How does he figure it could possibly be over by then? Fritz mentioned the same thing in a letter must have been quite a statement. That's the trouble the people back home have no idea as to what goes on & they believe the war is already won. A good many people are due for surprise, I'm sure. Likely to be a little painful, too . . .

. . . This is Good Friday. Doesn't seem like Holy Week at all. Naturally I've tried living the Lenten season but it's not at all like at home. Things keep interfering with your plans & it's lucky if you get to Church every Sunday say nothing about during the week. I feel like a heathen & I guess I should do better . . .

I was surprised that soldiers were hunting big cats with a tommy gun, which uses low-velocity .45 caliber ACP ammunition. One would think an M1 Garand with .30-06 high-powered ammunition would have been the ticket. Dad lit up the countryside shooting at jackals on the way back. Whoa! He never told me about this adventure! I guess he didn't want such a testament to be a bad example to his son who loved hunting. He did tell me about a more horrific event he witnessed while in his tent in an encampment. He heard a shot in the tent next to his and quickly went to the tent next door, only to see a man sitting on his cot with the stock removed from his carbine, and his bunk mate on the ground in front of him, kicking and bleeding from the head. As dad held the tent flap open, a medic rushed into the tent under Dad's arm, only to immediately turn around and walk back out. The man on the ground had been shot under the chin on the right side of his head, the bullet exiting through his temple. His bunk mate had removed the stock to clean his weapon, not checking to make sure there was no round in the chamber. He also failed to maintain muzzle discipline, when the gun went off, killing his bunk mate. From then on, that soldier was on suicide watch. It had a profound effect on my dad, and he used it as an example often during my youth to impress upon me the importance of gun safety. NEVER let the muzzle of your weapon point at another human being, even unintentionally. ALWAYS consider your weapon to be loaded, even if you're positive the gun is empty.

"Old Hank Ford" was probably a reference to Henry Ford, the CEO of Ford Motor Company. Henry Ford, as I mentioned earlier, was a leading proponent of the isolationist America First Committee. Although he later took on a role in the war production effort, he wasn't a proponent of that early on. He was virulently anti-Semitic, anti-union, and—many would say—racist. In the days before the US joined the war effort, he believed in appeasing Hitler and falsely gave Hitler credit for being a purveyor of peace. His book *The International Jew* was one of the most influential anti-Semitic books of the time. If this is who Dad was referring to, it's surprising that Ford made such an unrealistic prediction about the war ending in only a couple of months. He was in a position to know, and he should have known better.

April 9, 1944

Dearest Gloria

Easter Sunday morning. A beautiful Easter Sunday morning too & I'm in India where Easter isn't known or recognized. To the people here it's another Sunday & I guess to some it's just another day. Holidays have lost their meaning since I've been in the Army. These holidays used to mean plenty . . . Easter Sunday & I'm in the office, not much to do but it's a good idea to be here . . . Ordinarily I come down to the office without hardly thinking about you but I can't keep my thoughts from you this morning . . .

Guess some people in India don't know it's Sunday, three bullock carts are passing in front of the building. They look just as dirty on Sunday as during the week. There are a lot of people passing dressed up as though they might be going to Church. I guess some of them are going to the movies. Sunday morning is when Movies are shown for the natives. I guess they must have Hindu sound for them or something. Another peculiarity of India

I've never mentioned before.

The day hasn't started for you as yet. In fact I guess you haven't gone to bed on Holy Saturday night. Anyway I hope you had a Happy Easter & that everyone liked the new hat or whatever new outfit you probably wore & I hope I'll be able to see you & be with you next year at this time.

I guess I'd better close now. Remember I'll always love you Baby.

As always

Jack

April 10, 1944

Dearest Gloria

Another day gone by and another day nearer the time when I can get out of this place. Or should I say a day nearer to the time when I'll be back with you. Nothing too much wrong with this place except geographic location. Not that I like it but it could be worse, some consolation in that.

Another alibi (I guess that's the correct spelling, sometimes I wonder how I got through grade school with my spelling. O.K. go ahead & laugh) on our little hunting trip. This time it was Bill. It seems he was sitting in a tree above this goat when a black panther came up, made a face at the goat, backed off & was set to spring at the goat when Bill pulled the trigger & nothing happened. The slide had gone forward in the tommy gun but the round didn't go off. This noise didn't seem to scare the panther so Bill started to fiddle with the gun & finally reached for his carbine & said "wait a moment" at the same time. There's where he made his mistake, the Sgt. With him couldn't shoot when he said "Wait a minute" & of course the panther got scared & was gone in an instant at the sound of a human voice. All I saw was two wild turkeys & wouldn't shoot for fear of scaring away any big cats. Guess we'll have to try again next month. The moon comes up too late to do anything anymore this month. At least we know they are there so—who knows . . .

April 11, 1944

Dearest Gloria

Another day without a letter, something so off the beam. I'm not the only one so I shouldn't complain. I'll get them all at once again like I've been getting my mail lately. Don't like that because I don't get to comment on your letters in such detail and would if I got one per day.

Went to a party last night. A little shindig for the Signal Section, turned out to be a rather stuffy affair. One of the boys was to fix me up with a date. Just hold your horses, I'll tell you all about it. When I got back from my trip I hadn't been in the office two minutes when the captain called up and asked me if I wanted a date. Well at that time I didn't even know there was a party or anything so I wondered what was wrong with him, now imagine having someone call you up to get anyone a date according to his specifications, in other words I was to tell him what kind of a gal I wanted & he would have supplied me with one. Pretty good I'd say. I told him not from him I didn't want a date. Not exactly in so many words, although he is the kind of a guy I would tell to go to hell if I didn't agree with him. I told him I'd let him know if I wanted date of course you know very well I never went back to him. No one asked me why I went stag & I didn't tell them but I certainly would have if anyone asked me. There is just one girl I want & want very much but at present she's just a little bit too far away. I'll get there sometime, though. As I mentioned, the party wasn't too hot, I'm sending the menu. It was actually a dinner dance for officers. The music wasn't bad & the food was O.K. but if it hadn't been almost a compulsory affair I wouldn't have gone but it's good politics to be seen on such occasions . . .

And so it is in the backwaters of the war. Officers were expected to attend social events, which weren't necessarily for fun but for making acquaintances within the hierarchy. Hunting trips, parties—office politics. Although my dad never liked politics, he soon would have his fill. And although he was not yet involved in the fighting, it was never too far away.

April 12, 1944

Dearest Gloria . . .

. . . I'd better set you right on a certain point right now. I'm not on my way home yet & don't expect to be for at least a year or more. I'll let you know very definitely when I'm about to push off so don't read between the lines. I'll probably be Twenty-eight years old before I see you & you'll be twenty-four at least you'll be over twenty-three. Is that clear enough. I know it's a very brutal way of telling it. I'm sorry if I got your hopes up. That's just too good to be true & I guess you did know better but like the drowning man, etc . . .

. . . It's getting terribly hot here now. About as hot as it ever got at Banning. Still hot in the evenings. Up until the last few days it wasn't too bad but there has been a change in the weather. I'd say that it got well over 100 today. April 12 what do you suppose it will be in July? I dread to think of it. I can still sleep pretty well at night but later on the nights will probably be uncomfortable.

I hear a guy sounding off across the way. I guess the Army isn't treating him right. He should be at least a General by now to listen to him. They're not treating me right either, so what. Anyway I've got to quit for tonight. Good night, Baby.

With Love
Jack

April 13, 1944

Dearest Gloria . . .

. . .I'm sending a copy of our weekly program schedule of the radio station. Pretty good I'd say. We don't have a radio but intend to try our luck at renting one. Don't need much of anything because the station is right in Delhi & these programs are the only ones worth listening to anyway so—It's a tough war we're fighting.

Some battle, we'll be well pampered when we get back. The only thing they can't do for us & the thing missed most is the "Good Old U.S.A." Can try to make us feel at home but it ain't home & no matter what is tried it just won't work. As for the radio programs, I can hear one going on right now. Pretty good program.

Bought a huge knife today. The Gurkha guards wear them as weapons. It's a thick blade affair with a fancy bone or horn handle. I'll get a picture of it one of these days. Getting this thing to defend myself with when I get home. It just won't pay you to get rough, I'm liable to swing with this meat cleaver & leave you with part of your scalp missing. Tough guy, I'll have you know . . .

Kukri, Gurkha Fighting Knife with U. S. M-8

April 14, 1944

. . . You know I used to think the British women were sort of straight laced, poker faced individuals but since I've been here I've found just the opposite. A good many Officers bring British WACs late into their quarters & you've never heard such squealing & yelling in your life. They seem to be very silly & giddy at times. I haven't got much time for them & you might say the same for the men. As for the men I just mean I haven't much time for them. Most of the dealings I've had with them I find they are pretty slow thinking & acting. Pretty slow in getting things done or in changing their minds.

Radio going to town across the way on "Paper Doll" etc. Fibber McGee & Molly just came on now. Sounds pretty familiar to hear old McGee again even though you know he's coming off a record being played out at the station. You see they make recordings of broadcasts in the States & then ship these records over to us to be played over Public Address systems or over radio stations such as we have. This war is certainly not what you'd expect it to be. We have it a lot nicer than I had dared to expect almost to the point that I'm disappointed. It's much better than what we got at Banning as far as the Army is concerned, but of course we would make ourselves comfortable if we had the cash, with what the nearby town afforded which we could & do here. You know they gave us a tent to sleep in & B rations. I took neither; I lived up town & signed out of the mess & all in restaurants. Cost me plenty but I lived better. Here you couldn't do that very well. It all adds up to the fact that there they were training or trying for a tent life, etc., while here they try to make us comfortable because they want to be comfortable themselves. Here we find other things to grumble about & I believe we do have good reasons sometimes. I don't mean because of the fact that we're away from home & in India. I'll tell you about it sometime.

Tomorrow I've got to pay the officers in the Signal Station. This is their per diem or meals to you. Don't like this detail very much because I could make a slip & that would cost me rupees. That's one disadvantage of being an Officer. You never know when you might get stuck with something like this & any mistake you make you pay for yourself. It's an O.K. system but you can sure be the goat if you're not careful.

A helluva letter but I'll try to do better one of these days. Don't think for a minute I'm downcast. I'm just out of gas but I can still tell you that I miss you & love you very much. Good night, Baby.

Jack

April 15, 1944

. . . I'm pretty tired tonight, paid all the officers this morning & came out exactly right without any trouble. I thought for a minute I was going to have 150 rupees left over but found out I hadn't paid one officer that I thought I had paid. Anyway when I got it all straightened around I was correct to the last Anna. Feel pretty happy about the whole affair, as you can imagine.

I wonder how the weather is around Iowa these days, it certainly is hot around here. Around 100 in the shade & it doesn't get cool until early in the morning. We can expect about two & a half months of the same kind of weather & hotter. In July the monsoons start & then it should cool off some. I guess we'll just have to grin & bear it.

The fellows next door are getting noisy again tonight. Hope we don't have any trouble with them. They through or rather threw a good one a couple of weeks ago & kept me awake most of the night. They are discussing the European invasion now & it seems they expect it very shortly. I hope they are right. Maybe the European deal will close by the end of the year.

I just wonder how long this rat race will last. Sitting here in Delhi I wonder if it ever will end . . . Might as well stay comfortable.

Lt. Forster was getting impatient about the war and wondered if it would ever end. Boredom was setting in and petty frustrations were starting to build. But there were also positive things. Dad was happy about a new broadcast radio station in New Delhi that catered to the tastes of soldiers so far away from home by keeping them abreast of life in the United States and providing music and entertainment of the day. It also gave Dad something to write about to Mom and the folks back home since he couldn't tell them about his work due to censorship. He often complained about lacking subject matter for his letters, but he knew he was expected to write and needed to write.

> *. . . All my letters are about the same every day lately. Guess I'll have a stencil cut with blank spaces for the date & signature & just send one every day. Simple isn't it, about as simple as the thought of it, I guess . . .*

April 17, 1944

> *Dearest Gloria*
>
> *Got five letters today. Three from you dated 17, 23 & 24th of March. One from your Mother & one from mine . . .*
>
> *. . . Your Mother seemed a little worried about her letter to me but she certainly does O.K. considering everything. I was able to read everything O.K. & there were surprisingly few mistakes. I don't do so hot myself & I've been to school quite a little. I've gone to school since High School, you might say off & on until now. I imagine she feels self-conscious about it but let's not worry about it . . .*

Mom's parents emigrated from Italy, so her mother (my grandmother) was self-conscious about her writing in English. Her dad was dark-skinned and small (about five feet tall and skinny) with a thick Italian accent. Mom told me people would make fun of him at times, so she was a little self-conscious about her family. Something in Gloria's letter indicated this to Dad, and in a following letter he tried to let Gloria know that despite his occasional inappropriate kidding about her "dago" heritage, she needn't be apologetic about her heritage with him.

. . . Always seems like I haven't done my duty if I don't write every day. At least if I can't have a better excuse than I had last night. The book was a "Captain North Adventure," namely "The Singapore Exile Murders." All about an army officer in the Orient. The fact that it concerned the army & the setting being in our general vicinity made the story pretty interesting. Singapore is about 1500 or two thousand miles away but even so the city is enough like some of the coast cities of India that the descriptions of streets, natives, etc. were very interesting. Anyway I've finished it & all the other I've had laying around so I shouldn't have a similar excuse for not writing in the near future. I'll try to read "Readers Digest" or something like it where I can break off at any time.

I don't have much time left before I've got to get back to the office so I won't comment on [your] letters until tonight. I'll be able to give them more time . . .

April 17, 1944

Starting the letter I promised you this noon.

We still get them, I mean shots. After Penn & Miami I'd supposed we got all that was coming to us for a while but today we got some more. Same shots, but another dose of it. Most of the fellows needed them but I had plenty of time to go yet before I was due for some. In order to get everyone they simply said everyone that didn't get them within the last 30 days gets another jab in the arm. My right arm is pretty sore but I guess it will be O.K. in the morning.

Got four letters today. One from my mother, one from Fritz & two from you. The mail has been balled up because I got some letters from you yesterday with a later date on them. Those today are from 18 & 20th of March while those of yesterday with a later date on them. Those of yesterday are of the 25th & 27th of March. One of your letters had two pictures in it. When was the one taken of my family? Guess that's the first picture of your family I've seen. Your dad certainly is a small man by the looks of the pictures. That's O.K. if we ever get into trouble I won't get beat up. I should be able to outrun him in any case. I'm sure we will get along O.K. I can see you're almost apologizing for your family. Don't ever do that. After all your family is what made it possible for you to exist. As far as you're concerned, I know what you are & I'm not marrying the family, just you. Your family must possess the same qualities you possess & that is far more important than wealth, education, position, etc. I'm looking for a good wife not a social butterfly. You know I have no social position that you couldn't very well fit into so don't let it worry you. In the army you know pretty well what would be required of you socially & as civilians we will have to build a social position as I have no real social position as you know. I'm sure everything will work out O.K. so don't worry. I suppose you wonder why I went into such detail on the subject. Was done simply to put you at ease about something that would be a touchy subject but actually means nothing . . .

April 21, 1944

Dearest Gloria

Another hot day & a busy one at that. Didn't exactly have fun working but I rather enjoyed the day's work. Had not a bit of trouble today that I couldn't very easily take care of. Makes things much more pleasant than when you get bawled out or run up against a blank wall or something. Not that I run away from the hard jobs, in fact there is much more satisfaction to completing a difficult job than there is to completing a number of easy ones . . .

. . . Went to the show this evening. Saw "Guadalcanal Diary." A good show & it makes us on "Per Diem Hill" feel like slackers even though we are in a theater of operations. We still seem an awful

long way away from the war.

I wonder what Hank Ford thinks about his little forecast. About half of his time has passed now. I imagine the second front in Europe will start any day now but what could they do in 30 days? The second front deal certainly is keeping everyone guessing. Maybe they'll just worry the Germans to death & never start the second front. Whatever they do they can't do it too quick for me. Seems like a lifetime since I left you . . .

Soldiers all over the world were starting to wonder when the Allies in Europe would open that second front. The Soviets felt they were doing most of the heavy lifting in Europe, and although the US and Britain had invaded Italy, Stalin didn't think that was enough. He also wanted Britain and America to put pressure on the Germans from the west. Nobody outside the small group of top planners knew when or where the invasion would happen to open that second front.

The Allies waged a great deception to make Hitler believe it would occur in Pas de Calais, the closest point between France and Britain. This deception was successful and caused the Germans to spread their defenses throughout the coasts of France. This made them less effective when the invasion finally occurred along the beaches of Normandy on D-Day. Because of the need for secrecy and deception, it's no surprise that Dad and Allied soldiers worldwide were clueless about when and where the invasion would occur. It's also unsurprising that they hoped it would happen sooner, not later.

April 28, 1944

Dearest Gloria

No mail again today. It's getting to be an old story & a not very interesting one. This is about the longest time I've gone without mail except at first & during the time I was away. All the people here are complaining about the same thing. Someone is slipping

& I don't like it. I'm a month behind on things now where before it usually was about two weeks. Maybe I'll get some tomorrow but that doesn't do me any good today . . .

. . . I wish I knew what to write about tonight, I've talked about the weather, as much about my work as I can, I don't talk about myself or do I? I could talk about you but it's a very "small" subject so what can I do? So I sit here with a cigarette a glass of ice water (a little Canadian Club added) & the radio wondering what to say. I supposed if I think long enough I think of something I might even put my foot in it by saying the wrong thing.

. . . There is one item I haven't mentioned that came up today. Seems like after six months duty here we become eligible of 15 days leave. Might get a chance after a while to get away to the hills to do a little hunting & fishing for a couple of weeks. They send you to a rest camp for a couple of weeks to keep you from going "nuts" in this place. I'm thinking very seriously about this as yet because I haven't been here 6 months yet. Won't be long though, time has flown & it won't be too long before I'll have 1/4 of my time in. Talking of spending time here & getting back, I guess it's just as well not to get back right away because if I did get back soon I'd be very likely sent out to another theater very soon so I guess my best bet is to stay here for a while. At least until they begin to decrease the number of men they send overseas. In a year from now the picture should be different, I hope . . .

April 29, 1944

Dearest Gloria

Got some mail today. One V-mail from Fritz dated April 9 & a letter from you dated April 13. Lot of it still missing I'm sure. I'm also sure you still love me enough to write every day . . .

. . . Although my mail is sent back by plane it could never make it in one day. I doubt if it always gets out of New Delhi the same day it's mailed & you know the record time from here to the states

by cargo plane is something like 3 or 4 days. It probably is more like a week or more before my mail reaches the States. As you know it has to go by air in order to get back to you in less than a month. The fastest boat takes a month or more for the trip . . .

So you didn't write to Jake yet well here's his address so let's get on the ball.

1st Lt. C. H. Jackson
Hq Com Z, C A M A
San Bernardino, Calif.

He might not be there anymore but it [will] certainly be forwarded so don't worry. If & when you write give him my regards. I wonder if I'll ever see him again. I've got him to thank for a lot of things although I didn't much care for the guy when I first met him . . .

Clyde Jackson was one of my dad's first and best army buddies. They served together in Banning, California. Dad didn't see him again until after the war, but they corresponded through the war and after. Jake even sent Dad an 8x10 picture of British General Francis Festing, the commander of the British 36th Division from whom Dad's unit was destined to be detached in the Burmese jungle, months later. Years later, my family also visited Jake at his home in Colorado when I was very young.

. . . We are listening to the "Hit Parade" & I see that the tunes popular when I left are still pretty well on the top. Four months isn't so long I guess but it seems like an awful long time when I look back to the time I kissed you Goodbye at the station.

I'm on the spot again tomorrow. Sunday & its payday & I'm to pay all the officers. Seems funny to dole out a lot of cash to a bunch of fellows that outrank me by so much. This includes a couple of full colonels or buzzard colonels. All on a Sunday morning. I wonder if I'll get to go to Church or not. I certainly try . . .

May 3, 1944

Dearest Gloria

Got lots of mail today. 4 from you & one from my mother. Those from you were dated 7th, 9th, 10th & 11th of April & the one from my mother April 6. The stuff kept drifting in all day long. Made me feel pretty good. Also got my footlocker today but I wasn't so happy about the condition it was in. My clothes was wet & everything in it was in pretty bad shape. The bottom of it was punctured & apparently the rain got in. About half of the locker got wet. My ink was O.K., some athlete's foot dope & some other items were O.K. The film I was telling you about didn't do so good. I've tried a couple of rolls in my camera but it was all stuck together. About three rolls seem to be O.K. Some of the rest might be O.K. but I'm doubtful. The trouble with it was that it wasn't tropical pack. This reminds me if you can get the tropical pack on film you send it might be a good idea to get it. I guess coming by mail might be much different than this stuff had to go through. You've got to realize that this stuff has been on its way for 5 months. I hope the film you send doesn't take so long. All in all I guess everything isn't so bad but it was pretty messy . . .

Haven't had any news today. Every time it's time for a news broadcast they give some excuse and start playing records. I wonder what's up? Could be that something big broke or maybe there just is no news. Burns & Allen show coming on now so I'd better close or my letter will seem a little disconnected . . .

. . . P.S. I love you & miss you every day.

May 5, 1944

Dearest Gloria

Received two of your letters today. April 2nd & 5th. A little old but nevertheless welcome.

Looks like I've got to move out of my home one of these days. They are moving all of the Junior Officers to another building. First I didn't like the idea but I took a look at the new place & I'm beginning to think it's a better deal than the place we are in. The rooms are larger & the whole building seems to be better as a whole . . .

. . . The boss got back yesterday (I don't mean Riordan) & things have been popping today. There is a lot of political business going on & I'm getting fed up with it. The boss has friends & the friends have friends. I get along with them swell but some of the fellows don't & you can see how some of the boys get pushed around because of it. This war has been going on too long, I guess. The boys are getting like a bunch of old women with their friends. I'm disgusted even though I'm on the good side of this thing—I hope . . .

Office politics is something that always frustrated my dad. "The boss has friends and the friends have friends" is the type of thing that pissed Dad off, and the intrigue that swirled around it threatened the serenity of his workplaces. Dad was probably worried that he might get embroiled in these office politics—as some of the guys had already experienced. A month or so before this letter, he'd noted that the "boss" was the kind of guy who could make things unpleasant for those who weren't careful.

May 6, 1944

Dearest Gloria

Am writing a little late tonight so it probably [will] be very short. Received six letters from you today. Dated 3,6, 15, 16 18 & 25th of April. The one of April 25 did O.K. but you can see how scattered out they are.

I'm writing late tonight because I went over to Central Vista where our new quarters are & looked at my new room. Bill & Lt. Petrie live next to me there, [or] rather will live next to me. Each of us will have a separate room & the rooms are quite a lot larger than the ones two of us are living in now. Can't quite figure it out. It is a better building with larger rooms & still they are moving the

Junior Officers out of here to the new place. Right now our room is pretty crowded because we don't have our beds double decked. Over there three of us would live in one room & still have more room than we have here. Enough for the quarters . . .

May 9, 1944

Dearest Gloria

. . . I still haven't moved to Central Vista but I expect to move any day now. I'm not in any hurry because the mess won't be open for sometime yet. We'll either have to come back here or eat downtown.

Did I tell you Riordan is out of town now? Have to go directly to the Boss with my work & I'm still a little timid about it. He has been swell to me but I've heard him with some of the other boys & he really cuts them down. I had to write up some extra dope including a personal letter & everything I've done so far was O.K. even though when he gave it to me I didn't have the slightest idea as to how to go about it. I hope I can continue to please the old boy. Not that I'm crazy as to whether he likes my work or not but I certainly don't want him cussing me out like I've seen him do some other people. He's just a little guy about my size but I've seen him make some full, real old timers really go into action when he got done with them . . .

May 16, 1944

Dearest Gloria

No mail again today. This is getting to be an old story . . .

. . . Changed places or rather changed to a different place to eat tonight. I've been eating at Curzon Officers' Quarters since I moved to Central Vista (Central Vista doesn't have the mess opened up yet). Tonight I signed out at Curzon & paid my bill. I'm going to eat at the Taj Hotel until they open the mess here. The food is better there & its on my way to work [but] Curzon is five or six blocks out of my way. At least it gives me a change . . .

. . . Lot of wild rumors floating around about the rotation plan & rest camps, etc. I guess the rotation plan is going into effect O.K. Some of the boys are leaving & as far as the rest camp I guess that's on the level. I'm not eligible until July 9th & I guess I won't get to go until about 5 Aug. By that time I should be plenty ready for a rest. Time will fly though. It has flown since I've been here. Almost five months since I left. Seems like an awful long time in one way & still it seems like I've just arrived. Five months over & about 19 more to go. Almost 1/4 of the time gone by if I have to stick out the time according to the rotation plan. Who knows what might happen. I hope it does & the time will be shorter or else you might get tired waiting. What would I do then?

Life in New Delhi was pretty normal, or at least as normal as it could be for a young American in a faraway land. Regular job, days off, office politics. But Dad was in a war zone, and his assignment was bound to change eventually. Soldiers don't often know what's in store for them or when their roles or assignments will change until they do. I'm sure this was the case for my dad. He was a skilled radioman who was well-trained in communications and the ways of the US Army. By May 1944, it was obvious the Allies were in the early stages of a push into Northern Burma. As for rest camps, it would take a long time and a radical change of scenery before Dad would see one. Although he didn't know it, things were about to get real for Lt. Forster.

5

The New Assignment

The nine-to-five life Dad had been living continued for the rest of May. Things went on as normal, but—whether he knew it or not—he wouldn't be in New Delhi for much longer. Petty frustrations grew, and there were signs that those troublesome office politics were starting to get to him.

While Dad was living his mundane life in India, things had been happening in Northern Burma. Stilwell and his Chinese troops, with the flanking action of Merrill's Marauders, had taken Walawbum and Shaduzup. The Marauders then continued to move on Myitkyina regardless of their casualties from enemy action, sickness, and jungle fatigue. And in March, despite the stubborn Japanese attacks on Kohima and Imphal in Northeast India, the Chindits had begun a second operation in Japanese-controlled rear areas south of Mogaung; there, they had built strongholds complete with landing strips. In contrast with the first Chindit operation, this one was coordinated with Stilwell's main thrust into Northern Burma and Merrill's penetrating force. The Chindit operation exacerbated the supply line troubles that plagued the Japanese plan to invade India. These deep penetration units played a significant role in confusing and frustrating the Japanese in Western Burma. Thanks to the Allied efforts, the once-masters of the Burmese jungle were now being challenged in their own backyard. But May brought the monsoons, and most of the Chindits were withdrawn from those bases at that time.

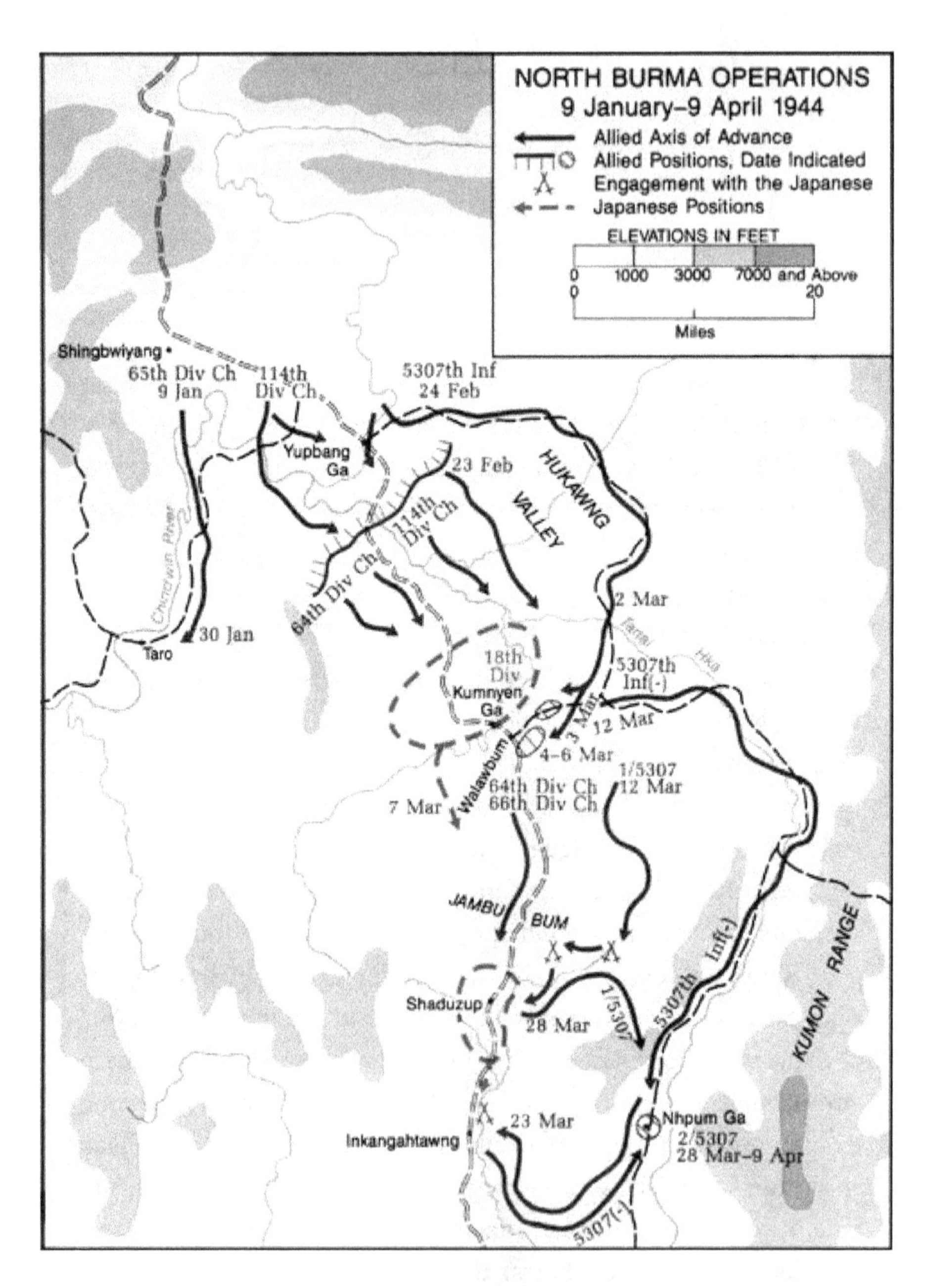

"Stilwell's Push into Northern Burma opening a path for the Ledo Road."
(War Department Map)

May 15, 1944

Dearest Gloria

Another day without a letter. One of these days I [will] get a flock of them. I got absolutely nothing today not even an old newspaper.

As I told you last night I paid the officers again today. Came out right on the button. The Finance office made a mistake & gave me 8 annas too much. I counted the money up before I started paying off & found an extra 8 Anna piece & I still had it left over when I got finished. Being too honest I turned it back to them when I returned the rest of the money. A lot of people would call me a dope for this but I guess I'm built that way, maybe I was brought up wrong. I feel pretty proud of my record of these pay days.

My cold isn't very much worse today but I don't feel quite as good otherwise. My bones hurt a little but I guess I'll get over it without too much trouble. Everything has been a little foggy today & it probably is being reflected in the letter.

I'm out of material again tonight. Just don't know what to talk about. Did get involved in a little argument with the staff car driver & a bicycle rider. I got the car to pick up the cash & on the way this one Indian riding the bicycle gave a signal that he was turning off & then didn't. Anyway the native driver yelled at him when we passed & the boy on the bicycle yelled back for him to shut up. Anyway when I got out the driver parked the car & I went in to get the money, the man on the bicycle came into the area & picked a fight. When I got out with the money the driver was all excited & wanted me to do something about it. He said the other guy came up to him & blowed (he meant hit) him on the face & hands. I couldn't very well do anything about it with a bag full of money so I just told him to report it to the motor officer & I'd be a witness if necessary. I've never seen an Indian so burned up but he cooled off after a little. I wanted to get the thing straightened out but I'll be darned if I'll go & settle an argument holding a bag of money. I'll bet all this is very interesting to you.

I'd better cut this thing short before you think I'm completely nuts.

This is one of those days that I miss you so very much. I wrote a letter to my Mother last night (Mothers Day) & told her more about you so you'll probably hear from her one of these days . . .

May 20, 1944

My Dearest Gloria

One V-mail today & it's from you. O.K., so you haven't written any V-mail lately. This one is dated Jan 20. Plenty old but better than nothing . . .

. . . Had a peculiar request today. One of the women working in the building called up & asked why there was no soap & towels in the wash rooms. I almost hit the ceiling. First of all towels are against Army regulations & where do you suppose I'd get any towels? A British woman, I'll get her fired if she doesn't quit fooling around. She called me twice & insisted on having her way, someday I'll see her face to face & I'll tell her to get the hell out of the office. I've told other people & they got out. I can't think of anything as silly as that. If she wants towels & soap she'd better bring her own. I've not much use for these British women anyway. They are so damn lazy & worthless. The American girl & woman is so far above them there is no comparison at all. They try to take their place in business but expect a lot of special consideration. I'm getting awful tired of pampering the delicate little things. If they can't take it why in hell don't they admit it. If I had my way I'd fire all of them & get some Indian men in their places. Why I tell you all this I don't know but I got so burned up & I knew that only one of these good for nothing limey women could think of something like that. I hope to God that our women are not like that. I'm sure you're not. I guess that's why I love you so much. A partner rather than a dependent person who cannot share trouble and hardships. You've done a swell job so far & I'm sure you'll be able to carry on for years to come.

I'm raving tonight. Can't explain why but I guess maybe it's because I feel being away from you more strongly tonight than usual. I do miss you so terribly much. I remember when I was home the folks maintained some family mentioned the fact that they hope the war would last a couple of years longer in order for them to pile up a little more money. Can you imagine anything like that? I'm afraid if I had that guy here now he would be in for a pretty rough time. I know the guy personally & I'm sure he would be ready for the operating table after I got finished with him. Maybe I was imagining things but I've been in spots where I wasn't sure whether I'd live through the next few hours or not & when I think of people wanting to have people continue through such moments it makes my blood boil. Again I wonder why I tell you all this except for the reason I always write what I am thinking about.

It's about time I ending this griping letter, told you that I loved you & bid you Good night.

As always

Jack

P.S. As I told you before I miss you more tonight than usual & I love you more than I can say.

Alrighty then. I guess it was one of those days. He may have been right about the fact that he was missing his girl and was unhappy with some of the things that were beginning to bother him at the office. Culture shock can be an insidious thing—sometimes it's not a shock at all but creeps in over time as frustrations build. It was a lot like that for me in rural Honduras during my time in the Peace Corps.

Dad may have been writing about a case of one woman feeling British colonial privilege, but it seems that the issues were larger than that. Lt. Forster was frustrated, and he'd had his fill of British women at that time. It was also obvious Dad was pissed off because of one man's crack about wishing the war would go on a little longer so he could make more money. The circumstances under which Lt.

Forster had found himself in danger are unclear, but being so far from home, it was possible that he'd already felt threatened, whether during plane flights, truck rides, or something else. He would have been unlikely to have told Gloria about such things—he didn't want to worry her—so they didn't appear in his letters.

May 24, 1944

Dearest Gloria

I've got a confession to make tonight. I'm sorry I didn't write last night after getting two letters from you yesterday. I worked a little later & then we had a continuous string of visitors until almost midnight. First, Petrie & his girlfriend came and then a Lt. of the Air Force and later another Signal Corps Officer. The Lt. of the Air Force is a graduate of Ft. Monmouth about the same time I got out & has been or is with Col. Cochran. Cochran is the guy who inspired the comic strip "Flip Corkin." Ever read it? Anyway this guy was telling us about the guy & I can see why he would inspire a guy naturally inclined to write. He must be quite a character. I suppose you've read about this guy Philip Cochran being in Burma & what he has done in that area. I just wonder what it would be like working for a guy like that & how the war would be getting along if all the commanders were like him. Enough of that & I'm still sorry I didn't write . . .

The mention of the air force personnel under Colonel Philip Cochran is worth examining, since Col. Cochran had already played a significant part in the Burma campaign. In his letter to Mom, Dad alludes to the fact that Cochran was a rather colorful character. This may be an understatement. In addition to being the inspiration for a character in Milton Caniff's *Steve Canyon* comic strip, he also inspired the Flip Corkin character in Caniff's comic strip *Terry and the Pirates*. In the widely acclaimed comic strip, Flip Corkin was Terry's flight instructor and mentor.

Despite the real-life Cochran's colorfulness and charisma, he was a no-nonsense natural leader who often came up with creative solutions to difficult problems. Once, while witnessing one of Cochran's creative solutions—a low-flying C-47 snatching a stationary glider full of wounded soldiers from the ground in a small clearing—the theater commander, Lord Louie Mountbatten, exclaimed in wonderment, "Jesus Christ All Bloody Mighty!"[7]

In Burma, both air superiority and supplying troops by air were essential to the war effort, especially in light of the terrain and the essential nature of long-range penetrating forces such as the Chindits and Merrill's Marauders. Roads were almost nonexistent in Burma's sparsely populated, mountainous jungle areas, and most existing roads were impassible during the monsoons, which lasted from May into October. General Wingate's reliance on supply by air during the first Chindit operation highlighted this need for supply by air.

When the second Chindit operation was conceived, it was decided that it would be on a much larger scale than the first. In addition to supplying the operation by air, this force would be inserted primarily by air. The exception was Brigadier Bernard E. Ferguson's British 16th Brigade, which in February began its 360-mile trek from Ledo southward, through the jungle. Cochran, along with Col. John Alison, was put in charge of the 1st Air Commando Unit, which would carry out the air operations and insert five of the six Chindit brigades, behind enemy lines. Several sites inside Burma were considered for the insertion point, but in the final analysis, the Broadway airstrip, located on a plain southeast of Hopin, was selected. On the evening of March 6 into the early morning hours of March 7, engineers with equipment were inserted in this area by glider, along with a small defensive force. The initial landings were rough since reconnaissance flights had failed to reveal logs in the

7 John Masters, *The Road Past Mandalay* (New York: Bantam Books, 1979), 197–198.

landing area. Some soldiers were injured, and others were killed during insertion. Despite this setback, the logs were removed, the ground was improved, and additional transport planes landed by evening on March 7.

Broadway and another jungle airstrip, White City, near Mawlu, became strongholds for Chindit operations behind Japanese lines from March 1944 up until the monsoons started in May. Col. Cochran's creativity and charismatic leadership were key to the operation's success; he not only arranged for inserting the Chindits into Japanese-held areas but also organized their air support in addition to bombing and strafing the enemy. He was lauded for using small aircraft to evacuate sick and wounded personnel from behind enemy lines, giving soldiers confidence that, if they were wounded, they would not be left to die under some bush in the jungle. During that first insertion operation into Broadway, newsreel accounts show Col. Cochran addressing his personnel, telling them their whole reason for being was to get those soldiers onto the scene, and saying the operation would be "jammed up into a couple of minutes . . . Nothing you've ever done in your life means a thing. Tonight you're gonna find out that you've got a soul."[8]

Unfortunately, on March 24, General Orde Charles Wingate, the creator of the Chindits, was killed when his plane, a US Air Force B-25, crashed into a mountainside in foul weather. Overall command of the Chindits was then handed over to Major General W. D. A. "Joe" Lentaigne. As a historical note, Wingate often flew in an American B-25 bomber with an American crew. It was not possible to distinguish between the victims of the crash, as they had all been burned beyond recognition. Because the majority of the victims of the air crash in which he died were American, he was buried in Arlington National Cemetery in Virginia, along with his British aide-de-camp, and the American crew of the B-25.

For the next couple of months, Chindit forces battled Japanese

---

8 Army Pictorial Service, "The Stilwell Road," U. S. Army Signal Corps. 1942

troops along the railway between Indaw and Mogaung, with almost constant fighting between the Chindits at White City and the Japanese out of Mawlu, just north of Indaw. The Chindits' main objectives were cutting the rail line, which was key to supplying the Japanese at Mogaung and Myitkyina, and disrupting the supply line to Mutaguchi's troops, who were attacking Kohima and Imphal. But when the monsoon started in May and the airstrips were rendered inoperable, the operations behind enemy lines were called off. Even so, Mountbatten and Stilwell wanted the push through Burma to continue through the monsoons—but from further north, with more direct action from a larger, more complete force. In May, when the Chindits moved out of White City and Broadway, most of the soldiers were evacuated and relieved. These strongholds had successfully disrupted Japanese General Mutaguchi's supply lines—a valuable accomplishment. The Chindits had achieved their purpose, and leadership deemed their operations untenable going forward. However, British Brigadier J. M. "Mad Mike" Calvert and his 77th Brigade were ordered to march north to attack Mogaung. In early June, they moved north to begin their attack.

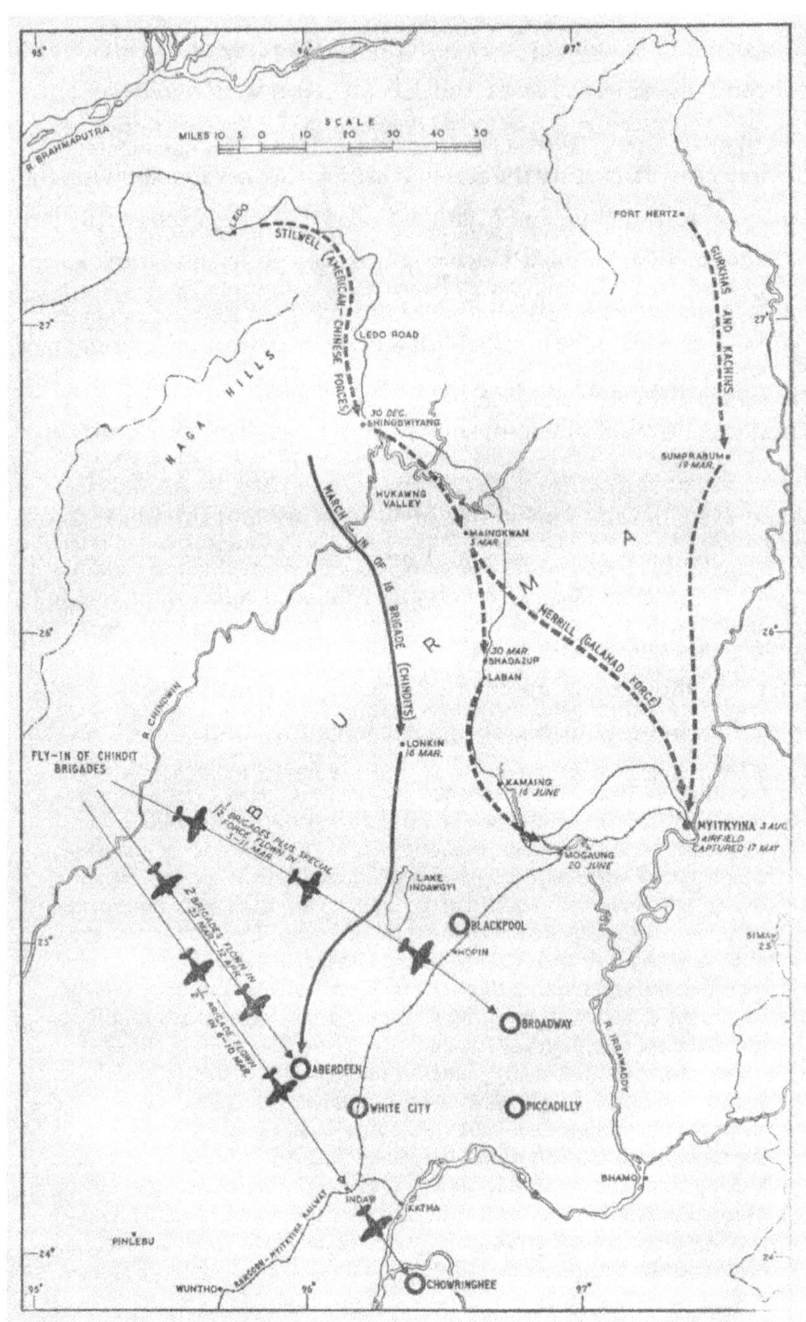

THE SECOND CHINDIT EXPEDITION AND THE NORTHERN FRONT IN BURMA, DECEMBER 1943—AUGUST 1944

War Department Map

May 29, 1944

My Dearest Gloria

No mail today again but I'm still writing regardless.

Been shooting the bull all night so it's getting late again. Pete had his girlfriend around & some of the fellows dropped in from time to time . . . so the place is getting to be pretty homey. Guess I'll stay (as long as they make me).

I still sort of marvel at this place. Going down the street & just consciously looking around for things & comparing them with things at home really brings out the fact that you are in a strange land. Here in New Delhi you can see most any means of transportation known to man. Cars, buses, bicycles motorcycles, tongas, carriages, airplanes, trains & in Old Delhi they have street cars. No boats, because it's so dam dry you'd have to float it in a bath tub. Wait a minute I guess they do have row boats in the river on the other side of town. One thing sort of beats me is the British women who ordinarily are pretty soft like & wouldn't think of doing some of the things the American girl does but they do ride the back end of a motorcycle. You often see what looks like man & wife riding a motorcycle & they don't have a side car either . . .

Dad's comment about his place getting to be "pretty homey" and his comment "guess I'll stay (as long as they make me)" may have induced the intervention of karma. As it turned out, his stay in Delhi would not continue.

May 30, 1944

Dearest Gloria

No mail at all today but I do have a little news. I don't think my address will be New Delhi for very much longer. Yes, getting a new job & I believe it will be something a little bit more up my alley. The one I had was about to drive me nuts so maybe a change will do me some good. Another thing I've been told that the new job will get me a promotion. In fact Capt. Riordan promised me faithfully that he would see to it that I got it. Finally. I don't trust him too much on that but who knows. I know it won't be quite as comfortable as I have been. I guess New Delhi is the most comfortable spot in India & another thing I'm pretty sure I won't be able to tell you exactly where I am. New Delhi is the only place you can mention but I guess it really doesn't matter. In any case, don't worry. I'll be perfectly safe, I won't be fighting the Japs. As yet I don't know just what my duties will be but I'll find out & I pretty sure I'll be able to give you some idea as to what it's all about. Right now I don't know whether to be happy about the whole affair or not but a change will make the time seem shorter at least. Besides there is that ray of hope as far as promotion is concerned.

Anyway you know I will be moving. I don't know when & if I knew I wouldn't be able to tell you so— . . .

. . . One thing I am worried about is your birthday gift. I'm afraid I won't get it in time. I had it made & I gave them almost a month so maybe all I'll be able to send you is my love unless I'll be able to pick up something else. I'll try my best.

I guess I'd better end this tonight. I love you so very much, Baby. Good night & I miss you.

Sincerely

Jack

May 31, 1944

My Dearest Gloria

No letters again today. I'm afraid I won't be getting any from you for a while. How I miss those letters.

I don't know an awful lot of news tonight except that I still expect to be moved shortly. Can't tell you where because New Delhi is about the only place we can mention in this theater. The only thing I can mention is that I have a friend in the place I'm going to & he might be able to do something about getting me a good job. I don't know whether I'll like the new place but you can be sure I'll make the best of it. I told you that Riordan promised me a promotion yesterday. Well, today he wasn't quite as promising. Don't know what the score is on this I might still be coming back with gold bars. Maybe it's not important but I am getting plenty anxious after twenty months [since my last promotion] & feel I've got a right to be anxious. I'm more anxious to get back than anything else. Won't be long now I'll have 1/4 of my time in here & I've got great hopes that it will be more than 1/4. As I said before I can't tell you very much about my new assignment but I expect to be able to see Florence Brunner, (the relative & school mate of mine) & my new APO will be 689. Write to me as follows:

Lt. Louis J. Forster 0-1637436
Sig Sec HG NCAC – CBI
APO 689 c/o PM NYC

This is a little premature but by the time this gets to you & your letters return this should be it . . .

June 4, 1944

Dearest Gloria

Well, I'm now out of New Delhi as you probably suspected.

I haven't written for the last couple of days & I probably won't be writing quite as often as I have been before this. Another thing I won't be able to tell you exactly where I am but I can tell you that I am now in Burma. Yep, it looks like my days of lazy living are over for a while. This jungle life is not exactly a snap but it is a change from the past which should make time pass more rapidly. Another thing is that I certainly will learn a lot more of the customs & habits of the people of the world. I'll certainly have plenty to tell after I get back.

Something about the Burma jungles. First of all this is the beginning of the monsoon season & it's plenty wet. Everything is just dripping wet. Even the cigarettes in my pocket are damp as hell. They don't taste the same that way. The country is beautiful as far as that goes. The hills or rather mountains are plenty rough & steep but just as green as you can imagine. It's not as hot as Delhi. Not near as hot but being as damp it does get a little uncomfortable during the day. The clouds are beautiful as any I've seen.

Another thing I might mention is the Chinese driver we have. What a sense of humor the boy has. Can't quite figure out what makes everything seem so funny to him. I get a big kick out of the boy, though. One thing is sure & that is he has the ability to drive. I was really surprised at how well he handled the truck in tight spots. Every bit as good if not better than most American drivers. He can't speak English but by hand motions, etc. we can get him to understand what we mean. He does speak a few words such as "Let's go" & "O.K. Joe". I repeat I get a big kick out of him & I wouldn't ask for a better driver.

The driver and his friend just came in & they are giving us a lesson in Chinese & it's really something. Get a big kick out of it.

I'd better close now & try to get at writing more later. Don't worry about me even if you don't hear from me every day. I'm not in any danger.

Good night, Baby. I love you more every day.

As always

Jack

I had to laugh when I read Dad's comments about the Chinese driver. Obviously the driver had made an impression because it fit my dad to a T. When I was growing up, he would occasionally use a Chinese word or short phrase, and he would laugh as he was doing it. Later, when he visited me in Honduras, he would somehow communicate with the locals despite not knowing more than a word or two of Spanish. He'd combine what little Spanish he knew with gestures and hand signals. Sporting a ready grin, he would get his point across and make friends along the way. Maybe he learned to do this from his encounter with this Chinese driver.

June 7, 1944

Dearest Gloria

It's been several days since I wrote & I've got a free moment so I'd better get on the ball.

Well, I've seen Florence Brunner, in fact I'm now in the same camp. I expect to see her this afternoon or evening. She really was surprised to see me. It's been about 6 or 7 years since I saw her last & I was almost afraid I wouldn't recognize her. I almost didn't, she's lost quite a little weight but she claims she lost it in the States. She's been over here in the jungle for 17 months & still going strong. Yep, it doesn't seem to bother her too much. Of course she is anxious to get back but as I said before it doesn't seem to trouble her very much. Anyway if she can take it & stand up under it so well I'm sure I can.

As you might suspect I haven't received any mail for some time & I'm afraid the mail situation will be worse than ever now. Can't do anything about it but hope it does come through. I can see a good reason for it to be slow here so it won't trouble me too much.

I suppose you have visions of me sleeping on the ground & living off the jungle but that's not the case. I've slept on a cot every night since I've left Delhi & had either a tent or a basha[9] *for cover. In either case there was always a good roof & a floor to the thing. It's really not bad at all. Even if I did have to sleep outside I've got a jungle Hammock. It's quite a [gadget]. The darn thing keeps you off the ground. Has a roof over it made of rubber & sides made of mosquito netting. You climb into the thing & zip it shut & you're as snug as a bug in a rug. I got the thing but I don't know if I'll ever use it. I suppose by the time I get through dragging it around for a few months it won't be in very good shape but I would like to bring*

9 The word "basha" is an Assamese word (from the province of Assam in India) meaning a hut that is typically made of bamboo and grass. This term was adopted more generally for a makeshift temporary shelter by the British military.

one of the darn things home with me. Maybe I'll be able to buy one.

Well, baby I've got to write to some more people so I'd better close now. I should be able to write a little more often for the next couple of days. Have trouble keeping dampness out of the envelopes. Don't know how I'm going to get around this.

Don't worry about me, just remember I'll have plenty of things to tell you when I get back.

All my love
Jack

Dad was a rookie at being in the jungle, but he was about to get an education in jungle living. As he said, it was the start of the monsoon season, which usually lasts into October. When he arrived in June, he was in the Hukawng Valley at Shingbwiyang, a camp in extreme Northern Burma where construction of the Ledo Road was beginning. It was also where he met up with his cousin and former classmate, Florence Brunner. Both my dad and the road crews were following the path of General Stilwell's Chinese divisions and the 5307th Composite Unit, Galahad force. As said earlier, by this time, Galahad had helped take Walawbum and Shaduzup and was already knocking at the door of Myitkyina. Galahad had completed its difficult and dangerous crossing of the Kumon range, setting them up for a surprise attack on the air field at Myitkyina. Chinese troops flew by glider to the airstrip, allowing them to take the airfield. In typical fashion, Stilwell, jubilant over his success despite British skepticism, wrote in his diary, "WILL THIS BURN UP THE LIMEYS!"[10] Taking this airstrip was significant since air transport over the Hump from Assam to Kunming and Chongqing in China had been difficult due to Japanese fighter interference from the air base near Myitkyina. Furthermore, planes were not able to carry full

10 Center of Military History, *India-Burma: The U.S. Army Campaigns of World War II* (Washington, D.C.: Center of Military History, 1992), 18, https://archive.org/details/IndiaBurma/page/.

cargo loads at the altitudes they had been forced to fly. Taking the Myitkyina airstrip was a game changer. It allowed the Allies to fly in reinforcements for their effort to take the town of Myitkyina and eliminated the Japanese fighter threat from the Myitkyina airfield to the airlift to China. Meanwhile, Stilwell, after cooperating with Galahad to take Walawbum and Shaduzup, had turned south and was now knocking at the doors of Kamaing and Mogaung.

When Dad wrote his June 7 letter, he may have been traveling the Kamaing Road to catch up with Stilwell's Chinese force. He was not yet in the combat zone, but he was headed in that direction. Living conditions were becoming more rugged—and wet—as he got deeper into Burma.

The jungle itself was a formidable obstacle, especially during the monsoons. The terrain was complicated by precipitous mountains and rushing torrents of streams and rivers. Roads were scarce, and those that existed became mostly impassible. Mud was everywhere. Climbing mountains and crossing rivers and streams were the hallmarks of life in the Burmese jungle. The foliage was so thick that major armies could pass within a short distance of each other and not know the other was there. But one of the jungle's worst features was the disease. Most people traveling through the jungle during monsoon season ended up with malaria, and amoebic dysentery was also endemic. Soldiers took the anti-malarial drug atabrine prophylactically. There was also scrub typhus, dengue, cholera, and a number of other tropical diseases. During the monsoons, casualties from sickness were more prevalent in Burma than casualties from battle wounds.

June 11, 1944

My Dearest Gloria

Haven't received any mail for a couple of weeks now but I guess I'd better keep writing.

Went to Church this morning, received Communion & after Church visited with Florence for a few minutes. The last half hour or so I've been working on my envelopes. The darn things are all stuck shut, every last one of them. This is going to be a problem unless I buy a half dozen or so & write that many letters immediately. Just from the moisture in the air everything gets soggy. A cigarette gets all limp as a rag & doesn't taste the same. From one extreme to another. New Delhi was so darn dry & this place is so darn dry [wet]. Frankly I can't say which extreme I prefer.

News is a little slow around these parts. We didn't hear about the European deal [D-Day] until a couple of days later. I was glad to hear about it or did I tell you that in my last letter. The news I'm waiting for about now is the end of the thing but I'm a little afraid it might take some time before that day. Won't it be something to go back to living a normal life. For me it will be a tough job. The period of readjustment will be horrible. It's a period I'm trying to prepare myself for. You realize that after moving around so much & seeing practically the whole world it will be difficult to resign myself to stick in one place. I'm sure you will be able to be a great help in this period. You should be better able to understand the trouble a person had in getting settled after being away from home as you were . . . What do you suppose it will be like to the fellows that have been away for much longer period & the conditions under which they lived & worked? I'm counting on you for plenty, I guess, when I expect you to be with me then. It won't be easy . . .

. . . Back again but nothing to write about except that it's raining again. It rains at least a little every day & sometimes just a little more than a little. Only about 5 or 6 inches in twenty-four hours. You just can't imagine how damp it can get . . .

June 13, 1944

My Dearest Gloria

Still am not getting any mail but I'd better write or you might disown me. I couldn't very well afford to have that happen. Wouldn't know which way to turn. I guess I know I haven't been writing as often as I should but writing is getting to be quite a problem. The paper is all damp & envelopes are almost impossible. There is no possibility of it letting up for a couple of months at least, in fact I guess it will get worse. Don't get the idea because I'm talking about stationery getting damp that I'm living right out in the weather. At present I've got a good roof over my head, a cot on each side of me & a bamboo floor under me. Besides that there are four walls lined with [coarse] sack cloth & screens at all openings & electric lights. Nope the rain doesn't fall on the paper but it just draws dampness out of the air. I've just never seen so much rain. Getting used to it, if I get wet it doesn't seem to matter, it's not cold enough to make it uncomfortable, besides we have stoves in the basha so, we get along.

One week from today I'll be twenty-seven. I'm getting old fast. Don't feel any older but time slides by awful fast. I hope the time I spend here isn't wasted & I guess it won't be. Almost 1/4 of the expected time over here gone by. I can't hardly believe it and yet it seems ages since I left. Let's just hope the rest of it seems short & that it will be shorter than we now expect.

Haven't heard much about the European Theater the last couple of days. I wonder how they are coming along. If the news service keeps up like this the war will be over & we won't know about it. News does come into camp every day but unless there is something unusual we just don't get it & don't bother to check up either . . .

June 15, 1944

My Dearest Gloria . . .

. . . Got some new stationery today. I happened to find a stray P.X. that had some. This P.X. was some place. I'm glad I had my rubber boots on because I sure needed them. The mud was over ankle deep all around & in it. Speaking of stationery, I'm going to write or should I say I'm going to use ordinary envelopes & send them free.[11] *I don't think it will make much difference in the*

11 Airmail envelopes cost more to buy and send. Soldiers could send plain envelopes at lower cost, and they supposedly could arrive at their destination almost as fast.

delivery time & [it] is pretty rough trying to keep stamps or air mail envelopes. In fact it's tough to keep any stationery but when you buy air mail envelopes most of them go to waste anyway so being a thrifty soul I'm going to try to get along with some that cost less than six cents. I hope you don't mind. If it makes very much difference in the delivery time let me know & I'll change back regardless of cost. All this should show you that I'm not a cheapskate & that I'm perfectly willing to spend six cents on you anytime. How about it. This might not sound so good on paper but it's supposed to be funny.

It's still raining plenty. For the last couple of days it rained almost constantly. Just a drizzle some of the time but every once in a while it pours down in sheets. I've never in my life seen so much rain at one time. There is one advantage & that is that it's not as hot here. We've got a fire in the stove most of the time. Not so much to keep warm but to dry clothes . . .

. . . I guess I'd better wind this thing up now & get to bed. I went to the movies last night ("Destination Tokyo") & didn't get to bed until late so I'm sleepy. By the way, this theater is something. Outdoor type with ground for seats. It rained last night but we just stayed there & saw the show, rain or no rain. I've known the time when I wouldn't go to a show if it was raining & the show was in a theater but out here it's different. A lot of things are different, some of which you won't believe when I tell you.

Good night Baby & I love you so very much.

As always

Jack

June 22, 1944

My Dearest Gloria

Almost a week has gone by since I wrote last so I'd better get on the ball. This past week it was pretty tough trying to write but it should be better from now on.

Had quite a birthday surprise. Got about twenty letters, a newspaper & two rolls of film. I was really glad to get those letters. It took me almost twenty-four hours before I got them all read. Of course I read yours first as usual. Yep those letters were O.K. Should make me realize all the more how letters are appreciated & make me put out a little more effort as far as writing goes. I should be able to get more time for writing now since I'm in a more permanent spot. Up until a day or so I was on the move quite a little but I've got an idea I'll be staying in this spot for at least a little while. It's not exactly the most comfortable spot in the world but I believe the work I'm getting into will be up my alley. Something I've been looking for since I got my bars. I believe I'll like the people here better too. That makes a big difference. I'm writing this early in the morning but I won't be able to finish now. I'm due to see the C. O. now so I'd better sign off until later in the day.

Well I'm back but it's a day later It got a little late last night & we don't have any lights, so need I say more.

I'm getting set in my job now & I guess this job fits me better than any I've ever had since I've been commissioned. Signal supply & repair. I've had quite a little experience in both & it's the kind of work I like. A safe job & it has regular hours. The first couple of days I was here they had me in operations which meant taking a shift during the night or at least odd hours. Not so good. I'd rather take my meals at regular hours & sleep at night. So I'm pretty well satisfied.

The war news is getting better every day. If things keep going as fast as they have been in the past month the war will be over before the end of the year. Yep, it really looks good.

I suppose you have been worrying just a little about my being in Burma but that's foolish. I don't ever expect to get close to where the fighting's going on in my job. Single or a small groups of Japs get all over this territory but usually they are absolutely harmless. Most of them starved to a point where they give up without a struggle. So I'm not worried a bit.

The weather has been a lot better for the last couple of days. It did rain a little this morning but this afternoon the sun was out as it has been for the last four days. Helps a lot to get clothes dry & keep the moisture down in bedding, etc.

All in all everything is pretty good. It's not near as comfortable but I can take it. We are a long way from nowhere & it can get awful tiresome but I guess we'll have to take it & just say "This is war" . . .

Dad had been moving from the Indian border through the northern tip of Burma across areas that had been taken by Stilwell's Chinese army. As he passed through those places, he stayed in the buildings that were left behind as Stilwell moved south. He even found a PX, indicating that he was in an already established area along Stilwell's route. But things would become more rugged and untamed as he went deeper into Burma.

Obviously, Dad was heartened by the war news from Europe. Although there were still rough spots to go through in Normandy—the infamous hedgerows and the city of Caen, for example—it was a sign of progress that the invasion had not been repulsed and the boys were moving forward. Things had been moving forward in the Pacific, too. MacArthur had mopped up the New Guinea campaign and the marines were invading the Marianas, which would give the air force B-29s a base from which to attack Iwo Jima and the home islands of Japan. Despite this, the Japanese were making progress in Eastern China; as a result, the Americans were losing bases in China for their B-29s. But overall, the war news was good.

By the time Dad arrived in Burma, things were moving there, too. The CBI had been last in line to receive troops and resources throughout the war, and it took the British and Americans a long time to figure out how to fight in the jungle. But by June 1944, the Allied forces were beginning to get the measure of the Japanese and beat them at their own game. They were now better equipped, better supplied, and controlled the air over much of Burma. Things were moving forward.

Given all the different countries, cultures, and languages represented among the Allied forces in Burma, it took a while to get things coordinated. In the first place, the British were at loggerheads with the Chinese. They had different views as to how to fight the war. The Chinese had been fighting the Japanese in China for almost eight years, and much of their country had been taken over by Japan. In the middle of all this was American General Joseph Stilwell. He had been hesitant to take the command that Army Chief of Staff General George C. Marshal gave him, and his hesitancy was well-founded. To illustrate the convoluted nature of his position, Stilwell was second in command to British Theater Commander Lord Louie Mountbatten in the CBI. Stilwell was also Chinese Generalissimo Chiang Kai-Shek's Chief of Staff as well as the administrator of Lend-Lease supplies to China. As a result, he was caught up in the politics of Chongqing, China's wartime capital. He once wrote of that situation, "What corruption, intrigue, obstruction, delay, double crossing, hate, jealousy, skullduggery we have had to wade through. What a cesspool. What bigotry and ignorance and black ingratitude."[12] Stilwell was not a diplomat and was often overtly blunt in his dealings with both the British and the Chinese. In addition, the relationship between the British and the Chinese was poisoned with a long history of enmity and hate. Stilwell wrote in his diary, "What a mess. How they hate the Limeys. And what a sucker I am."[13]

As noted in an earlier chapter, Stilwell considered his to be the worst command of the war, and his lack of diplomacy made him less than ideal for his position. He had earned his title of "Vinegar Joe" in his dealings with Chiang Kai-shek and made no bones about referring to the Generalissimo as "Peanut" in external communications. I once heard my dad refer to the Generalissimo

12 Eddy Bauer, "The Allies in Burma," in *Illustrated World War II Encyclopaedia* 19 (Westport, CT: H. S. Stuttman,1978), p2579.

13 Dwight Jon Zimmerman, "Stilwell in China: The Worst Command in the War," *Defense Media Network* (March 6, 2012), https://www.defensemedianetwork.com/stories/stilwell-in-china-the-worst-command-in-the-war/.

as "Chancre Jack," an even less complimentary term that no doubt had been influenced by Stilwell. Stilwell was always suspicious that Peanut was hesitant to fight the Japanese and believed he was saving his army and the US-contributed Lend-Lease supplies to fight the Communists under Mao Zedong after the war with Japan was over. The multinational effort in Burma was mostly designed to keep China in the war against the Japanese. However, Chiang Kai-shek had conflicting interests, and it was Stilwell's job as Lend-Lease administrator to China to be a watchdog and ensure that Allied interests were served. In essence, he was both watchdog and underling to the Generalissimo—a strange position indeed.

Stilwell's bluntness and his position as Lend-Lease administrator meant the Generalissimo almost constantly asked for Stilwell to be relieved. However, General George C. Marshall was protecting Stilwell in the summer of 1944. British General William Slim, who had been the commander of the British 14th Corps throughout the Arakan campaign, had a slightly different take on Stilwell: "He had strange ideas of his loyalty to his superiors whether they were American, British or Chinese, and he fought too many people who weren't his enemies; but I liked him. There was no one whom I would rather have had commanding the Chinese army that was to advance with mine. Under Stilwell, it would advance."[14]

So this is the setting under which my dad entered the fray in the Burmese jungle—a multinational army under an American general who commanded Chinese, Indian, Gurkha, and British soldiers who were often aided by Kachin tribesmen native to Northern Burma. Additionally, it was a constant fight against nature, especially during the monsoons, and danger and disease were a constant threat. This was a challenging setting, to be sure, but for the time being, there was no one better than Stilwell to get the job done. Things were heating up in Burma, and Lt. Forster was about to get into the thick of it.

---

14 Eddy Bauer, "The Allies in Burma," in *Illustrated World War II Encyclopaedia* 19 (Westport, CT: H. S. Stuttman,1978), 2579.

Chindits near Mogaung

6

The Jungle War

June 27, 1944

Dearest Gloria

Just finished a letter to my folks & I guess I've to a few minutes to start one to you before it gets dark & the movie starts. I hadn't written home for over a week so I guess it was about time. My letter writing has gone to pot with this move but now that I'm more settled I should be able to get back in the groove again. We don't get mail very regularly here. About once a week is about all we can expect . . .

. . .For a couple of weeks while I was on the move I didn't miss you so much but since I've arrived at my destination I miss you more every day. I guess it's getting news, etc. that make it. The war is going so well that I'm beginning to anticipate a little trip home. Don't get me wrong I'm not on my way but it looks like this war will be over before we know it. We're doing plenty O.K. here & the European theater is doing plenty good & the South Pacific isn't doing so bad either. All in all it looks like we've got them on the run & I'm pretty sure we'll keep them on the run until it's all over. If Hank Ford made his prediction now it wouldn't sound quite as foolish. I don't expect it to end as soon as all that but by the end of the year it could very easily be over. What a day that will be. I'll certainly try to get out of here in a hurry then . . .

. . . Just put on a little insect repellent. Have to keep the mosquitoes away. You know that certain types of them carry

malaria & malaria is no fun. People usually get over it O.K. but they are never sure that they're cured. I certainly wouldn't want to come home to you & come down with a fever & chills every so often. Besides being pretty sick it can also leave some weakness so that's why I use the dope.

One of the boys shot a snake tonight. Pretty good sized one, about 8 feet long. Even though the guy got a little excited because the snake was on his bed he still got it with the first shot. No he didn't shoot it while it was in or on his bed. That was the first snake I've seen in India [and Burma] except some of the snake charmers used to carry around. There are supposed to be lots of snakes around but I guess the Chinese have killed them all. They eat them so thanks to them no snakes. Speaking of Chinamen, these boys really like to shoot. They bang away all the time. Just shoot to hear the noises a lot of time & the bigger the gun the better. They love the tommy gun because it makes a lot of noise . . .

Dad had been in India until June, but he was now in Burma. He would eventually meet the last of the Chindits as they were withdrawn. As for the snake one of his boys shot, he didn't say whether the snake was a python or a king cobra—maybe he didn't know the difference. But because he was with the Chinese, he must have been with Stilwell's force. At about that time, Stilwell's headquarters were in Kamaing, a little more than twenty miles northwest of Mogaung, so it's safe to say that Dad was in that area.

Dad was settling into his new job, if only temporarily replacing another officer, and he seemed to believe conditions were stable and safe—an impression that he was always quick to reinforce with Gloria. As for disease, it was rampant. Almost all soldiers in Burma eventually contracted malaria, and most had bouts with dysentery, scrub typhus, and just about every other tropical disease. There were also leeches, some of them up to a foot long, that would chew right through a soldier's clothes and cause infections.

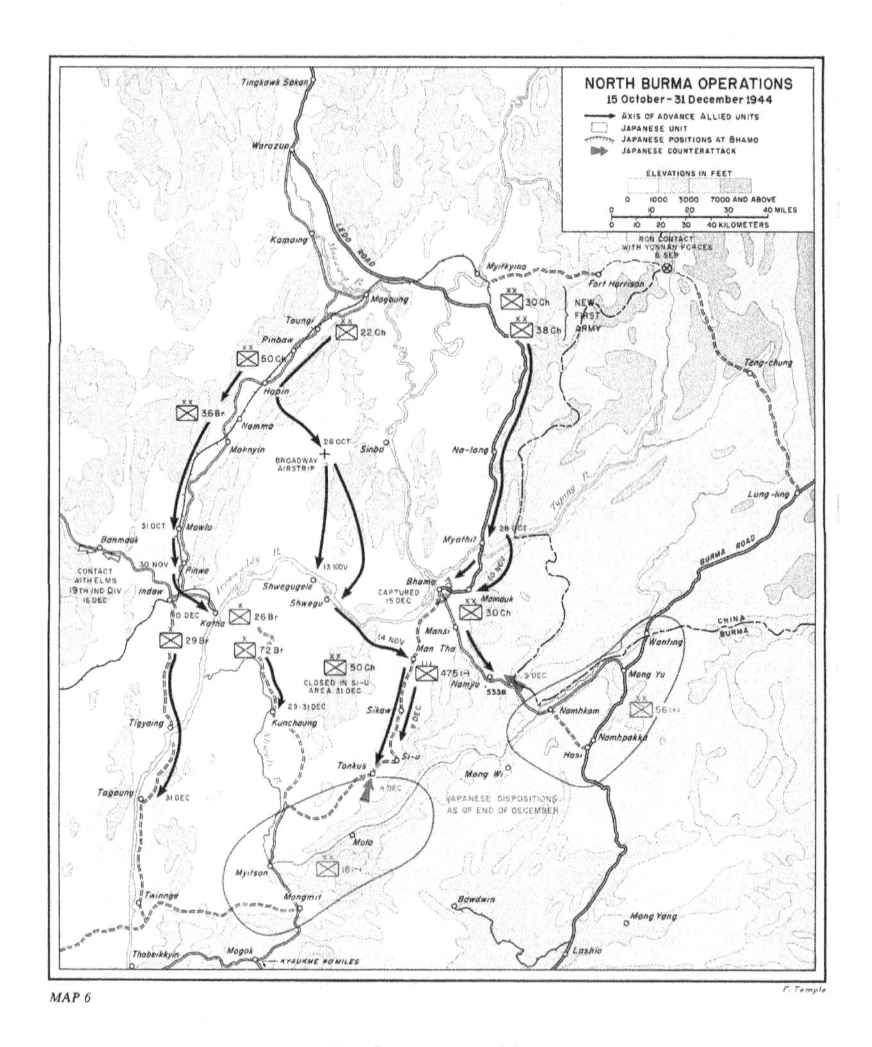

War Department Map

After Broadway was evacuated in May, Stilwell had ordered the last Chindit unit, the British 77th Brigade under "Mad Mike" Calvert, to take Mogaung. The Chindits were light infantry and weren't structured for such an assault, plus they had a long way to go northward through flat, monsoon-soaked ground to get to their objective. Stilwell was mopping up Kamaing, north of Mogaung, and Calvert's force had suffered from exhaustion, disease, and lack of rations before finally beginning an all-out assault on Mogaung on June 24, 1944. Calvert was reinforced by a Chinese battalion from Stilwell's camp and finally cleared Mogaung of all resistance by June 27. After suffering 1,500 casualties from battle and disease, Calvert was left with only 300 men who were still fit to fight. When Stilwell announced through the BBC that his Chinese troops had taken Mogaung, he didn't mention the Chindits' contributions under Calvert, which Calvert took as an affront. He communicated to Stilwell's headquarters, "Chinese reported taking Mogaung. My Brigade now taking umbrage."[15]

Stilwell then ordered Calvert to move on Myitkyina, after which Calvert turned off his radios. Instead of going to Myitkyina, he joined Stilwell at Kamaing. The last of the Chindits had become a depleted force by that time due to illness and injuries. At first, Stilwell was angry at Calvert for not proceeding to Myitkyina, and it was thought that Calvert might be court-martialed. Once Stilwell met with Calvert, however, Stilwell realized the 77th Brigade was unable to continue due to attrition.

A similar and possibly worse story was the case of the 5307th Galahad Force, the other long-range penetrating force still operating in theater. After participating in Stilwell's drive through the Hukawng Valley and taking Walawbum and Shaduzup, he had sent them over the rugged and dangerous Kumon range toward Myitkyina, aided by Kachin tribesmen who were native to the area.

June 30, 1944

Dearest Gloria

Just finished oiling up my guns & got a little time so—

I built me a little light yesterday so I could read & write a letter at night & I was doing O.K. with it but just as I got finished with my carbine & pistol the bulb burned out. Can't quite figure it

15 Louis Allen, *Burma: The Longest War, 1941–45* (London: Phoenix Press, 2000).

out. I've got the right voltage on it & I didn't bump it or anything. Anyway I'm writing this with my flashlight & it "ain't so good." . . .

. . . I spent 5 months in New Delhi where the "big shots" hang out but I had to come to Northern Burma to see the two "big shots" of the theater. In other words I've seen Lord Louie Mountbatten & General (Uncle Joe) Stilwell. Uncle Joe is around a lot in these parts but "Lord Louie" doesn't come around so much . . .

. . . Six months gone by & it seems like a lifetime. Not that the time has passed slowly but it seems such a long time ago since I left. I guess the toughest part of this separation is over. I'm sure I haven't spent half my time here as yet but every day brings me closer to home & you. I believe I have spent about 1/4 of the time I'll be here at this place already & it could be 1/3 or even 1/2 but the last is very doubtful . . .

I take note of the fact that Dad called Stilwell Uncle Joe. It wouldn't be likely that soldiers under Stilwell would call him Vinegar Joe, but Uncle Joe is more of an endearing term than Vinegar Joe, the nickname Chiang Kai-shek had given him. It seems that Stilwell treated soldiers under his direct command (whether they be American, Chinese, or Indian) with more kindness than he treated those outside of his immediate area—like the Chindits and Marauders.

July 2, 1944

My Dearest Gloria

. . . Guess I'd better get some repellent on before the "bug" gets me. Just a minute please. Well I got that over with. Messy stuff. I try to keep it off the paper but I don't do so good. It's powerful stuff. I've put some on me & then used my flashlight & the paint came off on my hands. Doesn't seem to bother the skin much except it burns a little when you put it on your face . . .

Been having a rainy spell again. For the last couple of days it's been pretty wet around here. I caught it just right, I washed a bunch of clothes about three days ago & it's still not dry . . .

. . . I've got an idea I'm going to gain some of the weight back. Been eating like a horse. The trouble is I don't ever seem to get enough to last me from one meal to another. I guess it's the outdoor life I'm leading. It's really outdoor too. Just a canvas roof on some bamboo poles with no sides. It's plenty good enough. All you really need is a roof . . .

[July] 5, 1944

Dearest Gloria

I guess I didn't do so good on my writing. It's been three days since I wrote the last letter, I'm sorry . . .

. . . What a place to celebrate the 4th of July or rather a place to celebrate. The day was no different from any other but I did get a sunburn. I went down by the river to wash some clothes & take a bath. It took me awhile to get my clothes washed and for once the sun was really hot. The sun was bright & there I was in the nude getting burned & I didn't realize it. It's not bad though, it feels a little warm & itches a lot. Maybe I'll get a good tan for a change. It should be very even, no white edges showing under swim trunks. It will probably will be all worn off by the time I get back.

Feeling sort of lonesome today. Being out here in this stinking jungle is no fun. I only hope it won't last too long. I guess the crack about the jungle isn't a true way of expressing myself. I'd feel the same way not matter where I was & in this frame of mind. Maybe it's because I miss you so much. You'll never know just what you've done to me. I don't regret it a bit, though. It's rather peculiar how things work out. Something that started so innocently has changed things for me so very much.

We've had two pretty nice days now, but I guess we can expect a lot more rain tomorrow. As I said before, I can take it pretty good now. I guess you can get used to most anything. I guess I could even get used to living with you. (supposed to be a joke) Forgive me, will you?

After such a queer collection in this letter you'll be wondering whether I've gone crazy & expect to see me in a strait jacket someday. I'd better get to bed now the rest of the boys are already in bed. So good night Baby & remember I love you so much.

All my love,

Jack

July 11, 1944

My Dearest Gloria

Several days have passed again since my last letter. Just can't get myself to write these days. Something always comes up to interfere. Last night I was Officer of the day, first time here. A good many evenings the fellows just sit around & discuss the war, etc. Just one interruption after another.

Seems like we're having a slack period in our monsoon. Hasn't rained much for the last several days. It did rain hard this morning for a while but it stopped in the middle of the morning & the sun came out. It's really a relief to get a little dried out for a change.

How do you like the war news these days? Good news all over for the past month or more. Too bad they can't see the handwriting on the wall & give up. A lot of lives would be saved & the cost of the war would be much less. Let's hope they will get wise pretty soon. It can't be too soon for me. I'd be ready to leave tonight for home. I know it's just wishful thinking but I listen to every news broadcast almost expecting to hear that it's all over. Seems like I miss you more every day. It's not that I dislike my work or am uncomfortable because I've got an easy job & it's work that I like. In fact I guess I'm just as well satisfied here as I have ever been. I wanted to come overseas & I wanted to get out into the combat zone so I couldn't be called a U.S.O. Commando & I got both. I won't have to be ashamed of my service in the Army on that score. I'm about in the worst spot in the world, will be glad when it's all over but I'm glad I'm here. I get filthy dirty so bad I can hardly stand myself but it will probably help me appreciate a few things better someday.

Being in a Signal unit we have good radio receivers, the best in the world, I guess & we take full advantage of what they have to offer as far as news & entertainment broadcasts are concerned. We're not too fussy who we listen to. Japanese, German, Indian, British, US and all. It's really funny to listen to the Axis broadcasts of news. They're still winning & have a good story for any defeat. I must say the music of the Axis stations is better than the Allied music. Seems funny to hear a piece come over the radio from a Japanese station played by one of the popular U.S. orchestras. Haven't heard any from Germany but they have good music & musicians of their own. The boys really get a laugh out of these Axis broadcasts. We hope they keep it up. They certainly help moral & not harming it any. So much for that . . .

Dad's letters came a little less frequently in July 1944. He also had the occasional assignment of being "officer of the day," a duty that was assigned to officers within a command on a rotating basis. It required that the officer handle administrative tasks and incidents that needed attention regardless of the time of day—all in addition to the officer's normal duties. The officer was typically assigned such tasks for a period of time such as twenty-four or forty-eight hours, after which he was relieved by the next duty officer listed on a roster. Additionally, there was plenty to do during the day, both in supply and repair, and keeping clothes clean and dry.

At night, it was difficult to write because of the lack of light. Dad often had to avoid writing after dark because any kind of light might become a beacon for an enemy attack or artillery fire. But although he was in the jungle during the monsoon season, supply and repair was a nice job for him and he wasn't up front like the infantry soldiers were—at least for now. He was also fortunate that, as the leader of a signal unit, he had access to a radio and the news—even broadcasts the Axis powers used to target GI listeners. These Axis broadcasts used improvised characters to deliver their messages. The Germans had Lord Haw-Haw and the Japs had Tokyo Rose. The purpose of these broadcasts was to demoralize soldiers in the field with negative spin and propaganda, but the GIs tended to disregard the disinformation and just listen to the music, as Dad indicated in his letter.

July 12, 1944

My Dearest Gloria

Mail came in today but none for me. Why all my mail comes in one bag about twice a month is beyond me. So I was turned away with my tongue hanging out while the rest of the boys read their mail.

Went for a ride yesterday over some of the roughest road I've ever been on. My back is still sore. You'd hardly believe your eyes when you see these G.I. trucks going through the Burma mud. No self-respecting truck would attempt some of the mud holes we went through. I had a driver from Minnesota by the name of Johnson & he was good. Good & rough but he got several tons of wire over this rugged path O.K. Sometimes I thought he would break the truck & myself in two. He used to drive a six-ton semi north of Minneapolis, so he knew just when to give her the guns. At times like those I'd think of how wonderful an invention the airplane is. Besides being almost crippled I got my arms sunburned (had my sleeves rolled-up like the farmer I am). Doesn't hurt much but it does spoil the lily white skin until it wears off. What a pity to be maimed by the sun when I could have avoided it simply by keeping my sleeves down in military fashion. I suppose you're wondering about me after an outbreak like that. Must be the jungle has got me already. They call it "getting jungle jolly" here . . .

July 20, 1944

My Dearest Gloria

Another period of several days has gone since my last letter. Don't seem to be able to arrange my habits to write every day.

The rain or monsoon has taken a turn for the worse today. It started to rain last night & it's still raining. It doesn't bother me much anymore. I've got a new method of keeping my stuff dry. Got myself a big wooden tight box & put a couple of bags of Silica Gel in around my stuff. It's a sort of a or rather a perfect drying agent. I'll probably have to dry the stuff out once in a while so it can gather up the moisture. I just hope it continues to work as good as it has. Can you smell the stuff on the paper? It's pretty strong now but it might air out before it gets there. All that about such a small item. At that rate I should be able to write a book . . .

Believe it or not, Dad, you did write a book.

July 22, 1944

My Dearest Gloria

Well, I only skipped one day this time. Who knows I might get back on the ball as far as writing goes . . .

. . . How about the war news these days? Almost too good to be true. If things keep happening as fast as they have in the past thirty days it won't be long now. This little Hitler deal although not unexpected is almost unbelievable. This uprising will either be stamped out in a hurry in short order or it will gain momentum. I've got an idea that it will develop into something because I believe the people are getting pretty receptive for something like that. Like a man drowning grasping at straws. I don't believe we've got the whole story as to what's going on as yet but here's hoping the next few week sees the Hitler Crowd wiped out . . .

Dad was referring to the attempted assassination of Hitler through a plot instigated by a cabal of high-ranking German officers. When Claus Schenk Graf von Stauffenberg placed his explosive-laden briefcase under the table next to Hitler at a meeting in Hitler's Wolfsschanze (Wolf's Lair) in East Prussia, many hoped the war would soon be over, but alas, events didn't turn out that way. Hitler received only minor injuries, and if anyone expected it to be part of an uprising, it never happened. Mass executions were staged all over German-held Europe, along with a well-publicized show trial, which discouraged anyone with seditious ideas from making any similar attempt. Even Field Marshal Erwin Rommel, arguably Germany's best commander, failed to escape retribution. He was forced to take cyanide in order to save his family.

Unfortunately, Dad was wrong about the "Hitler Deal," and his optimism about it gaining momentum was unwarranted.

> *. . . Things are also looking up "in the Pacific." With Tojo [Japanese General Hideki Tojo] gone & Guam invaded plus a few other developments it looks plenty good. Not entirely impossible for the war to be over by the end of the year. The only thing about it is that if it does end as soon as that I don't believe the Army of the two countries will feel they were really beaten. The military leaders will maintain they were sold out. Of course they will be kidding themselves & as far as I'm concerned I'd say "So what." I'm interested in getting the war ended & will do everything I can to do just that & in a way favorable to us but I'm also very interested in getting back to the good old* U. S. A. *& you. I never dreamed a person could miss something so much. It could only be another person & in my case, of course, it's you. As it looks now I might have been wrong as to the time I'd be back. It could very easily be that I've spent half of the total time over here already. How do you like that?*
>
> *The last couple of days it's been pretty wet around here. Looks like our little break in the monsoon has ended although it was pretty nice this afternoon & it's still not raining now (8:30 PM). Hope it lasts . . .*

Japanese Prime Minister Hideki Tojo had resigned on July 18, 1944 in the wake of the fall of Saipan. The big question was always how long the war would last. The final outcome was becoming clear, but when would the guns go silent? Dad made an astute observation: "If it does end as soon as that I don't believe the Army of the two countries will feel they were really beaten." This had been the case at the end of World War I; many in the German military had believed they were winning the war when the armistice was called, and harsh terms were issued to Germany. Never mind that in July 1944, the Japanese were already preparing their home islands for an invasion that would have killed millions, had it come to that. It was becoming obvious that neither Germany nor Japan would ever give up. They would have to be crushed.

July 24, 1944

My Dearest Gloria

I skipped another day so don't expect a letter dated July 23. I was going to write but just before I sat down to write I went out to check the boys working on our projector to see if they had everything working. Well it's the old story the machine went on the blink. We fixed it & were about to start the show when it started smoking again. By that time I was too disgusted to write. Tonight we got us a different projector so we should do O.K.

The first couple of weeks I was here I didn't know what to do with my time but the last week or so I've been plenty busy. Not too busy, just enough to keep me happy. Yep, I'm pretty well satisfied with the job now but I'm afraid I'm going to be idle again one of these days when the officer whose place I'm taking comes back. I'm just beginning to work into it too . . .

. . . My letters are getting worse every day. The jungle has got me for sure. I'll get over it quick though once I get out . . .

July 26, 1944

My Dearest Gloria

Skipped another day. I guess I'll never get back to the old habits on writing.

I'm starting this letter just before the movie & probably won't get it finished until after the show. Of course I'll take time out to see the show. I believe I'll stay in my basha & watch it from my bed. It's much more comfortable than sitting on the ground. Two nights ago we had "Show Business" here. A pretty good show. Eddie Cantor & Joan Davies. It was really a treat to see a good show for a change.

I'm writing with pencil tonight. Lost my pen. Yes, the Parker "51." I didn't lose it exactly. I was robbed the other night. Lost the pen, my billfold, a pen knife & nail clippers & I didn't lose any money to speak of but things that were more valuable than money. My billfold contained my A.G.O. pass, a [unintelligible] , Foreign money of all the countries I've passed through since I left, the darn thing was about ten feet long. Besides that it was signed by a lot of my friends & some pretty high-ranking officers. Tickets to my weapons, picture of you & several other articles I'll never be able to replace. If I ever catch a guy going through my stuff I going to shoot the bastard & I'm not kidding. I would have no trouble to get myself to do a thing like that out here. I might kill him but so what, he wouldn't deserve to live. Show started see you later Baby . . .

. . . In your letter of June 25 you break out with several questions. I'll try to give you the answers. You wonder what it's like here. I couldn't possibly tell you but it's not so good. No place for a white man at any rate. No, cigarettes are not giving me much trouble any more or maybe I'm getting used to them being damp. The mosquitoes are plenty bad. I've got bites all over me. I cover myself with dope, spray under my mosquito bar before I go to bed but I still get stung all over my arms & legs. I hope I don't have malaria in me. It wouldn't show up now because we take dope every day to prevent it from showing up. What do I do in the evenings. See show, join a bull session, once in a while I write you, listen to the news, etc. Is the camp close to town? What a silly question. Baby <u>we are in the jungle</u> & I mean the <u>jungle.</u> No women no

wine and no song out here, just plain work & we get only the bare essentials out here in this God forsaken hole. The movies & radio is the only things that keep us going. No P.X.s & the only thing we get that's not absolutely necessary is cigarettes and maybe once in a while one or two bottles of beer or a little candy. It's not so hot but we get along.

I'm getting terribly sleepy so I'll sign off for tonight. Remind me to ask you to send me a pen one of these days also to send it first class otherwise it will follow me home on the return trip.

Good night Baby. I miss you terribly tonight. I just can't tell you how much.

All my love

Jack

P.S. I [will] put a request for the pen in my next letter. A request that you can take to the Post Office without showing something personal.

From time to time, something got under Lt. Forster's skin and he went off. Having his stuff stolen was obviously one of those things.

Once Dad started writing his letters in pencil, they were harder to read. No one was looking forward to him finding a new pen more than I was. As for being in the jungle, he was in it for sure at this point. His job replacing another officer in supply and repair appeared to be at an end in late July, so he was transitioning into something else. Riding through the jungle with a load of wire a couple of weeks earlier may have been an indication of things to come for him. The Burma jungle was unfriendly to radio communication at times. The mountains and flora absorbed signals, especially during the monsoon. Plus, having messages intercepted was always a possibility with radio. In some situations, wire communication was the best and clearest way to communicate, especially while directing fire between forward observers and artillery units. It was an indication of what was to come for Lt. Forster.

July 27, 1944

My Dearest Gloria

I'm doing better on letter writing. I wrote last night & am at it again tonight. I'd better or else a certain little girl I love very much will start writing less letters. I hope she doesn't. I miss them so. Anyway, here goes with the second letter in two days.

Of course I told you about getting some things lifted the other night. I guess I can kiss it goodbye for good. It doesn't look like it will be found or the guy that lifted the stuff.

I've got something on my arm that's about to drive me crazy. Some sort of itch & I do mean itch. I've never had anything like it before. It's something like poison ivy I guess. Hope it will go away in a day or so. If it don't I'll be ready for a strait jacket in a few days. I'm writing in bed under my mosquito bar because I don't want to wear my shirt over the messy junk the pill rollers put on my arm of course I don't want to expose myself to the mosquitoes. Unhandy as hell writing this. Makes my neck sore.

What to write about. I can't tell you every move I make like you can. Even if I could there would be very little to say. Will I be glad when I don't have any more letters to write.

I suppose you've heard of the new Super Bomber the B-29. I saw a couple fly over the other day & believe me they are something. They make other ships look like toys. All silver & shiny. Quite a sight & I'm glad they are on our side.

The news is still good but I expect something unusual to happen one of these days. It's been about a week since the last spectacular news & it's about time for something to break loose again. It seems to run that way.

This position is getting so darn uncomfortable I'm going to cut it short for tonight.

Good night Gloria.

All my love

Jack

After this letter, it was more than ten days before Dad wrote again. In his next letter, he mentioned that he had been suddenly shifted to another job, which kept him extremely busy. During this period, he worked sixteen to eighteen hours a day. At one point, he became so exhausted that General Stilwell noticed and told him to take a rest on the General's own cot. Dad told me about that years later. War often requires men to give it all they've got, and this was one of those times for my dad.

About this time, Dad entered a phase where he was more engaged with the front and began following the railway that came northward from Rangoon and Mandalay, then northeast to Mogaung and Myitkyina. He started just southwest of Mogaung and headed southward along the rail line toward Mawlu and Indaw. Stilwell's Chinese were to the east of the railway and British General Francis Festing's 36th Indian Division was to the west—both headed south. Years later, he wrote, in a sheet intended for the veterans' publication *Ex-CBI Roundup*, "Had various assignments in the combat zone. The most memorable one was with the British 36th div. as artillery communications officer. A pretty tough assignment, as seldom a day went by when I wasn't subject to enemy fire. The reason for my being assigned there is I was able to do repair work myself."

He didn't tell Gloria about that assignment until it was all over. Years later, he told me about being ambushed by a Japanese machine gunner, bullets rattling in a bamboo stand just behind him and over his head. That time, it was a good thing he was short. Fortunately, his boys were able to liquidate that threat. But there was more to come, much of which he kept from loved ones back home.

Aug 6, 1944

My Dearest Gloria

I suppose you are slowly going mad wondering why you haven't heard from me. I am not at fault this time. I made a move out of my last job in sort of a hurry & since then I've been busier than I've ever been before. I can't tell you much about my job but I've worked miracles several times since I've been here. It's all communication out here. Wire, radio, messenger, everything but pigeons are used & I'm the only Signal Officer around. I have a small detachment of wire & radio men & when I say small I mean small. I guess no one anticipated the job or should I say the size of it when they sent us because I've never seen any soldier worked as hard as these boys are working. I'm putting in 16 to 18 hours per day myself. It's funny what you can stand once you get used to it. I don't mind much because I can clearly see where I'm helping to get the war over. I'm up forward now & can hear the big guns but am in no real danger. It's funny about this sort of work that is I didn't anticipate it to be like it is. I've probably said too much & will probably worry you but there is really no danger.

I've received no mail since I left but am expecting some any day now.

I've got to close now. I haven't written to my folks for some time so I'd better get at that. Good night Baby & I love you. I write as often as I can but don't expect too much. Please don't worry.

As Always—Jack

I don't believe the US Army Signal Corps trusted their pigeons' loyalty, although I do have a picture suggesting their use was being contemplated. In the photo, Dad stands with some other officers as they gaze at a cage full of pigeons. As it turns out, pigeons were indeed used effectively in Burma.

Dad finally admitted in his letters to being "up forward." Months later, when this job was over, he admitted that he had occasionally been ahead of the infantry, often stringing wire to forward observers who'd call in artillery barrages onto Japanese positions. Still, he took great pains to reassure Gloria. At this point, however, he'd probably said too much, and I'm not sure his attempts to reassure her were working anymore.

Signal Corps Pigeons

Burma
Aug 18, 1944

My Dearest Gloria

I must write on your birthday even though I'm out of spare time. I've had practically no time for myself since I've been on this new assignment. I really don't mind it very much because time goes by so quickly. Something that helps a lot when you're away so far. I wouldn't like to miss this phase of my military career but I'd hate to have to go through it all again.

Getting back to your birthday. I'm sorry I cannot send you some little gift but the rice paddies & jungles have very little to offer. I'll do my best to make it up to you for the rest of my life.

I'm really seeing things out here these days. I've seen all kinds of dead Japs & some not so dead but captured with guards over them. Am also picking up a few little items which I intend to bring home in memory of this little tour of duty. I'll really have something to tell after I get back. I hope people will be able to believe it. It's all so different than I had anticipated. Not near as terrible but it is plenty tough & hard work. I've improvised & studied to make communications better & am really pleased with the success we have realized from all the little things I have added to our original setup. Sometimes we have almost worked miracles out here. Sometimes I would have sworn the system would break down but by hook or crook we would keep it operating.

I haven't received any mail since I got out here. I believe you are still writing. I shouldn't even doubt that, I know you are. Won't it be swell when we won't have to write letters.

The weather around here has been plenty hot. It's O.K. though. I'd rather have the hot sun than the rain. The rain makes it pretty rough when you haven't got anything but a jungle hammock over your head. The darn things are a lot more comfortable than you would think. I've never heard of anyone falling out of one.

I've got to cut this short. I've been interrupted too often. Sometimes a phone is not so good.

So long for now. I'll write when I can & I do hope I get some mail. Don't worry about me, I'm O.K. Remember I love you Baby & am just living for the day when I can return to you.

All my love
Jack

There were no letters between August 6 and August 18, and none between August 18 and August 30. Working up to eighteen hours a day during the monsoons in a place where using lights at night can give away your position to enemy artillery was not conducive to frequent writing.

The phones Dad referred to were not from any established civilian network—they were only for use within the local command structure. Radio communication was always part of the communication repertoire but is not necessarily a good thing in terms of reception and security, so Dad and his boys strung a lot of wire every time they moved.

An ad in LIFE Magazine showing the Signal Corps in action, stringing wire. (LIFE Magazine)

Burma
Aug 30

My Dearest Gloria

By now you must surely suspect I've forgotten about you. I've never seen anything like what we've been through the past month. A full gallop pace all the time & believe me I'm tired. Absolutely played out. From morning until night there were constant calls, requests & details to be attended to by a certain young (getting older fast) Lt. Actually I've been right up where the fighting was going on & being the only Signal Officer here the load was terrific. I can tell you all this now because it's all over so there is no need to worry.

As I said before I have a small detachment of men here to keep communications available for a certain unit. Believe me these boys have gone through hell for the past several weeks. I've had to work but was comparatively safe. The boys on the other hand did hard physical labor in addition to being sniped at, run into machine guns, mortar shells & even hand grenades. By the way five of these boys are getting citations for different things they have done since they have been out with me. Another one is being recommended for a promotion of two grades which will make him Staff Sgt. As for the danger I've been in there isn't much to say. I was under artillery fire several times but the nearest one to me was about 75 yards. It's funny but it didn't seem to scare me at all. Actually I've been too damn busy to let it bother me. Can't quite understand it now that it's all over. The little yellow devils were trying to kill us & we just kept working along as though it was a ball game & we had nothing to lose except being humiliated with a lower score. Several times at first bullets would cut grass all around us, strays I guess but no one was hit. Surprising how much stuff can fly around without anyone being hit. As I mentioned before we are getting a rest now & all the danger has passed. I still can't figure out why some of my boys were not killed but they all came out of it without a scratch, just tired & scared. One of them was in pretty bad shape one day when a British boy lying right next to him was killed but his nerves are back to normal again. Why do I tell you all this when it would be better left unsaid. (Borrowed a pen which ran out of ink & now the color changed when I refilled, must have been different ink).

Getting back to writing letters, I can honestly say that time was almost entirely lacking. I mean spare time in the daylight hours & after dark I couldn't very well write because lights had to be kept down low & used only where necessary. Even so I used to have to censor mail by flashlight.

This letter has been written in several different parts during the afternoon. Right now I'm just finishing my chow. Got a cup of tea here (I've been drinking lots of tea since I've been here. We get mostly British rations & K rations).

Anyway I've seen my share of mud, fox holes, dead Japs (God how they stink) & everything. Had a good time though. I can't truthfully say I'm glad to have gone through it all, at least I won't have to be ashamed of my service overseas.

Well I've got to close now & get a letter off to my folks.

Good night Baby & don't worry about me. I'm plenty safe & fairly happy now. I'd be much happier if I were with you because I love you so much.

As always
Jack

Reading that he didn't seem to be scared by bullets and artillery rounds landing near him, I remembered something Dad had said several times over the years. He would say that when those things were happening, his attitude was more like "ha, ha, you missed me"—those would be his exact words—and then think nothing of it. He said it became real to him as he reflected upon it months and years later. That's when he realized that he could have been killed—much like how one of his boys "was in pretty bad shape one day when a British boy lying right next to him was killed" but soon got over it. It's strange how the human mind can make accommodations to danger in the moment, allowing a person to function. But post-traumatic stress is a real thing, and such events can come back on a soldier years later with frightening effect.

Burma
Sunday Sept 2

My Dearest Gloria

Not quite so long between letters this time. Maybe I can keep it that way for a while. Stationery is going to be a problem one of these days. It just doesn't grow on the trees out here. Although I'm in a Burma village now things like that are unavailable. None of these villages are anything but bamboo huts huddled together. Each one has a name & when you look at them on the plots & maps you'd swear there was something there but when we get the Japs out we find the same old story, dead Japs by the dozens, bomb craters, shell holes & practically everything destroyed. You just can imagine what our shells & bombs do to these places. Some of the bomb craters are about thirty feet across & about twenty feet deep. Those babies really make a racket when they go off. I've been within about 500 yards of where they were dropped & added to the explosions there is sort of a ripping sound. Once you hear a bomb you remember the sound, it's much different from shells or mortar fire. The shells whistle overhead & then explode with a bang distinctly different from the bombs. We have had a little shelling (ours) at night & those old babies sound like a freight train as they go over (Sometimes our guns are behind us & fire over our heads. They sound good when they go that way but when you hear them come the other way it's not so comfortable) Had that experience the first night I came here. I've got a carbine & pistol & was just cleaning the guns when I heard a gun in the distance & several seconds later a sort of a wobbling whistle & an explosion. Didn't quite know what to make of it but finally it dawned on me that the bastards were shooting at us. Well for about a half hour I'd get up, start cleaning again, hear a gun, listen till I heard a whistle & then duck. The funny part of it is it didn't scare me just about getting up to bat at a stiff baseball game, in fact I believe I've been a lot more nervous at a ball game. You listen to a few of them and before long you can about tell where they will hit. Nope they are not near as terrible as I imagined them. Anyway it's all over now & I can't say I'm too sorry although it never did worry me much. I was a little peeved one night when they opened up in the middle of the night & kept me awake. We finally got a bearing on them & sent a couple of big ones back in the general vicinity of the gun & they shut up in a hurry. Lovely when you're on the winning side. Actually this whole business is so much like a ball game or some other competitive sport. My place is in a command post & as the reports come in you sort of add up the score, watch the plans being made for the attack & then wait to see if everything goes according to schedule. The timing is really something sometimes a matter of seconds between incidents in this game. Between bombing , artillery fire & of course at a certain moment the Infantry rushes in to take the area just blasted. All very interesting & bloodthirsty. You get hardened to all sorts of things. Dead bodies don't phase anyone anymore. There are any number of Jap skeletons within 100 ft of where I'm sitting now. They did stink a little when we moved in here so we buried the newer ones & left the ones pretty well on the way lying there. They seem so much like animals that only the smell is the only thing that bothers you. Enough of that, I've probably upset you now but it's really nothing, we joke about these things as you would about any everyday occurrence at home . . .

. . . This letter had an interruption in it tonight, had to take time out for a steak. No kidding, I did have a pretty fair steak. One of the boys went out & killed a water buffalo & it was plenty good after K rations. I'm going out one of these days with a bunch of hand grenades & see if I can get some fresh fish. Just throw a

couple in the water & let the concussion bring the fish to the top.

These Burma nights are beautiful, the moon is just coming over the hills & the Burma moon is like no other. I like to watch it come up & start dreaming like we all do these days. Which reminds me the war news is wonderful. It looks like the war with Germany will be over in a few days or no more than a few weeks.

Well, Baby, I'm writing this with my flashlight & the mosquitoes are about to eat me up so I'd better end this.

I can't tell you how much I love you Baby & I miss you terribly. Good night, Baby & please don't worry I'm in no danger.

All my love
Jack

Burma
Sept 6, 1944

My Dearest Gloria

Doing O.K. now as far as letter writing goes, or am I. Not quite every day yet & I'm afraid those letter per day days are over for the time being at least.

I'll try to make this letter a bit less gruesome than my last one. I don't know what to talk about other than the things happening around me & now there isn't anything happening. I do anticipate going back to my base to see my boss one of these days. At that time I expect to be able to pick up some little items like stationery, flints, a couple of quarts of liquor, etc. for my boys & myself. Help the [morale] a lot. The boys are O.K. though, seem to be enjoying themselves O.K. In fact I believe they like it better out here than they did with their regular unit. I get a big kick out of this job here. Most of my work in the past has been in staff work & I never had more than a clerk or two working for me but this is different. You can never appreciate what it is like to have a detachment or unit more or less to yourself. Enough of that for now.

We've been having our share of rain in the last couple of months.

It should start letting up but as yet there are no signs of it doing that. Seldom a day passes that it doesn't rain, sometimes just a drizzle & sometimes a downpour. It doesn't bother us too much anymore. We have gotten used to the weather & how to get along more comfortably. These jungle Hammocks are a life saver. They have rubber tops to keep the rain out, mosquito bar on the side that zips shut & a couple of loops underneath for the rifle & clothes. They are more comfortable than you'd imagine, in fact I guess they are more comfortable than a canvas cot. Guess I'll have to have my picture taken in one to give you an idea of what they are like. Speaking of the rifle, I have mine under the darn thing but I keep my .45 Automatic inside with me. I wouldn't like to have to reach under it to get the gun in a hurry. There is a story going around that an army photographer was sleeping in a Command Post of one of the Chinese Divisions when a couple of Japs woke him up. They were getting a little too hungry so they decided to give up & picked this guy way inside of a camp to surrender to. They also picked an American because the Chinese would have polished them off. Anyway even though they are ready to give up, I still would feel better if I had several .45 slugs available in case I needed them. (I borrowed a pen & it ran out of ink so I finish it with this stub).

Mosquitoes are terrible tonight. I've killed a half dozen within a few minutes. Hope none are carrying malaria & if they do I won't come down with it. There isn't much of it around but once in a while I do lose a boy for a week or so with malaria. Hope the US Army has this malaria pretty well under control. I'd say 50 years ago it would have been impossible to carry on a campaign here during this part of the year. I believe that is what is knocking hell out of the Japs here because I haven't seen a really healthy Jap out here. I saw one that wasn't so bad but most of them are too far gone to really know what's going on. The healthy ones don't surrender, I guess.

I haven't received the package you sent about four months ago or the fountain pen you mentioned but I've got another request to make. How about getting some flints for my lighter. Just send them in a letter. I expect to be able to pick some up but I'm not sure about it & I'm almost out. I don't know how I'd get along without my lighter here. Matches never stay dry long enough to work . . .

Mosquitoes and malaria were always a concern in the jungles of Burma. Dad mentions that it was "knocking the hell" out of the Japanese, and indeed I saw in a documentary once in a postwar interview with a Japanese soldier who confirmed that they didn't have the medicines to combat malaria that the allies had.

For Dad, this was everyday life in the jungle. Reading what he writes about, it sounds mundane except for the dead guys, the malaria, and getting shot at, not to mention the incoming and outgoing artillery passing overhead—and learning to distinguish between the two—and distinguishing between the explosions of bombs and artillery. All very . . . normal?

Burma
Sept 13, 1944

My Dearest Gloria

Well, Baby I just received some of your recent letters & feel that I've been told off in pretty good shape. I realize now how selfish I've been. I'd really go up in the air if you would write the same kind of letter that I wrote you. You probably did too but sort of toned it down in your letters. Anyway I'm terribly sorry & will make an honest effort to do better. In any case don't get the idea because I don't write every day that I love you less than before . . .

. . . You were right about my getting close to the Japs. I was within a couple of hundred yards from the front lines for a while but now I'm quite a long way from any fighting Japs. Even when I was close I never saw a fighting Jap. Just dead ones & prisoners. I never was in much danger but there was a chance in a hundred maybe not even that much. We have no American casualties, no man even wounded. I will say some of the boys were lucky but as

far as myself I guess I've been closer to getting hurt or killed at home. A lot of stuff can fly around & hit no one. Then again a little splinter of steel will knock off a man. The story is told around here of a shell hitting right in a large group of men. Lot of fragments flew through the air but only one man was hit & this one killed instantly. At first they thought the concussion killed him but they later found a tiny particle of steel in his heart. He could have been hit in any other part of his body & probably would never have gone any further than an aid station to get fixed up but I guess his number was up. The same could have happed at home or in the rear area. The only real mean thing about being up so near to the front is the living conditions & you move so often . . .

. . . Now for the war news. The boys are doing O.K. Ten miles inside the Siegfried Line is plenty O.K. This line was supposed to be like a stone wall but maybe we've got something to break down walls. Japs also took a pound yesterday. How they can have anything afloat any more seems pretty hard to understand. The whole war seems to be well planned & the plans are working. Another week or two for Germany & no more than a year for Japan. Japan could fall any time because this is the first time in their history that they were up against it. We have no way [to know] how they will react under these circumstances. So if things end quickly & I'm not stuck on some Army of Occupation job it might not be too many months before I'll be back . . .

I can't say Good night because it's only 3 o'clock & the sun is still high in the sky so I'll just say so long until my next letter.

All my love

Jack

P.S. I guess I'll have a bottle of beer with one of my Sgts. Yep got my first case in three months yesterday.

Burma
Sept. 22, 1944

My Dearest Gloria,

Got a little time to spare so I might as well waste it on you. I'm glad I'm 15,000 miles away after a crack like that. Can't quite reach out & hit me can you? This is almost as much fun [as] making faces at people along the road as you drive by. That's alright you'll probably forget about being sore by the time I get back. At least I hope so . . .

. . . I'm lazy today. No ambition whatsoever. I'm glad I don't have anything rushing to do because I just don't feel like doing anything. Nope I'm not sick so maybe I <u>am</u> sick. I certainly am sick of Burma & the jungles. What I couldn't do now in any good old U.S. town. I've been bored to death in some of the spots I've been in but I certainly would like to be bored a little one of these days again. We're located in a little village in Burma & the fellows kid each other about going down to the "Blue Goose" & tearing up the place. They dream up imaginary incidents that supposedly happened in this imaginary "Blue Goose" the night before. They dream up some good ones. The jungle's got the boys. They are getting "jungle Jolly" as we call it out here. Nothing serious but they have been out here eight or nine months & that's pretty long . . .

Burma
Sept 24, 1944
Sunday

My Dearest Gloria

Here goes for another one of those crazy letters. Probably will end up like yesterday's letter. Yep, been writing three days in a row now. Am I forgiven now? Can I come home & walk in without throwing my hat in first? You'll probably say yes & then be waiting with a club. No I guess I'll stay in Burma for a while yet. Who knows, you might cool off a little in a couple of years (I'll probably get a good reply to this one). By the way I haven't received any mail for about a week now. Who's slipping now? Don't give me that stuff that it's probably held up some place. You know that in the past that I've been getting my mail regularly from two weeks to two months or more old. All kidding aside the mail has been pretty slow at times but in the last month or so I guess it's better than ever before.

Burma is beautiful today. Sun is shining & everything is fresh & green. Beautiful? To hell with it. I guess it would be beautiful if only one thing weren't lacking. A four lane highway with a town every couple of miles & a large city less than an hour's ride away. All little things that people take for granted in the States. The boys certainly ought to learn what they really mean.

I missed Mass this morning. We called & they told us Mass would be at 8:30 but instead it was at 8:00, so—. Don't get the idea that because we have Mass here regularly that we're living in town some place. A couple of weeks ago the Japs had this village & everything we have, except a couple of broken down bashas, we brought with us.

End of the paper coming up, so I'll have to quit. Take it easy Baby. I still love you as much as ever if not more.

All my love
Jack

There was a slack period of fighting in the jungle, and Jack, after being chastised by Gloria, once again tried to be more faithful in his writing. It appears that fighting in the jungle was all about five days of boredom punctuated by ten minutes of terror. Who could blame the soldiers for getting a little "jungle jolly" during the boring times?

Burma
Sept 28, 1944

My Dearest Gloria

I skipped a couple of days again. Nothing to write anyway but I suppose you'd appreciate them even if I don't say anything . . .

. . . I finally got that package you sent for my birthday. First of all I want to thank your Mother for the cigarette case. I didn't need it for the awhile after I made my original request but now it's coming in handy. My old one is getting worn in spots. Yep a very thoughtful & useful gift. Everything else was plenty O.K . . .

. . . The subject of leave is starting to be brought out into the open. Maybe if I'm a good boy I might get to go back to Delhi or someplace for a couple of weeks. They won't give you enough time to go home & even if they did I'd almost hesitate a little. It's a helluva trip & how I'd hate to leave again to come out here. Maybe the end of the war will come soon enough so we won't be too old to enjoy life together . . .

. . . Well Baby I'm about out of subjects so I'd better end this thing. I've got to clean my guns today. They get rusty fast out here in this damp jungle.

Take it easy baby & I hope you'll continue to like your new place. Also thanks again for the package. I'm sorry I couldn't return with me a little item for your birthday. I'll make it up some day. All I can do now is say that I love you.

As always
Jack

Burma
Oct 1, 1944

My Dearest Gloria

How do you like it? Pretty good isn't it? I mean my new Parker pen. Yep it arrived last night. I really tickled pink when it came. I'm really fixed up now. A darn good pen, pencil & all kinds of leads. I can get ink here for the time being. I actually like this pen better than I did my "51." The darn things are not all they're cracked up to be. I showed the set to the officers around here & they were surprised that stuff like that was still available & wondered how I got it. I came back at them saying, "Aw she's a great girl." I really appreciate this an awful lot & I don't know how to thank you . . .

. . .Got some more "shots" today. Didn't bother me much as yet. I don't expect to have much trouble with them. It's better to put up with the shots & some of the preventatives than put up with the diseases that you run into out here. I guess it's the worst place in the world as far as living conditions go. There has been quite a little said about troops serving out here & that rotation is to be really put into effect. Two years is a great plenty & I believe it should be cut down a lot more. About one year or at the most eighteen months is enough. I've already got 9 months. 8 or 9 months wouldn't be too bad. Of course I'm ready now but I'm afraid that's impossible.

Well, it looks like the monsoons are about over. The sun is out real bright today & it hasn't rained much during the last couple of days. The only difficulty or should I say physical discomfort is the heat. It gets hot as hell when the rain stops. You should see me today. I've got a pair of British slacks cut down for shorts. A pair of British canvas shoes & nothing else. Looks like hell but I'm comfortable & simplifies the clothes-washing problems. Maybe I shouldn't complain about washing clothes because at present I'm not washing my own clothes. Yep we got a native that came out of the hills after the Japs left to do these things for us. Yep, we're getting pretty fancy now. The boys are even building an Officers mess tent this afternoon. Just give us a little time & we'll at least try to make ourselves comfortable.

The news has been sort of slow the last week or so. Not doing too much right now. That's the time to start expecting something. The boys in Europe will probably start rolling again before long. Seems like the war isn't quite over yet. I have a feeling I'll get home before the end yet. I'd rather have it the other way but—.

Burma
Monday
Oct 2, 1944

My Dearest Gloria

It's getting so I've got to write you about every day. I sit down to write letters & it never fails, I start one to you. The trouble is if I only write one the rest of the people have to wait.

Got three letters yesterday. The latest one dated 19 Sept. And by the way I see you're starting to flirt with strangers. Bad enough to start things with old friends but strangers. Looks like I'll have to go AWOL to protect my interests at home. If it wasn't so impossible I guess a lot of fellows would go over the hill to keep the gals at home straightened out. I feel I can trust you so I won't take the chance. It's a pretty long swim anyway. So considering the fact that I can't swim, you're safe . . .

. . . Read an article in the July 3 issue of "Life," the issue with all the color tricks, etc. in it. There's an article in it "Joe is home now." I think it's pretty true to life & the things he experiences I believe are typical. Of course all of us won't be maimed. I don't expect to be . . .

Dad wrote Mom about an article he had read in *Life* magazine describing the story of a GI who had been in Africa, lost his left arm in combat, and was returning home. The article follows "Joe" on his train trip to his hometown of Onteoga, New York. It describes his fear of going home in his condition, his worry about how his family, his girl, and the town will react, what he'll do dealing with people and life, in general, and how he'll make a living. He suffers bouts of bitterness and anger, especially at first. The story is a bit dark and shows the struggles, both emotional and physical, of a man maimed in combat.[16] It is a stark account of what many soldiers faced upon returning home, whether disabled or whole. It also shows the

16 John Hersey, "Joe is Home Now," *Life* 17, no. 1 (July 3, 1944):p 68–80.

frustrations of dealing with civilians and the difficulties of trying to communicate what war was like—what it all meant to the soldiers who fought it. The article shows how impossible it was for returning soldiers to relate their stories adequately. I'm sure Dad read that article and wondered what it would be like for him when he finally returned home.

Burma
Oct 8, 1944
Sunday

My Dearest Gloria

I guess I'd better dash off a note today. Haven't written for several days now. By the way I haven't received any for about a week either. I've been fairly busy the last couple of days so Baby got left out in the cold. Yep the Col told me the other day to build a couple of showers, etc. so I built a super duper. Getting pretty classy. Used to go down to the river but the river we have here is always muddy & washing out of a helmet is not so hot. It's funny what you can do with an old gas drum & a few bits of pipe & tin cans. I'd say we've [got] the best showers in this neck of the woods. After all look who built them.

Everything is about the same out here. It does rain a little once in a while but the monsoons seem to be ending. Gets pretty hot when it's not raining. I'm usually running around with just a pair of British shorts on. Getting a pretty good tan & you should see my hair, it's getting lighter every day. It's bleaching out not getting gray. By the way I didn't think it's getting any thinner in case you're interested . . .

Burma
Oct, 15, 1944

My Dearest Gloria

O.K. so I'm late about writing again. I have been pretty busy for the last couple of days again so—. I've got work to do now but I'll just let it wait. I probably will be pretty busy for the next couple of weeks but after that I'm getting a new job which should give me some free time . . .

. . . The mail situation ain't so good now. About the first mail I had in a week or more. It's a good thing we don't have a regular mail call every day. The hardest thing in the world is to be at mail call & not get any mail. As it is I usually get a couple of letters every time mail comes in. Makes me happy because as a rule they are from you. The letters arrived yesterday in the morning & I didn't get to read them all until late in the afternoon. Every time I get started to read them I'd be interrupted by some silly "Bloke" (British influence) That's BOO HOW (Chinese influence). BOO HOW means bad. Yes, I've worked with all of them British, Indians & Chinese. I do expect to get back where everything is strictly American before long. Besides that I guess I'll get my old repair job back. That will be tekha (Indian influence). It means good. Giving you a lesson on foreign languages this afternoon. Just remember them all and the lesson will be a success . . .

. . . Don't know what to say. Guess I'll talk about the war. Nice pleasant subject or is it? News still sounds O.K. The good news always makes me use it as a gauge for the end of the war. Not a good idea because as you probably have noticed, usually we make a big push & things look wonderful and you expect to have the armies keep moving for the next couple of months as fast as they moved during a few days. In other words if they move ten miles in one day you can't expect them to keep up a ten mile a day average until they get into Berlin. As a rule they don't or at least they haven't yet. So they make a big push & then settle down for a couple of weeks again Well one of these days it will be the last push & it will be all over. Do I make myself clear? I didn't think so. The Japanese situation in the Pacific looks very good but in China it's BOO HOW. Something stinks a little bit there. Sometimes these Chinese amaze you one way

& then the other. One day you'd say they are "bloody" good soldiers & the next day you cuss them out. I can't figure them out . . .

The Chinese had been fighting the Japanese in their own country since 1937, so the war was getting to be very long for them. Early in the war, the Chinese suffered one of the worst massacres in history at the hands of the Japanese in what was called the "Rape of Nanking." Aside from that, Chiang Kai-Shek was looking ahead to his eventual fight against Mao and the Communist insurgency he had been dealing with since even before the war. I wouldn't blame him for being both a little war-weary and for wanting to let the Limeys and Yanks do it as far as fighting the Japanese was concerned.

Japan, despite quickly losing ground in the Pacific and losing virtually its entire navy, was advancing against Chinese forces in Eastern China. The American 14th Air Force had been sinking Japanese shipping in the South China Sea and had even been attacking Japan's home islands from bases in Eastern China. Because of this, the Japanese dedicated about 250,000 troops to pushing the Americans out of those bases, and the US lost B-29 bases in China as a result. In a way, this vindicated the Allies' efforts to supply China with military aid and occupy Japanese military resources in places other than in the Pacific.

Many of the soldiers that Dad had fought alongside in Burma were the Chinese troops Stilwell trained at Ramgarh, India, after he was run out of Burma in 1942. There was only a small contingent of American soldiers with Dad, and a few Indian troops, including Chinese artillery units to support the British and Indian infantry. The vast majority of soldiers with Stilwell himself were Chinese, but there was also Festing's British 36th Division, composed primarily of British and Indian troops with British leadership. Dad spent much of his time in the jungle with the British 36th.

Although Dad's duty was not as severe as that of the Chindits and the Marauders, it was still necessary to receive supplies by air, and Dad told me that the brigade he was with was often resupplied by airdrop. Dad once told me of an occasion when the airdrop included bags of rice being dropped without parachutes and a "Chinaman" was killed while trying to catch a bag thrown from a C-47 aircraft. They were, after all, living and fighting in the jungle with limited roads, most of which were impassible during the monsoon. Fortunately, Dad was with Stilwell's larger main force and Festing's British 36th Division; unlike the Galahad Force or the Chindits, they were supported by bigger numbers, artillery, vehicles of different types, and all the other things that regular infantry units are comprised of. Therefore, they were much better able to face the enemy head-on.

Burma
Oct 22, 1944

My Dearest Gloria

Another letter for you today. It has been several days since I wrote last. Been pretty busy. I'm still looking forward to getting a little further back where the hours are a little more regular. I'm not close enough to be in any danger but just close enough to be unable to have lights at night, So—.

Almost broke my nose yesterday morning. In fact I believe I did crack a bone but it's still in place so I guess it's O.K. I might keep a little scar to remind me of it. I tripped over a telephone wire. I was carrying my helmet in my hand & fell on the darn thing. So much for that. It still is plenty sore & a little swollen. It really made me see stars for a few minutes. No, I wasn't drunk. The British linemen left the wire going to our exchange on the ground. Didn't do anything about it even though everyone was falling over it. Well it didn't take long for them to get it off the ground after I got done telling them to get the darn thing fixed. I got pretty hot after I came out of being stunned.

By the way you can tell your friends that I finally made the grade. Yep 1st Lt. Forster now.

Almost two years to the day, or should I say two years almost to the day [since receiving his commission]. I don't know what day I made it as I've not received the official orders yet, just a radiogram. I guess it's not impossible anymore to be coming home with Captain's bars on. Yes, it made me pretty happy even though I had been expecting it for some time. It's funny how those things leak out. I only hope the men I have with me get theirs. It's a little unusual for officers to get promoted before the Enlisted Men out here but it did happen. You just can't keep a good man down. Boy I hate myself . . .

Japanese Invasion Money – Shows the optimism of the Japanese Army for their invasion of India

Nov, 1, 1944

My Dearest Gloria

Quite a few days since my last letter. About a week I'd say. Been plenty busy again & it looks like it might continue for some time. I'm still with the same outfit as I was for the past three months but it's not as "hot" as it was. The Japs are not fighting back much. The bastards are running so fast that we have a hard time keeping up. This fast moving is plenty tough, believe me. Still I guess it's much better than when they fight back.

Got bad news again. I lost the top off the Parker pen. I'm afraid I won't find the darn thing either. I might be able to get some sort of a top off an old pen I hope.

Another piece of news I have isn't so bad. Yep, I won a medal. I've been awarded the Bronze Star. Nothing very much. Something like the Good Conduct Medal. They threw quite a number of them around in this little war we have down here. Nobody got anything more though. It might help me get out of this part of the world a little sooner. Also out of the army after the war with Germany is over.

By the way, I was made 1st Lt. on the 16th of Oct. Just two days before I had two years as a 2nd Lt. Can't say I was 2nd Lt. for two years.

I'm writing this by flashlight, sitting on a Jap "Bunker" (A hole in the ground with logs & ground over it. Hard as hell to see from a distance & hard to get the Japs out of. The place is full of these bunkers but the Japs don't seem to be using them anymore. I wouldn't either. They really smell & are full of mud & filth.

It's still getting cooler at night. I almost froze last night. I've only got one blanket with me & it gets pretty cold. I finally put my raincoat over the blanket & then it was plenty warm (Just had our artillery open up to sort of worry the Japs & I almost jumped out of my shoes. Had no idea they were about to shoot. Noisy devils . . .)

. . . I'm sending a little Jap money this time. They use this in

Burma. It has no value as it's invasion money & you'll notice the Japanese Gov. promises nothing on the paper. I've got a few other little things I've picked up but I hesitate sending them because they might get lost.

I guess I'd better close now & write my folks. Haven't written them for a week or more.

Good night Baby & don't worry if you don't get letters every day. It's pretty hard to get to write them these days. Just remember I love you & miss you.

All my love
Jack

Dad described his being awarded the Bronze Star as something akin to receiving a "good conduct medal" in his letter to Mom. I don't know if he was trying to minimize the danger he'd faced or whether such valor was so commonplace that nobody thought much of it. The citation was written on October 12, 1944:

Second Lieutenant Louis J. Forster, 01637436, Signal Corps, Army of the United States. For Heroic and Meritorious Service in Combat in North Burma from 29 July to 28 August 1944. During this period Lt. Forster was Communications Officer for a Corps Artillery Group. With Inadequate Personnel and at the almost constant risk of his life he maintained his organization communication system. His personal supervision and repair of the system at all hours of the day and night under enemy artillery and small arms fire was an inspiration to his men. As a result of his efficient leadership and heroic efforts, forward observers always had at least one means of communication available in order to give prompt support to the infantry. Lt. Forster's efforts assisted greatly in accomplishing a successful coordination of Infantry and artillery.

By command of General Stilwell:

Dad and his crew had worked very hard, often many hours a day. General Stilwell was widely known as Vinegar Joe in the press and diplomatic circles, and it was the "Vinegar" part that his superiors usually felt. But to men under his direct command, he was known as Uncle Joe. Although he achieved remarkable results in the field—some would say at the expense of many good men—he had ruffled the feathers of too many higher-ups.

Nov 7, 1944

My Dearest Gloria

Just a note before lunch. Hope I won't be interrupted too many times. Hardly five minutes go by without someone calling for me. So many little things. Someone wants two flashlight batteries or some darn fool thing & they call me away from what I'm doing because it's more convenient for them. What makes me sore is that they probably are not doing a thing themselves at the time & could come to me. Yep I'm really fed up with this crowd. The only compensation I've got is that they got me a promotion & were responsible for me getting the Bronze Star.

Got quite a little mail the other day. I didn't get to read them until about a day later, that is all of them (about ten) because I'm just a little too busy . . . I've moved so darn much since I've been in the Army that when I get a home to settle down I'll probably stay in the same spot for the rest of my life. I hope it will be soon. I've seen all I want to see of Burma & all the rest of the world except home of course . . .

. . . Did you see the news about "Uncle Joe" Stilwell being relieved? I wonder how it will affect us here. There probably will be a slight change in policies, there always is when a new man takes over. I've seen D. I. Sultan [Dad's new CO] many times in Delhi but don't know much about him . . .

As much as General George C. Marshall had wanted Stilwell to take the command in the CBI at the outset of World War II, Stilwell's negatives finally caught up to him. Chiang Kai-shek had almost constantly lobbied Roosevelt to relieve him, and Stilwell had worn out his welcome with Mountbatten as well—Mountbatten accused him of abusing and neglecting both Calvert's Chindit brigade and the Galahad Force. Col. Hunter, who had taken command of Galahad in General Merrill's absence, had called the Marauders "the most beat-upon, mishandled, most heroic, most unrewarded regimental-sized unit in World War II."[17] Although Stilwell's leadership in the field was the main factor in winning back Northern Burma and keeping China in the war, his negatives ultimately did him in. Peanut finally got his way and convinced Roosevelt to relieve Stilwell.

Nov 21, 1944

My Dearest Gloria

I've been putting this letter writing behind too many things again. Almost two weeks since my last letter. Every day I say to myself, "Well tomorrow I've got to write," tomorrow comes & goes & no letter. How do you put up with me? I still get your letters regularly. They always are very welcome but sometimes I don't get a chance to read them for hours after I get them.

Not much news here. I did get a touch of malaria the other day & felt pretty tough but I'm O.K. now. Can't hear so good but that wears off after I stop taking quinine. I was lucky I got it I guess. Some day you might ask me how getting malaria may have saved my life. Yep I'm fully convinced that if I was feeling well I would have been in a little Jeep incident in which the driver was killed & I would have been the driver, I always drive myself. Now I ain't got no Jeep & one man less. Good lad, too. I might have been able to avoid it had I been along but I don't know for sure. Someday I'll give you all the details. I'm sure I'll never forget them. Believe me it shook me plenty.

It's getting pretty cool these days. It's about five o'clock & I'm already wearing a field jacket & don't feel overheated. The rains

17 Jonathan Martin, director, *Secrets of World War II*, season 1 episode 22, "Merrill's Marauders," aired May 28, 1998, BBC Worldwide.

have really stopped, the dust is pretty bad but nothing like the mud . . .

. . . I've been transferred to another outfit. I'm now in the 988th Sig Operation Cr. Apparently it's just a paper transfer because I've still got my old job. I do expect to lose it any day now though, I hope. Expect to get a little leave after I leave here. That will be the day. I've been in the jungle so long that I'd better move out before I start swinging on trees. By the way I'm enclosing a negative of a Jungle fighter, do you recognize him? . . .

. . . It's getting too dark to write so I'd better close. Good night Baby. Please don't worry & as I've said so many times, remember I love you.

All my love
Jack

Lt. Forster – Jungle fighter!

I wonder if the incidents of the preceding days might have been the reason for his almost two-week lapse in writing. Many years later, while we were fishing with my dad on separate occasions, my son and I both witnessed the emotion he felt when recounting to each of us how malaria had saved his life. I still remember how he expressed it, voice quivering: "The only time I didn't go out and they got that boy." How do you process the fact that another man died in your place?

A few days later, Dad found himself on a train heading toward Calcutta and eventually back to New Delhi. He was exhausted and had lost weight. He was also carrying malaria and amoebic dysentery. After escaping death himself but losing one of his men, the accumulation of illness, tension, and malnutrition must have weighed heavily upon him. He had been moving with Allied forces in the Burmese jungle during monsoon season for nearly six months, and he needed a rest.

7

On Leave

Talk of going on leave had been circulating for a while, but after leaving the British 36th Division at Pinwe, just south of Mawlu, Dad was back in India. A couple of his letters from this time either didn't arrive or somehow got lost. I don't have them. But in the next letters I found, it was obvious he was back in India. He first landed at Calcutta, where he took in the sights—he hadn't seen Calcutta yet. He had to come all the way back to India to realize how tired he was from his time in the jungle. I guess that's how it goes sometimes.

Dec 6, 1944

> *My Dearest Gloria*
>
> *I made a mistake on the date of the letter I wrote last night. I still can't remember the day or date but give me time.*
>
> *Went on a Red Cross tour today & found it fairly interesting. I'm enclosing the program. Hope you get something out of it. There are a lot of similar places here & I'll probably see a few more of them.*
>
> *This place makes me feel homesick again, I haven't been homesick for a long time. Nothing reminded me of home & of course I was too busy. Here I've nothing to do & music, people, automobiles & everything makes you think of home. I felt it very keenly this evening when the orchestra played "Miss you." I believe that's the title. An Indian sang it & he wasn't so good but the tune brought back memories, makes me want to stow away on the next Liberty Ship. I do miss you so these days, we could have a wonderful time*

here or any other place. I wonder how long it will be yet. I wouldn't want to come home now because it would only mean leaving again.

I think I needed a rest more than I had realized. I feel so tired at night & just don't seem to have quite the pep I had. I'll get it back though. I will probably be changed a little but I guess I was old enough so that it couldn't change one too much.

The bugs are bad tonight so I believe I'll make this a short one, besides I wrote quite a letter last night & if I don't get too involved there will be another tomorrow night.

Good night Baby. Take care of yourself & don't worry about me. Remember I love you & miss you.

All my love
Jack

Dec 7, 1944

My Dearest Gloria

Dec 7 what a day in my life. I wonder how our lives would have been changed if that day had been different. You know I hadn't met you & didn't until almost a year & a half later. Even then if it hadn't been war time, etc. things might have been different. War is not so terrible after all. Who was it that said there is nothing so bad that there is nothing good about it. Thinking of the past years brings back some wonderful memories.

I'm tired tonight. I don't know what causes it. I don't work now you know but I guess we did pound the pavement quite a little & it seems I need more rest now. I guess I never realized I was very tired. It's much different from getting tired because of a hard day's work. The nervous tension seems to keep you going never realizing you actually are worn out. By the way did you get the negative I sent you. I hope you were not too shocked with the way I looked. I did lose weight & maybe I looked a little frayed around the edges but it's all over now so I'll get my weight back & get back in the groove again.

I wish I could spend Christmas with you. Next year I guess will have to be soon enough. I'm quite sure I should make it by then. I haven't even done any Christmas shopping. Burma had nothing to offer & I haven't been here too long. It's getting pretty late I guess but maybe being late is better than nothing at all . . .

. . . Good night Baby. I love you & wish I could be with you . . .

[December] 11, 1944

My Dearest Gloria

Guess what—I'm writing on the same desk I wrote you so many letters last spring. Yep same desk, same room, same place & under the same conditions generally. Remember the picture I sent you of myself writing you? Well, everything is the same except I have a bottle of beer & I believe I had a can in the picture. It's really good to get back to civilization. You can't imagine it. Just to get away from where the bullets fly is enough and when you take all the discomforts away it's really something. You almost stop to live, you just exist, I wouldn't have missed it but I don't need a second helping of that. Enough of that for now.

I suppose you wonder why I didn't write the last few days. Here's why. Two nights on an Indian train & last night I just had too many questions to answer. I still have a lot of friends here & they all are swell to me since I got back. News travels fast & I'm one of the few that has had a comparatively rough time of it. By the way, I haven't mentioned it before but the Japs have your address. I don't think anything will come of it but I thought I'd let you know in case. Remember when I told you about malaria saving my life? Well, that day my jeep ran into an ambush & they wrecked it & took everything in it including all my clothes I had with me, my field bag which had some of your letters in it & also my pistol belt. Nope they didn't get my gun, I had it. It's all over now & I'm sure I won't ever get another assignment like that again. I'm one of just a small handful of officers of my type to draw one like it. I might possibly even stay here but I'm not strictly in favor of it except that it would make you feel good. Something that really matters. Yes I guess I still love you more than anything else. I had sometimes wondered what was coming over me in the jungle because I didn't seem to feel being away from you so keenly. Funny then not so funny if you think about it. I'm sure now but I often wondered. Now I'd love to get back to see you but wouldn't want to ever leave you again & if I did go back now I'd never get to stay there so—. I wonder if it will be long but in any case it will seem long.

I was going to do quite a little traveling while on leave but I guess I'll just stay here & rest. I can rest and still have a nice leave. About the nearest thing here that is like home to me. A very poor substitute but so is writing letters to being with you.

It will probably be Christmas by the time reaches you so I want to say I do hope you have a nice Christmas & that with God's help I'll be there to spend Christmas with you next year. With that I guess I'll say Good night Baby & I love you & I mean it.

All my love
Jack

Once he left Burma, Dad wondered why he missed Gloria more when he was back in civilization. My guess is that he had been distracted by his life-and-death struggles in the jungle.

When he was on leave and pending reassignment, Dad could tell Mom more about what had happened when his jeep was ambushed with some of his boys. He told me years later that a grenade was involved, one of his boys was killed and another was wounded. Dad had left a lot of his personal items in his jeep when he went to the infirmary with malaria that day. Among those items were some of Mom's letters, which had her address on them.

13 Dec 1944

My Dearest Gloria

I missed another day. I'm a bad boy. I'm sorry. With nothing to do but just visit I don't even write every day. I expected to write last night but I met Capt. Knickerbocker & Major Hinemon, two old Banning boys just about 5:30 & of course they insisted that I spend the evening with them. Had a nice quiet time. Just two drinks, a steak & a movie but we did a lot of visiting. Talked about old times & of course they were very interested in what's going on "up front." They were very much surprised at some of the things & they surprised me too when I found out about some things they didn't know about. All very interesting isn't it?

Guess I'll have to go back pretty soon. I don't get any mail while I'm gone & miss it. I'm also a little curious as to what kind of job I'll get when I do get back. I thought I would like to be stationed here again but I'm not so sure. It's all so very comfortable but that's the only thing good about it. Added to that I believe I'll get a pretty good job out of it at 218. At least a job where I don't get shot at. I've got all the medals I want. Don't get me wrong, I didn't try for any, the boys that do get killed or don't get them . . .

. . . I guess both of us are not accomplishing much toward our future life together but of the jobs we have mine is the most interesting. All I can say for myself is that in my little way I'm helping to win a war, saving a little money & getting a good collection of stories to tell our children & maybe grandchildren. I can see how bored you will be with those stories already. No, I think I'll be bored with them myself before you'll ever hear them. I'm beginning to realize why the boys don't talk much about their experiences already. You are asked by so many people about them that you get tired of telling people about them. All the questions are the same & most of the people soon forget the answers. Do I sound bitter? If I do I want to say I'm not. Some famous General said "War is Hell" & I guess he's right. It's not only hell for the boy up front but everyone connected with it in some way. I take the attitude that it's a job to be done, a mean job but no use in becoming bitter about it all, it just makes it more unpleasant for

yourself & those around. The Chinese have a good word for it but I don't know how to write it. It means "never mind" or "it doesn't matter."

I felt so relaxed tonight, more relaxed than I've felt for months. I also feel lonesome, very lonesome for you. It's beginning to really dawn on me again as to how much I miss you & how much I love you. I can tell you how much. I repeat with the General "War is hell." You must feel the same way many times . . .

What Dad said about recounting his experiences is spot-on: "I'm beginning to realize why the boys don't talk much about their experiences already. You are asked by so many people about them that you get tired of telling people about them. All the questions are the same & most of the people soon forget the answers." My dad was an expert in the art of reflection, able to look back on the events he survived and observe how they may have affected him—and how they continued to affect him. He could philosophize about it all and put it into perspective. I guess I got that trait from him. Two different priests in two different schools—one in sixth grade, one in twelfth—gave me the same nickname, "Socrates." But experiences such as those my dad had gone through are not part of everyone's life. Some are costly, but they are all priceless—if you survive them. They also do leave a mark. Feeling relaxed at long last, Dad realized how much tension he had endured and was now trying to adjust to the pace of being off the line.

15 Dec 1944

My Dearest Gloria

Another uneventful day & of course nothing much to write about. They sent me out for rest & I'm really doing that. To bed early & get up late. All day long I just loaf around from place to place with no regard for time at all. Can't say I'm having a roaring good time but I am enjoying doing just plain nothing. I don't even do any drinking. A couple of beers at night or maybe a drink or two of gin or whiskey but never enough to bother me. Nope I'm a good boy these days. Maybe I should watch myself. I did take a second look at a British service woman. A gal another Officer next door brought in, she was rather attractive but much too tall & her type wouldn't suit me. Seemed very spoiled & of course very British. Don't worry it's not for me.

I did a little shopping today. Got a few things for certain people. I remember you asking about some of the things you might like but I don't quite remember what it was, so I got a few things I thought you might like hoping one of them might be O.K. It's a little late for Christmas but I got out of Burma a little late. Maybe it won't be quite that way next year . . .

. . . I'm using a Captain's room who is spending 30 days in the States. I understand he got home at 4 o'clock in the afternoon & was married at 9 o'clock the same evening. Fast work wasn't it? How would you like to pull a stunt like that? If I was only going to have 31 days I'd be all for it. In fact I wonder why it took five hours, but when I get home I expect to have lots of time. I don't want to drag it out too long but it does look as though this couple was a little over anxious. I really wonder how it actually will be or where. It's just too far away to make any plans as to details . . .

. . . I didn't tell you I've got Angus for a bearer again. A pretty good boy. He wanted to know all about my past experiences, etc. I told him a few things & he just remarked "You very lucky." I don't know whether he meant I was lucky to get the chance or that I was lucky to get back . . .

Dec 20, 1944

My Dearest Gloria,

I'm still doing it. Another few days have passed since my last letter. But then I haven't received any for almost a month or at least three weeks. Yep I'm still here with Johnson but I guess I'll shove off shortly to spend Christmas at Calcutta. After that back to Burma & to work again. A leave is a wonderful thing even in India. I get up when I please & do as I please when I do get up. I had expected to go back before Christmas but as long as I can stay away as I like I might as well take advantage of it. After Christmas I'll be ready to get back to the job again & get my second year over with. . .

. . . I've often wondered what I'd do if I heard from you saying it was all off. It may sound silly but it has happened to some of my friends who thought everything was O.K. Some have recovered O.K. & some didn't ever get over it. The trouble seems that the gal strings the fellow along until one day a letter arrives saying she married some other guy. That's about the most cruel way of letting a guy know that I can think of. I can see why a girl might change her mind, it's only natural, but she is absolutely selfish if she pulls that kind of a stunt right out of a blue sky . . .

Dec 24, 1944

My Dearest Gloria

Christmas Eve in Calcutta. I'm sure to remember this one for a long time. I don't say it's the worst Christmas Eve I've ever had because I believe last year was much worse. Actually I feel quite satisfied. I just got back from Confession & I guess that makes up for a lot. The Church is really the only place a Christmas atmosphere is present. It's a beautiful Church, St. Thomas, & the decorations very similar to our own at home. The pews are not like ours in style but otherwise it could be a church in the U.S.A. By the way I went to Confession to an Indian priest. It's really wonderful how the Catholic Church can break down difference between races. Ordinarily the British have little to do with the Indians but here they confess to an Indian. I thought nothing of it until after I left the Church. I just began to realize that he was Indian. I told Filiak about it and he couldn't believe it even though he was Catholic at one time. I tried to get him to come with me but I didn't do so good.

He has promised to go along to Church in the morning. How about saying a prayer for him sometime. Apparently he left the Church some years ago for some reason & still thinks about coming back. No my Christmas is not too bad even though I am so far away. Last year I didn't even get a chance to go to Church, I spent practically all of Christmas on the train.

I'm going to say Good night Baby. I do love you so & I have a feeling by next Christmas we'll be together.

All my love

Jack

P.S. Although it will be late, I want to wish you a Merry Christmas.

December 25, 1944

My Dearest Gloria

Just a note tonight. I don't know what to write about except that I had a pretty fair Christmas. I got up at 4:40 this morning and went to Mass. Got Filiak to go along too. When we started back he said he was glad he went. The rest of the morning we went shopping around town looking for a few little items we wanted. I got myself a pair of sandals & a set of ivory pistol grips. I tried to get a top for this pen but not too much luck there. Some of the stores were closed so I'll have another look around tomorrow. Went to a Chinese place for lunch & then saw a show, "Take it or Leave it," and tonight we went to dinner downtown & came right back after dinner. Got back & met an Officer I knew while I was with the Artillery in Burma. Had quite a session with him & now that it's ended I'm writing to you. A blow by blow account of what I did on Christmas day in 1944. Actually I'm pretty tired tonight because it has been a long day & we did a lot of walking. So I said it will be just a note.

I hope you had a nice Christmas this year. You certainly didn't do too good last year, thanks to my interference. I'll try to make up for it someday. In another twelve months I hope to be able to make a real start towards that end. I miss you a lot these days . . .

Christmas was a hell of a time to head overseas, and for a prospective bride, a hell of a time to watch your fiancé march off to war. But that was the situation that millions of soldiers and their loved ones had to endure at that time. Dad's two Christmases away from his loved ones were part of the price to be paid for our freedom.

I think that Dad's leave in India was just what the doctor ordered. It was a time of year that brought out the Catholic in him, and the holiday season helped him to remain connected to his faith despite being half a world away from home. A year earlier, he had been roommates with Lt. William Filiak. Since that time, they'd both had had their baptism by fire—Filiak with Merrill's Marauders and Forster with Stilwell and British General Festing, the Chinese, the Indians, and the Chindits. Dad had already been in theater for one year, and as far as he could tell, he'd spend one more year there before he could go home.

8

Back to Burma

Dad had been away from his first assignment in New Delhi for about as long as he had been there in the first place, and most of that time away was spent in the jungle. He undoubtedly felt he'd become a little "jungle jolly." As he discovered when he arrived back in India, he had been under a lot of pressure and had lived under tension and poor living conditions for much of his time in Burma. His diet had been primarily K rations or British rations, and he had lost a lot of weight. He had also contracted malaria, as most soldiers in Burma did at that time. While on leave, he still carried the remnants of that illness—along with a bottle of atabrine to suppress it.

His leave time in India highlighted the contrasts between life in the combat zone and the relatively normal existence of his life in India. But he would soon discover that a month of leave wouldn't end his health issues, and he knew it would still be a long time before he'd get back home. Yet he had the feeling his job would no longer take him to the combat zone. He was still in Burma after his leave ended, but he was nowhere near the Japanese. He had gotten his belly full of that, and by early 1945, the Japanese in Burma were on the run. He was glad to have had a part in helping to win the war, but he was also glad that part of his life was over.

Jan 1, 1944 [1945]

My dearest Gloria

Again I've waited to write. I guess it's been a week again. I do have some sort of an excuse. I spent the big part of it traveling. I'm back at my unit now. Came in the night before last. Another thing is that I'm not feeling so hot. Went to bed last night right after chow, New Years Eve at that. Lot of drink floating around but not for me. It's nothing serious, just my stomach acting up. I guess the rich food I had on leave is something I can't stand. I didn't go to the Doc until this afternoon so I could hardly expect to get over it. He did fix me up & I'm sure I'll be O.K. again in a day or so . . .

. . . I forgot to wish you a Happy New Year. In fact looking at the heading I see I've set myself back a whole year. Too bad about that because on Jan 1st 1945 I've only eleven months more to go before I'm due to go home. Yep. You're time counts from the first of the month in which you left the States. Gives me almost a month gratis. I'm glad to get it & I guess you won't mind to much. Would you take me back as a First Lieutenant? You might have to you know. Myself I just want to get back to you & stay there . . .

Jan 4, [1945]

My Dearest Gloria

Skipped a couple of days again. Reason? I've moved again. Hope I get settled in one spot for a couple of weeks. Looks like I will. The job looks pretty good. Supply & Repair for a change isn't so bad. It's a new place & of course there is a lot of fixing up to do. When we do get it all cleaned up it looks like it will be O.K. Right now there is quite a little rubble lying around . . .

. . . In one of your letters you were telling me to give you a few more details about different things, particularly about this malaria deal. I guess I explained that in my last letter. Don't worry about it. Malaria is not pleasant but it's not near as horrible as the movies make it. In other words you don't just lay panting in your

bed until you die like the jungle pictures show. Most everybody gets it sooner or later out here but they get over it quickly. I don't know anyone that died from it but I guess there has been a few . . .

All my love

Jack

P.S. I believe I mentioned I wasn't feeling so well when I wrote my last letter I'm O.K. again so don't worry.

Dad mentioned that after returning from India, he had been in Myitkyina, but only for a few days as his unit was sent to Bhamo. Myitkyina had been taken on August 3 and Bhamo had been taken on December 15, less than three weeks before Dad's unit was transferred there. Myitkyina was just ten miles or so off the new Ledo Road, so Dad may have traveled the Ledo Road from India back through Burma, where his trip back would have caught him up to his unit at Myitkyina as they prepared to move on to recently captured Bhamo. In the summary he wrote for the *Ex-CBI Roundup* years later, he mentioned that he was sent to Bhamo to oversee a supply and repair shop; that's the unit he was in after his leave. In his letters, he mentioned that there was still some rubble lying around, which is consistent with the fact that Bhamo was taken by Allied forces only shortly before my dad arrived there. That progress also indicated that the Allies would soon complete their new land route through Northern Burma to the old Burma Road leading to China.

Jan 7, 1945

My Dearest Gloria

Do you like it? I mean my writing every day. What a silly question after you've been complaining all summer & fall about my letters. Yep, I'm once more in the groove. Now I'm complaining. I haven't had any mail for well over a week. Of course I had about forty letters all at once then.

Still raining or at least it did all day long. It has cleared some tonight & maybe tomorrow we'll have a change. We're operating rough out in it putting up a warehouse & it makes it pretty bad. We have got some of it completed so we can move in now & I guess things will be a bit better. I suppose you're very interested in all this, about as interested as I am in whether you cleaned your nails at 10 o'clock this morning. I'll behave & try to write about more interesting things.

We don't get too much news these days but the Burma deal looks plenty good. As I understand it we have the overland route to China completed now. I mean we have the Japs out. The road of course must be repaired & put into condition for heavy traffic. Still a big job but it's really surprising how fast the engineers go on it. A year ago or even less I found out what had to be done to get this road through & I expected it to take a couple of years but it's amazing what has been done. It's a better road than I had pictured & a lot more to it. You've got to see it & then you can't believe it . . .

. . . Here's something though. I miss you. An old subject. But I do love you a lot & could really go for an evening or two with you. The days are flying by and maybe it won't be so long any more.

I've got to say Good night again Baby & I repeat I love you.

All my love
Jack

Jan 10, 1945

My Dearest Gloria

First of all I've got a confession to make. I didn't write the last two nights. The night before last I went to visit the HQ boys to get acquainted with them & the Commanding Officer here. (It's always good to meet these boys during off hours). Last night there was a movie & of course everyone went so I went too. But tonight I don't have anything special so—.

I've moved again. You can hardly call it a move though. I just moved about 200 yds. Am that much nearer to my business now.

I've taken over from a captain that didn't do so good so I've moved into his tent. It's a pretty nice setup. Electric lights a desk with a bakelite top, telephone & all the rest of the things that make life worth living . . . I do lack a complete floor, ash tray & waste basket. I'll get those tomorrow. Oh yes, I also lack a radio but I'll get one tomorrow. Being Signal Supply Officer has its advantages. All in all I'm pretty comfortable at that. Miles away from the Japs & expect it to stay that way.

Took a bath tonight. Warm water too. I got a can, put up a couple of bricks for a fire place & it only took a handful of chips to heat the water plenty hot enough. It's surprising how well you can wash with a couple of helmets full of water. I had more but two helmets full was all I needed. I'd like to see you try it though. Guess I'll have to take you out camping sometimes & see how you make out. That would probably be the last time for me as you'd probably be more trouble than fun . . .

. . . Three letters from you, one from Veronica [Dad's younger sister]& one from my Mother. Veronica mentioned that I was about to become an uncle again but of course I know that. It was you that broke the news to me. Hope she get along O.K. We were almost like twins as youngsters.

You still ask about my malaria. I guess I've told you plenty of times that it's O.K. now. I got over it quick like. I felt like it was coming back a couple of times but it went away again. I don't expect any more trouble now. I had been a little slack on my atabrine but am almost forced to take it now. I'm glad to take it but unless you have someone checking you all the time you forget. Down here everyone has to take it & it does keep malaria down. Yep I'm feeling O.K now & with all the rest & no worries I guess I'll be able to build up resistance to the stuff . . .

Dad may have been overly optimistic about being over malaria. As a small child, I remember looking into the medicine cabinet at home and seeing that little brown bottle of atabrine. I also remember Mom telling me about his occasional bouts with the disease—the fevers and the chills. You never really know that you're completely cured of it. Some years later, in his submission to the *Ex-CBI Roundup*, he mentioned at the end, "It took some time before I got over malaria, dysentery and jungle rot."

As for camping, Mom turned out to be a great camper, and it was one of the things that made life for us kids cool and exciting. Mom and Dad camped almost all of the rest of their lives, and our lives were fun and educational as a result.

Jan 12, 1944 [1945]

My Dearest Gloria

Just a note tonight. I've been working to get caught up with my records & I've still got a little to do. Have to make another call tonight to see what goes on up the line & then I guess it will be time to go to bed.

I wasn't feeling too hot today & I guess a little rest would do me good. Funny I've been resting for over a month. I'm feeling better tonight than I did all day. In the middle of the forenoon I was ready to go to bed. I just felt like I had done a hard day's work at that time. I took it pretty easy this afternoon & I sort of snapped out of it. I did work hard yesterday & rushed around quite a bit early this morning. I guess I'm getting soft . . .

Jan 17, 1945

My Dearest Gloria

Just finished reading two of your letters. Just got them in fact. I suppose by the date you'll notice I haven't written in several days. I should have written yesterday but I was too busy getting used to this place. Yep, I've moved again but this time into the hospital. Don't get excited, I wasn't hit by a truck & Lord knows no Jap was close enough to get me. In fact I don't even feel sick. It sort of makes me laugh to be here. I had been feeling pretty rough for several days & I had been having quite a few days like that so I went to see the Doc. The Doc gave me an examination & immediately asked me when I wanted to go in. At first I thought he was crazy but he finally convinced me so here I am. I'm supposed to have a little bug in me called the Ameba or something like that. It causes dysentery but I don't have it. It also enlarges the liver & that's the only reason I believe them at all. By poking around they can find a sore spot so—. I guess I'll be taking a series of shots to get rid of it & just lay around enjoying myself. I might add that this isn't anything to worry about. A number of the Officers here have it & they don't make much fuss about it. All of them did & have a lot of fun. Why not? It's a very comfortable place, with radio, all the books you want to read, games, nurses to rub your back, etc. Pretty soft I'd say. If I've really got the bug I'll probably be here ten or twelve days & I suppose I'll be glad to get out but in the meantime I'll enjoy it.

By the way this is my first trip in the hospital. Never before in my life. It's funny though I entered on the 16th. That seems to be quite a date in my life. I entered the army the same day, got my commission the same day, reported in Delhi the same day, had my first date with you. Also was awarded the Bronze Star the same day. I wonder what will happen next on that date. I'll probably leave for home on the 16th.

I've got an Officer on my left who got his hands badly burned & of course he's pretty helpless. He's a good egg though & is very cheerful. He had to be fed & everything.

I almost forgot to mention that I received a second package from you. It looks like you might be able to cook a little unless you had someone do it for you. You'll probably notice I'm using the stationery. It came just at the right time. I was wondering how I was going to get some because I was running low. I thank you and the cookies are good. No I haven't finished them yet . . .

Amoebic dysentery isn't a fun thing to have, and I can speak from experience. Another thing I have in common with my dad, I guess. In my case, I didn't go to the hospital, and the cure wasn't in the form of shots—not the fun kind, anyway. I was given carbarsone pills. The Peace Corps doctor didn't explain how to take them—he was probably distracted since he left the office sick on the day he saw me. When I started taking the medicine, I took too much. Since the pills are 27 percent arsenic, the poison built up in my system and almost killed me.

When he was hospitalized, my dad's situation was not as bad as mine. But in addition to dysentery, he struggled with malaria as well, and he probably still needed rest from his jungle days. Based on his letters, it almost seems like he reveled in his inactivity in the hospital.

As for events occurring on the sixteenth of the month, his son, Bob, was married on March 16, 1973.

Jan 18, 1945

My Dearest Gloria

Just a note tonight. I waste all day & then leave my letter writing until evening. So I have several to write tonight.

You should see me writing in bed. It works O.K. but I would prefer a desk. I'm not in bed all the time but I do manage to stay there most of the time. Naturally I can stay up all the time but somehow I prefer to just lie around on my bed. Pretty soft. It might not be so pleasant in a day or so when I'll be taking a shot every day. I never did like them but I guess I can stand it.

The radio is going full blast & the music is good. It's coming from a G.I. station right here . . .

Jan 18, 1945

My Dearest Gloria

Another day & another letter. I don't have much else to do. I do manage to pass the time without getting bored. Something is always going on around here, besides I do a lot of reading. Most of the people are not very sick here.

Had a rude awakening this morning. The ward boy came in with a little glass. About the size of a "shot" glass but there wasn't a "shot" in it. Just plain old salts. I certainly didn't need it but I got it anyway. Horrible tasting stuff to get at 6 o'clock in the morning. Anytime as far as that goes. I also got a capsule this noon & tonight. I also got my first shot. I found out it's not so bad . . .

. . . Just for something to write about I guess I'll start in on the news. Old Joe Stalin is on the rampage again. Also on the Western Front things are looking up again. I have an idea it's really the beginning of the end this time. Always after a lull in the battle something happens & it's started by us, usually the results are in favor of us. Even here things are looking good. By the way do we figure in the news as yet? Maybe it's a surprise to you that the first overland convoy is on its way to China. I haven't seen the convoy & maybe I won't. I really don't know whether it's passed here or not & I'd probably miss it anyway lying on the "sack" all day. What a racket I don't know why they keep us in the hospital but I guess this stuff is not to be monkeyed (is that right?) with.

Boy that radio is really O.K. Even listened to San Francisco this morning.

I'm going to say Good night now baby. I'm tired after my hard day's work. I did too work. I censored three letters. I'll always love you & I miss you lots.

All my love
Jack

After a week, Dad already felt the boredom of the hospital. And although he wrote about the war, he didn't mention Europe's Battle of the Bulge in any of his letters from December and January. Although it was the battle that almost upset the whole apple cart in

Europe, Dad described that time as a "lull." I don't know if he was unaware of it or if he just didn't want to talk about such setbacks. He also wondered if anyone back home had heard about the war in Burma or knew what was happening in China. It was significant that the Ledo Road was now connected to the Burma Road and the first land convoy was on its way from India to China. Much of the equipment accumulating in India's Assam Province couldn't be flown over the Hump, so the land route was important. The road was later renamed the Stilwell Road in honor of its staunchest promoter. Old Vinegar Joe, or Uncle Joe if you prefer, would finally get his due. The road passed about ten to twelve miles south of Myitkyina and right through Bhamo. The total route between Ledo in Assam Province and Kunming in China was 1,079 miles, and it took twenty-three days to travel. The Allies could carry ample supplies to China via the brand-new road even though the Japanese were now on the run almost everywhere. Allied supply columns first used the road in January 1945, but it could be argued that its usefulness was already outdated by then. Supply flights from India's Assam Province to Kunming and Chongqing, though less than adequate, had sustained China since the Burma Road had been cut off in 1942.

This was a comfortable although boring time for Lt. Forster. He didn't have much to say except to talk about when the Germans might "fold," in which case he might be home sooner than expected. He also had an "administrative change" that located him in a different outfit: "I'm now in Cr. B 988 Sig Serv. Bn. Not really a change just [a] little reshuffle for administrative purposes I guess." He also occasionally discussed the war and the goings-on in the hospital. On January 23, he wrote:

These shots I'm getting daily are beginning to take effect. Sort of makes you feel drugged, lazy sleepy like. My arms are getting a little sore too. I'll live though, I guess. The only thing that bothers me is that I've spoiled my record. Can't say anymore that I've never been in a hospital. Still it's another experience. I want to add that there is nothing to worry about, I'll be as good as new when I get out. At least I'll know there is nothing radically wrong with me when I get out. They put you through the mill O.K. I'm beginning to feel like I'd like to get out of here although I'm not getting too anxious.

I guess hospitals are supposed to be boring, especially for a soldier who's been in combat.

As always, Dad told his girl that he loved her and missed her, that he couldn't wait to get home and marry her—and not to worry. He also talked about what he heard on the radio and saw in the movies. It seemed that no matter where he was, whether in the city, in the hospital, or in the jungle, somehow the army could set up a projector and show movies. This was true for US soldiers and sailors in all theaters during World War II, and it has been true ever since. And in Dad's case, since he was a Signal Supply and Repair officer, he could always get ahold of a radio. And then there was this:

Jan 27, 1945

My Dearest Gloria

Another day almost gone & I guess I'd better write even though I've nothing to say. I'm getting into a rut, guess I'd better get out of the hospital.

I got a pass today & went back to the outfit for a visit. It sort of breaks up my stay here even though there is nothing I went back for in particular. I didn't stay long, I found out I was glad to get back & take it easy. Funny thing about these shots, you feel pretty good but it does make you weak. I found myself starting out to walk across the area at a good pace & wound up out of breath quickly. I didn't lack the energy but was ready to take it easy when I got there. They certainly seem to be the thing to keep you from doing anything that requires a great amount of energy. Nope, it makes you feel old & contented. I'm afraid if I had to run a block I'd fall dead before I got there. It'll wear off in a little while though. I guess I mentioned that I took my last shot yesterday. I'm glad of it because I was beginning to get plenty sore. As far as that goes I'm still plenty sore.

Had quite an experience this morning. Every morning for the past week we here had a pretty little gal from Chicago waking us up. She wasn't too little at that & I guess she isn't exactly a beauty but she was very energetic & pleasant. Well, this morning I felt someone tug on my mosquito bar & all of a sudden this creature's face appeared. What a goon! She didn't say a word & when I said Good morning she hardly knew what to answer. I guess she's a good nurse but they should bring her up a little later in the day because seeing something like that when you first wake up is bad for my nervous system. Not good for my morale, either. I've been shaky all day from that shock. Haven't you noticed all the mistakes I've been making in this letter. She'll chase me right out of this place one of these days. Poor girl, I guess it's not her fault besides I might cause the same effect on somebody so why do I talk like that.

It's pitiful what I have to put into these letters of mine. It's a waste of paper & your nerves. How do you stand it?

I'm going to break it off & say Good night Baby. Every day brings me nearer to you & I count them. I guess it because I love you.

All my love
Jack

Jan 31, 1945

My Dearest Gloria

I skipped a day again. Had visitors at first & later we fried a few fresh eggs so the evening slipped by before I knew it. I could have written during the day but I don't like to write except at night.

Well, I'm out of the hospital as of today. I was supposed to get out yesterday but the Doc forgot to sign me out so—. It was comfortable anyway. The beds have springs in them & a little more comfortable than a cot. I'm not too strong as yet but I feel fine. Those shots & lying around made me pretty soft. I rather enjoyed it. All the patients were in pretty good shape so it was a continuous madhouse. We had a ward boy who was a clown & kept us entertained most of the time. Of course the nurses were O.K. too . . .

. . . I received a letter from you yesterday but left it with some stuff that's following me tomorrow. This one happened to be the one with the pictures in it. You mentioned that you received the negative I sent & that you were horrified with how I looked. I believe I mentioned that I had been through a pretty rough four months & was getting pretty tired. Besides that I was just getting over malaria. I took some pictures lately & probably will have one soon of myself. I'm sure you'll see a big difference. After two months of idleness there should be. I gained a lot of weight & feel like myself again. So it's back to work again but none of this rough stuff again.

Time seems to be flying by. I'm actually starting on my fourteenth month now. By the looks of the war it might not take all of the two years. I certainly hope not. In any case I fully expect that I will leave as soon as my time is up. Most of the fellows are going home on time now.

I'm sort of tired tonight. As I said before I guess I'm still soft. I don't expect to do much of anything for a couple of days & after that I'll be going out to pay some of the boys. It should be a nice trip & I'm looking forward to it. After that I'm not sure what I'll be doing but it looks like I'll get a repair job. Suits me O.K. . . .

From here on, there was no more terror in the jungle. The Japanese had been pushed far enough to the south of Burma that the Stilwell Road was open all the way to Kunming, China, and Dad was far enough north that he felt safe.

Feb. 5, 1945

. . . Well, I'm quite comfortable now. Got my tent all fixed up. Got a

radio right in front of me, electric lights. Everything very much O.K. You should see it. The tent is divided. I sewed up mosquito netting to separate the cots & the rest of the tent. (No cracks about my sewing). I built a table & it looked a little rough so I put a blanket over it & it really looks O.K. I've still got to build a shower & a few little things before it's all finished but there's time for that . . .

Feb 6, 1945

. . . We're getting civilized around here these days. We're working on an Officer's Club here for the Signal Officers in the area. Can't say for sure whether it will be a success but know this "happy go lucky" crowd should be able to work it up into something. We do have a swell bunch of Officers in our outfit right up to & including the C.O. By the way he used to be in the same outfit I was in at Fort Leonard Wood, MO. He was a 1st Lt. & I was T/4, he's a Major now. Getting back to the Club, it no doubt will have a few things lacking, such a female visitors, "Juke box" & maybe a shortage of liquor at times but I'm looking forward to it . . .

Bhamo, Burma was about the most relaxing place Dad had been stationed in the CBI, and he was there less than two months after it had been taken from the Japanese. The Signal boys seemed to be creating their own environment—and an Officer's Club no less.

Feb. 16, 1945

. . . Well, the party is ended & I'm frozen. I'm shaking all over & I'm almost cold sober. I'd say the party was a success. Even had a little song fest. The entertainment included poker, craps, drinks, a dart game, etc. I lost 15 rupees, about five bucks. This included a Bingo game where I dropped something like four bucks. We have bingo games here a couple times a week. It is staged by the Enlisted men & the profits are spent for the mess. Fresh fruit, vegetables & eggs. With these little extras & with the way our excellent cooks prepare

the food we have the best mess in Burma. I'm sure of that so why shouldn't I contribute . . .

Feb 18, 1945

My Dearest Gloria

I missed last night again. I had planned on writing today but had a busy day. This morning I had some work to take care of & of course I had to go to Church, this being Sunday. This afternoon? Well, I went fishing. Got quite a few fish too. We had a good sized boat with an outboard motor. The funny part of it is we didn't have a rod or reel. We just got a net & dipped them out of the river. I'd say we got around 75 lbs of fish that way. I suppose you don't believe it but I swear it's the truth. Burma has it's points & T.N.T. is a good fish bait. You drop a little over the side & a little later it goes bang you wait a few minutes & the fish come to the top. Of course while [they] do come up & stay awhile you've got to pick them up pretty quick because they usually come to & swim off. So we have a change in our diet for tomorrow. Speaking of a change in diet, we really are feeding well these days. I don't believe I've ever had better food in my life than we have here. I don't mean that I haven't had better meals, I've had some a lot better. What I'm driving at is that I've never had such a continuous feast. Just to give you an idea, I had steak twice today. Mashed potatoes, fresh tomatoes, hot rolls, banana pie, etc. Of course I only had a steak sandwich tonight because got back late from the fishing trip. We do have steak several times a week, a lot of fresh vegetables, pastries, a few fresh eggs, etc. It's a bit different from the K ration diet I was on some months ago. I should be putting on all the weight I lost during those months & a few pounds more.

Yesterday we had a show here. You'd never guess who was here, I hardly expected to see the stars present out here. It was none other than Lily Pons & Andre Kostelanetz (I guess at the spelling). Actually they've been in the Theater for some time. They were in

Calcutta on Christmas when I was there. It was a pretty good show even though they are sort of long haired musicians. It was an afternoon show & sort of hot in the sun. I got a good sunburn out of it. A little entertainment & subject matter for a paragraph in a letter to you. How do you like that?

The stars did shine in the CBI at times. Lily Pons and Andre Kostelanetz did their best to show support for the troops. British singer Vera Lynn was famous for her rendition, "It's a Lovely Day Tomorrow," and she came to India and Burma to entertain the troops. The song is about optimism in the face of tough times and must have brought many a tear to soldiers far away from home.

Dad and the crew in Bhamo ate about as well as any soldier in theater at that time, with fresh vegetables purchased from the proceeds of gambling at their new officer's club or fresh fish blasted out of the Irrawaddy River. Life in Bhamo seemed to agree with Lt. Forster, and for the next month or so, he wrote to Gloria about the new officer's club, books he'd read or was reading, and movies he'd seen. He also teased her about his "Varga" calendar with the pinup girls and told her about bingo games, volleyball games, baseball games, and how the war was going—which seemed to be pretty good. Then, of course, there was the subject of most importance, the point system: how many points do I have, and how many points does it take to go home?

Lily Pons and husband Andre Kostelanetz entertain the troops at Bhamo. Dad was in that crowd. (War Department, Signal Corps photo)

9

Sweating it Out

March 5, 1945

. . . I got a new gadget tonight. It's a clock that turns my radio off & on at a set time. Now I can go to bed & let it play & also have it come on in the morning. I always say nothing is too good for the boys in the fox holes. I'm getting spoiled beyond help. I've got the best deal here that I've had since I've been overseas. Delhi was comfortable & all but I didn't care much for the work & the food wasn't very good. Here I've got about everything one could ask for.

I noticed today that the cards for the point system of discharges are coming out. Four things are being considered.

1. Length of service since Sept. or Oct '40.

2. Length of time overseas.

3. Citations awards & campaign stars

4. Dependents under 18

That puts me towards the top of the list around here if not on top. Over four years service, over 14 months overseas, a bronze star medal, a campaign star & Unit merit badge. I sort of run short on the dependents under 18. Should have married you before I left, who knows. Of course all this won't be any good at all until Germany folds up. About two months or so from now seems a logical time for that. In any case I believe I'll serve at least five years. I can't see it come any sooner, but again who knows. It will hardly seem right to shed the uniform after wearing it so long, but I'm sure I'll be able to stand it . . .

The point system. This was the topic of discussion for war-weary GIs all over the world. Nobody wanted to spend another minute in the mud of the Burmese jungles, or on an island in the Pacific, or in a frozen foxhole in Belgium. No one wanted to be that last GI killed or wounded in action—or, as in the story of the soldier from World War I, killed one hour after the German surrender but before word got to the front lines. Everyone just wanted to go home to their lives. And yes, it is true that all battles are fought by scared men who'd rather be somewhere else. Everyone thought, *Where and when will that last battle be? I don't want to be there!*

Although he was starting to get anxious about going home, Dad had it about as good as he'd ever had it since arriving in the CBI. He had good food, a great job, and a relatively easy life in Bhamo, Burma. Still, he missed home cooking—and his girl. The waiting was no good anymore. It was all about the points.

March 13, 1945

. . . My soft job makes me think of home & you a lot these days. I'm going on an actual 15 months overseas with credit given me for 15 or over. Only a third left now but it looks like an awful long time to wait. I used to think, a couple of months or the like left wouldn't make any difference but now I believe I'll feel it's eternity even when I'm on my way. I don't only want to go home, I want to be home in other words. So far I have no hope or seen no indication that will be before the end of the year. Still a month is making a lot of changes these days. Things are happening fast these days. Let's hope . . .

March 15, 1945

My Dearest Gloria

Looks like it's every other day now. Played Bingo last night & after the game got involved with a boy that left for the Good Old U.S.A. he was really a happy boy & why shouldn't he be after 25 months. I took him out to the airstrip this morning & gave him a little send off. He was a good man, a damn good man & I was sorry to see him go but glad that he could get back. I'm really sweating it out myself, seems like I miss home so much more than I did for the past ten months or so. The time has flown & I hope the next eight or nine months will be as speedy as the last ones. A number of the boys are ready to go & will leave before too long. I'll be losing some of my repair [personnel] all along but I've got a fresh bunch now to break in & they look like a pretty good group . . .

The war in Burma was slowing down and the Japanese were retreating to Rangoon. They had lost 53,000 dead and missing soldiers in General Mutaguchi's abortive attempt to invade India in early 1944. While he was in the jungle, Dad had written about the sick and starving Japanese soldiers who surrendered in the jungle without resistance. They may have been part of the force that retreated from Kohima and Imphal. As a result of those extensive losses, General Mutaguchi was relieved of his command and recalled to Japan, his career over. Japanese resources in Burma were greatly diminished, due both to the losses inflicted upon them and the fact that their resupply options were severely restricted because of Allied naval and air activity. For Dad and his unit, it meant that demand for their services was diminishing. The army didn't disband the unit, however—in a war, you never know when such services will be needed urgently. However, with little to do, young soldiers began looking for ways to kill the boredom and make life more comfortable and entertaining.

March 20, 1945

My Dearest Gloria

. . . I'm beginning to almost hate to write. There is so little to say & I guess the only reason I write is to let you know I still love you & because it's the only link between us now. Eight months or maybe more before things are apt to change. Sounds bad so far doesn't it? I'll try to make it better from now on. (I mean this letter) . . .

. . . In the meantime I'll sweat it out, I'm not particularly happy even with all the breaks I'm getting, I've got practically anything a guy would want. A swell job, a darn good bunch of boys under me and all but the inactivity is sort of getting me down. I'm almost wishing for a move again, funny isn't it, first I crab about moving so much & then about settling down. Frankly it's got me worried. I hope it's not like that once when I become Mr. Forster again . . .

March 28, 1945

. . . By the way did you get the picture I sent of myself sitting on the radiator of the C & R car? It turned out fairly well but nothing to rave about. I'm sending another one tonight of myself working in the shop. This was a candid shot. I didn't know about it until one of the boys gave me the picture. I'm winding a coil, using a low speed drill to turn the coil form. The picture shows only a small part of the shop & that part where we make all the gadgets. S/Sgt. York usually works here. He's a wonderful lad with a lot of good ideas & the ability to turn out fine work. Hope he is not a relative of the Sgt. Alvin York of the last war. He's a boy from Texas, well built & fairly handsome. Like all the rest of my boys he's good . . .

. . . What a life I'm leading these days. I get up about 7:30, get to work between 8:00 & 8:30, fool around the shop until 11:00 or 11:30, take off for chow, after chow sleep until 1:30 or 2 o'clock & then go to a ball game, I might stop in at the shop for an hour or so some time during the afternoon. At five we eat chow, fool around the shop, go to the Club, play bingo or write letters. Sometime I do a

Lt. Forster at work in his shop in Bhamo.

little of everything. It's just too good to last, still I wouldn't mind a little more business now & then. It makes time pass more rapidly . . .

April 1, 1945

. . . This afternoon I went out with the boys to try out a new (new to us) outboard motor. We picked up a couple 22HP (horsepower) Sea Horses & have been working on them for a few days. I had my boys on one & somebody else on the other. Well, they tried theirs first & the darn thing caught fire & burned up, so we go out with ours out & naturally it worked. Of course we had a little trouble with adjustments but all in all it was a success. Looks like we'll get a little fishing done. I'm going to try to arrange a little fishing trip Wednesday. A rough war, very rough. If only you were here, everything would be perfect.

April 5, 1945

. . . Speaking of boat rides we really had a lot of fun on our fishing trip. I guess I told you about the motors & boats we have here to keep us entertained. My section more or less takes care of them & of course I've got to go out on all test runs etc., so I get a lot of boating out of the deal. It's certainly is fun . . .

April 6, 1945

. . . Got a date with Gen. Sultan tomorrow morning. No kidding I'm to see him in the morning. You guessed it he is to present me with the Bronze Star Medal I was awarded last fall. I've got the medal here in the tent tonight & I'm to take it to the Gen's quarters about nine tomorrow when it will be pinned on with a ceremony including cameras, etc. Me & MacArthur have our medals . . .

April 8, 1945

My Dearest Gloria

I skipped a day but I'm not sorry this time. It happens it's after midnight so actually you will probably get two letters today. By the way I am going to make this short tonight. After all I've got to get to bed. Why am I up so late? Well my boys had a little party & after it was well on the way they called me & asked me to come over. I'd say it's the nicest compliment a group of men could pay an Officer. First of all to want him to come & after that to expect to have a good time after he got there. Most men usually don't want Officers around because they figure the Officer will hold them down. So I'm just a little flattered. They are a swell bunch of men & I believe they would do almost anything for me, the same goes for me doing things for them. Enough of that I can't imagine you being interested.

Well, I got over my ceremony O.K. today. Old Dan S. pinned the medal on me while [the] camera clicked, etc., I'm going to go down to the photo unit & see if I can get a print or two. Six men were given awards. Four officers & two enlisted men, one of the men was with me during the time when the award was earned & three out of these men were Signal Corps men. The third Signal man was a photographer who was out with the Chinese, came up to a pill box that had a Jap machine gun in it. The boy jumped up on the pill box, threw a grenade in the hole & killed the Jap gunner. Funny things happen in this war.

April 10, 1945

My Dearest Gloria

. . . Also listened to the news & by the looks of things the war with Germany is about over. 200 men taking a town of 400,000 people shows something is up. It does look like it may take some time before the German army will be disarmed though. I hope they make it snappy. I can't wait to get home to you. I can hardly wait but (you'll probably kill me for this) if I have a choice on how to go home I'll ask to go home by boat, maybe I can be in a better frame of mind & in better condition. Besides that the plane trip is a

rough one, it really wears you down. I'd also like to make a boat trip & if possible by way of the Pacific so I could say I've been around the world. Not asking much am I? I guess it won't matter, the important thing is that I get home safe & before too many months roll by. I do hope it's no later than December . . .

April 14, 1945

. . . We woke up yesterday to receive shaking news. One of the Officers came in to the mess hall & told us we had a new President, naturally no one knew what he was talking about. I guess it shook most everyone in the world. No one quite knew what to say at first. About the first thing everybody thought was as to who the new President really was & whether he could carry on as well as the man who died. No doubt he will be unable to do this but we all have confidence in his ability & are sure it will have no effect on the war. The plans no doubt have already been made for that & it's just a matter of time until they will be executed. It definitely will have some effect on the post-war plans as no two men handle a situation the same but who knows he may do a better job as the Ex-president would have done.

Dad didn't even mention the new president's name in his letter. Maybe he didn't know it. During the 1944 presidential campaign, Senator Harry S. Truman had been a surprise nomination out of the Democratic convention to be Roosevelt's vice president. He had maintained a largely separate existence from Roosevelt in the few months since taking office. He said, upon receiving the news of the president's death, "I felt like the moon, the stars, and all of the planets had fallen on me."[18] Later, he recounted that he had never felt so scared in all his life. As an obscure senator coming to the seat of power, it must have been a lonely and daunting feeling. He was called to the White House to receive the news, and upon arriving,

18 Tom Huizenga and Ashalen Sims, "Sing Out Mr. President: Harry Truman Takes the Lead," National Public Radio, February 17, 2011, https://www.npr.org/sections/deceptivecadence/2011/02/20/133755317/sing-out-mr-president-harry-truman-takes-the-lead.

he immediately asked Eleanor Roosevelt if there was anything he could do for her. She responded, "Is there anything we can do for you? You are the one in trouble now."[19] Truman didn't even know the atomic bomb existed until he became president—actually, ten days after—and now he would have to ponder its use.

About this time, Mom, who had been visiting Dad's folks in Durand, came down with tonsillitis. Dad's folks convinced her to have the tonsillectomy in Durand rather than returning to Iowa for the procedure. She had some complications and needed to stay in Durand a little longer than expected to get it resolved.

April 20, 1945

My Dearest Gloria

. . . I just got the letters telling me of your relapse, you really got the tough breaks. I know it must worry you to death. I suppose you wanted to make a good impression & it's making you feel that you've made a mess of it. At least that's the way your letters sound. Naturally I haven't had a letter from home since your operation but I'm sure everything is O.K. All the more reason I wish I was there. Maybe I could do something to cheer you up. But don't worry I will be but in the meantime don't worry too much about your illness at my home. My folks are not the kind of people to deal roughly with someone really sick. Besides that they don't usually say things they don't mean & I'm sure they are telling you not to worry. This must sound awful silly to you after it's all over . . .

April 21, 1945

My Dearest Gloria

Saturday night, a rainy Saturday night & I've been busy cleaning up my tent. I've got most everything sorted out but I've still got a few things to do in the morning. I had a little scare, not too serious but I did stop short for a moment. I picked up a shelter

19 History.com Editors, "FDR Dies," HISTORY, April 8, 2021, https://www.history.com/this-day-in-history/fdr-dies.

half & saw something move, which looked like it had a million legs. I got a club & turned the thing over & found a big centipede under it. The darn thing was about eight inches long with about twenty stinger like legs. It was sort of a red color & about 1 1/2 inches wide & stood about 3/4 inch high. Those legs looked pretty wicked, as I said before they were stinger like & reminded you of thorns. Need I say I killed it? That's Burma. . .

. . .Not much to say otherwise tonight. As I said it's raining & I'll probably repeat that a good many times from now on. It looks like the start of the monsoon. It does make it a lot cooler & we are set up so it won't bother us too much this year. Hard roads, paths, good tents & buildings & no jungle right close by. It still is warm but comfortable. I took a shower after it started raining & having no roof over the thing I got about as wet from the rain as from the shower. Felt a little funny being out in my birthday suit & having the rain hit me. A little cooler than my shower but I got used to it & rather enjoyed it. Try it sometime. Of course you'll have to have a screen or wait till after dark. What would the neighbors say. . .

April 28, 1945

. . . Speaking of pictures, how do you like the one of me & Dan I. Sultan I sent last night. Can't see what kind of medal he is pinning on so I'll be able to say it's the Medal of Honor or something. The picture is really good in my estimation. The photographer did O.K. Notice all the details like the hair on Dan's hand, his stars & also my need for a haircut.

Played another game of softball this morning. "B" company played "A" company & of course "B" company won. How could they lose with me on the team. Got on base twice of three times up. Once a walk & once on a fielders' choice. I never did score because the boys after me didn't get a hit. I was caught between first & second once when I deliberately ran toward second in order to draw the ball out there so a man on third could score. I was out but he made it. It was a trick & it worked O.K.

Got the news of the Russians & U.S. forces meeting today. Also hints that V-day isn't far away. They made it sound like it might come within the next couple of weeks. Another hint was made that the Germans might give up after all. I go for that, I also go for things like the men with four to five years of service getting out. I've got almost four & 1/3 years now. It might be like a drowning man grasping at straws but I'm hoping . . .

Bronze Star Medal Presentation
(Signal Corps photo obtained by Louis Forster)

May 8, 1945

My Dearest Gloria

Well, Baby it has happened. The war with Germany is officially over. Just heard the President make the announcement. Naturally we knew about it for a day or so but now we're sure it's absolutely done. It's funny there is no real celebrating done so far but I imagine it will pick up as the night grows older. Myself, I've got two radios busy. My communications receiver to pick up short wave broadcasts & a civilian type set for the local station. I've got a few drinks handy if I should happen to feel the urge. Maybe I will, do you blame me? It's been so long. No, the people here are not really celebrating too much & they aren't too excited about it. Everyone is very calm but happy. It's rather hard to describe the attitude the men are taking. I believe it can be laid to the fact that it has been expected & now that it has happened it's not shocking news. Actually they seem to be thinking more of how Japan will be defeated, how long it will last & last but not least when they will return home. —Was just interrupted by a couple of fellows who wanted me to go along to the club for a drink. Went along but had no drink & came back because things were pretty dead there. Maybe it will pick up later. Right now I believe it will but I don't know what I'll do. I'm too happy about the whole affair & wonder if getting lit would the most appropriate way of celebrating it. Yes, my dear little woman I'll remember this day for a long time. All the things that happened & how they happened. Not much doing this morning but there was a different day. First I censored the mail (I was alone & acting as C.O. for the outfit) & then I went over to the repair to see if everything was O.K. Nothing unusual going on so far as repair was concerned. I check on how the refrigerator we're building is coming along, censored a few more letters, picked up a dynamotor to make a fan motor for my tent. It worked fine. All the time I keeping close to a radio & feeling sort of restless. Got a call from an officer to use one of our boats to search for a body of a boy who drowned. Naturally I made all arrangements, etc. Lunch time. We had steak, dehydrated potatoes, a lemon drink that tasted like battery acid, & last but not least, cake & ice cream. After lunch I stripped down to my wrist watch & went to sleep. I was awakened when rain hit me in the face about 1345. I hurriedly dressed & then fought with my tent to keep it [from] blowing away. A few minutes later W/o Paul Goodman came in & told me that one of "B" Co.'s Bashas had collapsed. I dashed out to see if anyone was hurt & was relieved when I found everyone O.K. Wires were blown down & the rest or most of the rest of the afternoon I went about getting the boys under a roof & getting the electricity system working. Everything is O.K. tonight. Later I went back to the repair shop & found it almost empty because the boys were getting straightened out after the storm so I went out to one of the tents in the area to have a cold beer. (came out of an icebox we found in a foxhole when we moved in here) Came back to my tent & to the next tent to have another beer. At the same time I got my bronze star medal from an Officer who had taken it to Calcutta to have my name engraved on it. A few minutes later went to supper & found it pretty bad. Toasted Cheese sandwiches tomatoes & coffee. Came back, took a bath & shaved & started to sweat out a broadcast from our President at 7:30. Heard the broadcast & then sat down to write. I repeat I don't know how the evening will end. All this brings up another subject. The famous point system. I'm sweating that out more than the news of today. I wonder whether I'll be within the critical score. I hardly think so but will be up high enough to qualify before the end of the year. [unintelligible] we were given another campaign star yesterday so I now have a total of three decorations. It doesn't affect me as far as the organization is concerned but it does as far as the army as a whole is concerned. So keep your fingers crossed & I'll be home before too many months to become the father of your children.

I love you dearly & I miss you more than ever. Good night Baby

& wish me luck.
All my love
Jack

Lt. Forster stands on turret of M4 Sherman Tank next to a M3 tank

A rather exciting day—the end of the war in the European Theater of Operations. It was, however, tempered by the fact that there was a huge job to do with Japan still fighting. The boys wanted to celebrate, but the work still at hand put a damper on their excitement. At that same time, the Japanese expected the Allies to invade their home islands and were preparing the civilian population to resist alongside the military. If an invasion had happened, it would have been a bloodbath.

Dad also mentioned that he'd sent his Bronze Star Medal along with a buddy to have his name engraved on the back. I had never noticed the engraving before, but the medal was behind me as I sat at the computer typing Dad's letters. Up on a shelf was the wooden box he'd used to send it home to his mother, inside of which was a smaller, more decorative box covered in black leather with the words "Bronze Star Medal" stamped upon it in gold letters. Inside was Dad's medal with a matching ribbon. On the back side of the medal was a circle with raised letters saying "Heroic or Meritorious Achievement." Across the middle of the circle, in tiny letters, was engraved "Louis J. Forster."

June 1, 1945

My Dearest Gloria

. . . Had one of the boys in tonight. A Sgt. by the name of Ralph Anderson who is from Eau Claire & is going home to be discharged on the 40 year plan. I must admit I got him a little high but I guess he'll be O.K. he's leaving tomorrow & wanted your address. He says he will write you & tell you about me. Now if he tells you I'm having dates with the Burmese gals he's a damn liar. He was kidding me that he would write that but I guess he'll tell the truth. He's also going to visit the folks & deliver my medal. Yep, I had quite a session with him & I certainly will look him up after I get back.

The "40-year plan" was a concession to men who enlisted at an older age. They were allowed to terminate their service when they turned forty, especially after attaining certain milestones such as decorations and time in service. Many older men had enlisted beyond draft age in order to do what they felt was their duty, but at a certain age—usually forty—they were allowed to leave the military. It reminds me of a scene in the movie *PT 109.* When an older sailor is asked why he enlisted at his age, he recounts that his stepson had enlisted, and it wouldn't be dignified for him to hop onto his stepson's knee after the war to ask him about the war. Instead, he felt compelled to enlist himself.

Heard over the Radio tonight that the Burma Campaign is over as far as the Americans are concerned, so it looks like we'll be moving to some other place shortly. I guess the next stop for me will be China. I don't like the idea because I don't like the damn "Chinks" but if it don't last very long I'll be glad to have been there. The boys in Europe are getting a chance to go home before leaving for the fight against the Japs but I guess we're too close to it all to get such a break. I don't know whether it would be a break or not, when I go back I want to stay. I guess it doesn't matter because I'm almost positive I'll qualify under the point system before the year is out. I've wondered about how I stand as to the Army as a whole & when you stop to think it's only the guys with children or an unusual amount of overseas time that can beat me. Let's hope I'm in the top 10% anyway . . .

Dad spent a lot of time with Chinese troops in the jungle, and although they were good fighting men, I believe he suspected them of stealing his belongings.

By the beginning of May, British General Slim's forces had driven south to the outskirts of Rangoon and found it mostly evacuated by Japanese troops. Many had gone back to Thailand or were embarked onto troop ships to return to Japan. The Allies sank many of the troop ships evacuating the Japanese from the Burmese capital; by mid-May, British troops, including Gurkhas and Indian troops, were mopping up Rangoon and the last few areas of Burma. There were no more effective Japanese fighting units in Burma, so the war in Burma was essentially over.

Despite the success of American island campaigns in the Pacific, many places in China were still under Japanese control—and in some cases, the Japanese were still advancing. For instance, the American 14th Air Force had been rooted out of the bases in Eastern China from which they had been bombing Japan's home islands and disrupting Japanese supply lines in the South China Sea.

The Japanese used 250,000 troops to shut down those bases—troops that were taken from other places they were defending. In that way, keeping China in the war paid dividends for the Allied forces in the Pacific. So the handwriting was on the wall for the Japanese Empire. It would not be long before the main islands of Japan would fall under attack from bases in the Marianas. But Truman also had a less-publicized ace in the hole. The Manhattan Project was nearing its first test of the atomic bomb—the ultimate game changer.

The war progress put Dad into another reflective mood, and he began contemplating his postwar married life. As always, I am impressed by his foresight and his ability to anticipate the problems that the changes in him would present in his civilian life.

June 3, 1945

My Dearest Gloria

How to start? A good question because I don't really know what to write about.

The day was just another Sunday in Burma as far as I'm concerned. I can't imagine what Sunday will be like or is like back home. Although we do let down just slightly & go to Church on Sunday, there is hardly any difference between Sunday & the other days. I repeat, I wonder how it will be. It brings up the subject of becoming a civilian again. I can feel that I'll be dissatisfied for quite a while. Getting out of the Army will be every bit as bad as getting used to being in it. I'll miss the friends, the Army, the talks, the living in a large group, the feeling of anticipation of a new station change & hundreds of other things. Maybe because I realize what it is I'll be missing will make it easier but I'm afraid I might be a little hard to live with for a while. I picture it as being something like leaving school & getting out into the world but then it will be some difference because we left school with anticipation as to what's next. The trouble being that I sort of know now what it will be like. Still there will be another angle to consider & that's the *fact that I'll be a married man & building a home. Another phase of life I've never experienced. I wonder how I'd feel if I hadn't met you & expected to come back to you. When I got into the Army I had made up my mind not to get mixed up with any girls for fear I'd meet the wrong one, finally it dawned on me that it might be a long time & I wasn't getting any younger. If I was to have a girl somewhere near my age & still have a sweet young bride, I'd have to do something about it. It didn't quite happen like that but I believe that's about what was running through my mind even though I hardly realized it & probably wouldn't admit it to myself. So I decided to do something about it, still sort of being afraid that being away from home & all would make me make a poor choice. Maybe that explains why I took a long time before I took you out & why I was so slow in asking you to be my wife. I know the day I asked you to come home with me you hardly knew what to do because I had made no promises, etc. You actually were wondering whether I'd <u>ever</u> get around to ask you. Actually I wanted to but my family worried me. They hardly knew about you & something like this wasn't like me at all. I realize you were in a tough spot & were wondering what I had in mind & Lord knows I hardly knew what to do. Under different circumstances I would have proposed weeks before, I had thought of asking you or rather picturing you as my wife long before I even took you out. From the first time I met you I guess I was caught. This was before you knew I existed at least you don't seem to remember me as long back as I remember you. I guess you had a lot to do with my changing my mind about leaving women alone while I was in the Army. I'm almost convinced it was love at first sight but I didn't know it . . . just want to add that we've had some wonderful times together & I'm sure we'll have more wonderful time when I get back but I'm afraid I'm going to need help to get readjusted. Why I worry about it now, I don't know because I'm afraid it will be months before it will happen but I can't help thinking about. There's one thing for sure, you will* *make it a lot easier. I love you so.*

Not exactly a beautiful letter & maybe not very interesting but maybe I'll be able to do better tomorrow night.

Good night Baby & I repeat I love you & miss you so darn much.

All my love

Jack

Dad's letter on June 3 revealed that he had worried about how his family would react to his engagement. He thought it would seem sudden to them, and he worried they might think he was making a hasty or impulsive decision. His family didn't meet Gloria until he brought her home immediately before his deployment, then suddenly, he was engaged to her. However, his worries were unfounded—his family accepted her immediately.

The letter also showed amazing foresight as he wondered how his life might be after the war. He again put himself into a reflective mood as he tried to envision his future. He anticipated problems that many of his peers did not: "Getting out of the Army will be every bit as bad as getting used to being in it." That in itself is truly insightful. Although almost every soldier who experiences war wants nothing more than to get away from it, Dad knew there would be things he'd miss. For instance, there is never anyone in life as close to you as your comrades in arms; that comradery is the one thing soldiers truly lament after leaving the armed forces—no one understands you better than those with whom you've shared your daily life, with whom you've fought and bled. I am amazed at this bit of reflection and Dad's anticipation of what was to come. He was apprehensive about the new life he was about to experience even though he couldn't wait to get to it.

June 7, 1945

My Dearest Gloria

. . . I'm in a sort of a low mood today. Just disgusted with

everything in general. Nothing has really gone wrong but just a series of little things. First of all we have two Officers, the Bn. C. O. and my company C. O. that don't know the first thing about running an outfit. Both direct commissioned men & recruits at that. They are old men but not old in the Army. I'm almost the oldest Army man in the outfit. As far as that goes I've had my commission longer than most of them. It makes you so damn mad when you see them fumble around & then come out with an order that's absolutely silly. This used to be a good outfit but we certainly collected a lot of bums in the last couple of months. Actually they are nice enough but so entirely incompetent. If they'd only use a little common sense & let some of the junior Officers give a suggestion, the fellows who know & laugh at their mistakes it wouldn't be so bad but they insist on making fools of themselves. I'm in a job now that I don't know too many details of & I take suggestions & recommendations from the boys that worked there before. After all they are not children & a lot of them are good. Even a private can come to me with an idea & I'll consider it. I've seen the time when I said something & an enlisted man disagreed & when I thought it over I found I was wrong & admitted it, but not these boys, they know it all. I guess I've said my piece . . .

May 9, 1945 [June 9]

My Dearest Gloria

. . . Had a little stroke of good luck today. The Company Commander is being transferred out & the man we're getting is a good man according to reports. As a man I had nothing against the man but his inexperience made it difficult to work for him. Actually off duty we were good friends. He finally saw it himself & asked to get out. It didn't take long for him to get it when he made up his mind. I knew nothing about it until he called me & told me he was leaving. A matter of a day or so after he had asked for it. One or two changes yet would put this outfit on top again. It's amazing how important a certain Officer or group of Officers can be. They <u>*must*</u> *be*

good to have a good outfit. I don't speak about these things from my own experiences alone, most of the junior Officers will agree to what I say & have expressed themselves that way . . .

. . . Say, I heard a bit of good news today. Two million men to be released. I guess you know all about it as you seem to be watching for the same news items I do. You couldn't be sweating it out as much as I am. If so, you'd be [slowly] going mad. I believe Gen. Pershing once said "War is hell." I guess he really meant that being away from home & the ones you love is "hell." That is the thing that seems to bother the men the most of all . . .

June 12, 1945

My Dearest Gloria

I guess I should start the same way tonight as a man coming home & wondering whether to throw his hat in first. I didn't write since the 9th. Day before yesterday it rained like hell & I was almost flooded out. I started a letter to my folks & while I was trying to hold the tent down during a storm that came up while writing the paper got wet so I gave up writing for that night. Last night I had one of my boys in for a friendly beer because he left for China this morning. Naturally it was late & just one of those things. I hope you don't mind too much . . .

Just had an ally of ours in for a beer. A British Officer. A nice "chap" who is living with us now. I never told you before I guess but I spent four months with a "limey" division last fall. Remember when I told you I was being shot at fairly regularly. Well, that was the time. I was with the Artillery as communications officer. I enjoyed the British company but I didn't particularly like the job. The British "Tommy" or infantry man is about as good as you can find. Not at all like the Britishers you find in India. They'd do anything for you & are really swell to work with. Actually I had a dozen or so British Soldiers working for me at the time. Chinese artillery, with American headquarters supporting British infantry

& it worked. In addition to that we had some Indians mixed in. Three languages within one division but we got along & killed a lot of Japs. I'll never forget those months. My Grandchildren will hear about it. Maybe I should get started on children first . . .

June 22, 1945

. . . I see "Uncle Joe" got a new job. Might get to see the old boy again if I stick around long enough. Some time, somehow the forces on the continent & the forces on the Islands will meet. I sure would like to get behind an American fighting outfit instead of the "Chinks." The "Limeys" were O.K. but I would like to see how the Americans work. Who knows what may develop. We certainly won't stay in Burma until the war is over. Not a fighting outfit like the 988th. I'm still hoping to get away from the war within the next six months. Not that I'm close to it now but between 10 & 15 thousand miles would suit me better. I'm not afraid of it but I want to go home.

Listening to the "Hit Parade." "Rum and Coca Cola," "My Dreams are Getting Better," etc. The "Armed Forces Radio" is really O.K. I never dreamed of anything like this would be made available to us overseas when I first got into the Army. I didn't expect to get overseas, either, but here I am . . .

Although I have most of the letters Dad wrote to Mom while he was in the CBI Theater, I have very few letters from Dad to his folks. The one dated July 1, 1945, is the earliest that I have. I found it in the shoebox with Mom's stash, though. I don't know how it got there, although she may have gotten it during one of her visits to Durand.

July 1, 1945

Dear Folks.

Got two letters in a couple of days from you so I'd better send one of my own on its way. Three pictures this time. All good ones too. The "Old Man" really looks proud with his rig. I notice Tony & Fanny [horses] are really getting white. Tony was almost white the last time I saw him but Fanny seems quite a little lighter. Hope to see the box the horses & driver before the box is used too much . . .

. . . So Arthur Jungwirth is home. I wonder how he is. How many months was he a prisoner? Those are the boys that really had it tough. It's not for me, if I ever got into a tight spot I [would] fight until I got out or else. Of course in his case I guess he didn't have much choice . . .

. . . Not much to write about from here otherwise. Naturally I'm sweating out the point system. Most everyone seems to think I'll get out but I'm not counting on making it very soon. If I get back before the first of the year I'll consider myself lucky . . .

Anton Forster on farm with wagon and horses

I smiled when I read the letter Dad wrote to his parents. He mentioned Tony and Fanny, two huge workhorses his folks had on their farm. I remember them being there in the 1950s when I visited as a child.

I'd never heard of the former POW from the Lima area that Dad mentioned, Art Jungwirth. I did grow up with some neighborhood kids whose dad, Walter N. Gilles, had been a prisoner of war. He'd been captured in the Philippines at the beginning of the war and was lucky to survive the starvation treatment the Japs were infamous for, as well as the transport to Japan. Many of the ships that transported American POWs to Japan were sunk by American submarines and planes. I remember Walt Gilles as a pretty good guy. He was our insurance man.

July 2, 1945

My Dearest Gloria

. . . One letter mentioned your brother's opinion of my going home. With his points & overseas time I should beat him home & be out of the Army but who knows. I'm just a little afraid of being held up by that little phrase "Military Necessity." I'm not a hot shot operator but I do have two years rating as an excellent Officer & by the looks of things that doesn't pay. Something is bound to happen to hold me up. It would be just too good to be true if there were no obstacles. By the way I might be taking a little tour one of these days & you might not hear from me for a week or two. Don't worry, I won't be fighting Japs, I'm all finished with that . . .

July 3, 1945

My Dearest Gloria

. . . I'm really loafing these days. Funny thing about war it's a continuous cycle of hurry up and wait. Next week I'll probably find myself busy as hell . . .

. . . 24 hours later . . .

. . . This happens to be the 4th of July, at least it feels like the 4th even though it is after midnight. Had quite a time with our "Limey" Officer today. Naturally the 4th of July is not a holiday in the British Empire. Anyway I kidded him & he asked for his tea

back & I told him to go to the Boston Harbor, etc. Well finally it ended up with him rubbing a raw egg into my hair. We were both sober, too & eggs cost about 31 cents apiece here. I dared him to do it but I didn't expect him to do it. When he did get at me I had to laugh so I couldn't defend myself, sooo . . .

July 9, 1945

My Dearest Gloria

. . .Well baby, I said it was to be short & as far as news is concerned it was or is.

Remember what I told you about not hearing from me for a while. I expect to go on this business trip shortly so don't worry. Absolutely no danger . . .

That business trip turned out to be a transfer from Bhamo, Burma, to Kunming, China. Since Dad had been assigned a jeep for his job, he drove it all the way over the Stilwell and Burma Roads to Kunming, China. It was a long trip, 707 miles, over winding, bone-jarring switchback roads up the mountains of southwest China. I don't know how long it took him, but it was probably well over a week.

[Left] Driving the Burma Road – The Salween River Crossing in China.
Taken by Louis Forster, similar to Signal Corps photos.
[Above] "U. S. Convoy enters China over 21-turn switchback section of the Burma Road. (Shutterstock)

10

China

'Blood Chits', which consisted of a sheet of cloth or leather, were given to foreign service personnel in China, with the Chinese flag on top and writing below. The writing means, 'This foreign person has come to China to help in the war effort. Soldiers and civilians, one and all, should rescue, protect and provide him with medical care.'

Kunming, China, 1945

Dad had suspected he was headed to Kunming, and when he arrived, he told his folks he was in China—although he didn't specify which city. Bhamo had been his longest assignment in theater, and it had been a comfortable one for him, so he had some trepidation about leaving. But China was another country to add to his list, and it would be from China that he finally began his journey home. I never found the first letter Dad wrote to Gloria upon arriving in Kunming; it wasn't in the shoebox. But I did discover a long letter he wrote to his folks. He spoke in less-than-glowing terms about the Chinese.

July 24, 1945

Dear Folks

About time for a letter. Got news this time & it might be either good or bad. I am now in China. Yep the trip I was talking about was over the Burma Road to China. Well, there's a lot to say about China. I don't particularly like it but the weather is much better than Burma. A lot cooler & not so much rain. I say it's either good news or bad to be in China because I don't know as yet how it will affect my coming home. Maybe I'd have a better chance in Burma but it's hard to say now.

Getting back to China. The people are really poor & dirty. I believe that they are actually filthier than the Indians. You have millions of poor people & still there seems to be plenty of everything here. They have all the things in the store windows that you can't get in the States. Of course the prices are beyond reach, a Parker '51 pen costs around $100. I suppose that's why they still have them. How the stuff got here is hard to understand, new models of all makes of cars . . . Clever people these Chinese. The trouble with China is that there [are] too many Chinamen in it. Actually China is not too bad, there is a lot of beautiful scenery here & I suppose not every pretty Chinese girl is a prostitute (It almost seems like it if you get downtown at night) & only the cities & villages stink. Besides I just came through the poorest part of China, that is Yunnan Province. Maybe the eastern part is better. It's a funny war in China & I'm sure the boys getting back will be able to tell plenty that doesn't show up in print or heard over the radio.

The Burma Road is another matter. It's not bad but it does loosen the bolts on the trucks, make you nervous & takes fat off where it does the most good. It is by far the most crooked road & goes over the highest mountains I've ever seen. In places I guess you could spit two miles, straight down. You travel a half day & get only five miles or so, air-line. It will take care of a lot more traffic than I dreamed of but it's not exactly the same as our four lane highways. The scenery along the [road] is really something. Sometimes it scares you then you get along a stretch that's really beautiful. I drove a jeep myself every inch of the way & am glad to have made the trip but I wouldn't like to make it again unless I could make it part of my trip home.

I'm in China but I'm miles away from the front & of course the

Jap Air Force is a little shy these days so I'm as safe & comfortable as can be.

By the way, here's my new address. Lt. Louis J. Forster 04637436

Co "B" 988 Sig Serv. Bn.

APO 627 c/o PMNYC

Hq. C.C.C.

The C.C.C. doesn't mean Civilian Conservation Corps but Chinese Combat Command

I'm sweating out this darn point system. It's about time they got it out & let us know either, or. I'm quite sure I'll make it but it looks like I'll have to sweat out a replacement & that may take months. I'll feel lucky if I make it by Christmas . . .

July 27, 1945

My Dearest Gloria

. . . By the way, the mail situation is getting bad. No letters for almost a week now. That doesn't happen often. Everybody is in the same boat though so—. I have an idea something is holding the mail up. We had a period like this just before D-day in Europe & maybe another D-day is pending. As far as that goes everybody is expecting another big deal in the near future. Naturally I don't know any more about it than you but by listening to the news I feel something is brewing . . .

Still no points announced. Some of the fellows that came over with me have gone home but not all on points. One just left yesterday with 103 points. Anyone with over 100 can go home now even before the final score is announced & it seems that without a replacement being present. Getting back to the fellows who came over with me going home. You remember Lt. Filiak? Well, the boy has gone home. I don't know just under what plan he went home on but I believe it's some special deal he got through his Burma work. I don't know whether I ever told you that he had been with "Merrill's

Marauders" & as I understand it they were to be returned to the U.S. after they had completed their mission so he's stayed longer than he should have. As for me I don't know but I'm hopeful, but I'm afraid I'll have to sweat out a replacement from the States. You can see what that means . . .

Dad mentioned that the mail situation was getting bad again, and again it could be the move to China that was causing it. At the same time, he felt that something was brewing. Little did he know that something very big was, indeed, brewing.

July 29, 1945

My Dearest Gloria

. . . Got a job tonight. I caught Officer of the Day. I never like it very well because if something should happen things can be pretty unpleasant. Besides that I have to get up during the night. We really have to have quite a guard here. These Chinese would steal the eyes out of your head if you gave them half a chance. It seems like a Chinese national pastime. It seems as natural to them as going to the movies is to us & they are darn clever at it. They pull the most daring stuff you ever heard of, just like a fox in a chicken [coop]. Well, anyway I hope none of them give us any serious trouble tonight or he or she might be among the dead in the morning.

I'm sending a little gift just a little something for your birthday. Twenty-four on the eighteenth of Aug. I believe that's the right date . . .

Aug 3, 1945

My Dearest Gloria

I'm getting ahead of myself. Lord knows I should remember the date. The day I've been waiting for & counting on but really got slapped in the face. 85 points & me with 84. I guess it won't change my status much & I might even get home around New Years yet. I'm guessing of course . . . I guess it doesn't do much good to gripe about it.

This mail situation is bad. No mail for several days again. I like to get it every day & not all at once. By the way still no picture.

I think I'll check into the hospital in a day or so to get a check-up. This dysentery I had might still be in my system even though I seem to be O.K. They recommend it because a person can become a carrier & give trouble later, at home. Can't have that . . .

Aug 5, 1945

My Dearest Gloria

. . . I might tell you about my new camp. We live in pyramidal tents (the same kind of tents we had at Banning). We have electric light, I have my radio & a tarp as a floor. I'm all alone in the tent now & have too much room. How about moving in? It won't cost you anything. Anyway it's comfortable enough & it keeps most of the rain out. Sometimes I could use a stove though. Gets pretty chilly around here. The wind blew a lot today & it kept blowing through the tent so It wasn't so good. I got into bed & slept almost all afternoon . . .

. . . I'm still a little out of sorts about that "Point System." 84 points, so near & yet so far. It'll take months before they lower it & then I've still got [to] sweat out a man to replace me. I'll live through it I guess but I don't like it one bit. I keep thinking of how much time I've already given & how you sit back there just marking time . . .

Signal Corps Camp

Aug 9, 1945

My Dearest Gloria

. . . The news is getting better every day. Russia finally decided to come into the war before it's too late. It certainly indicates that it won't last long now. In fact I'll be disappointed if it lasts another 30 days. Then what? Yes, I don't think Russia was quite ready as yet but was forced to come in for fear that the Japs would quit & they wouldn't have any word at the peace table. It all looks good to me & brother am I anxious to get it over with. I can see now where it is very possible that I could be home by Christmas, maybe even sooner. The war will certainly be over by then. Of course it will take a little time to even get started home when it does end. Things don't happen fast in the Army unless it's something unpleasant. No, I hardly expect to get started home within 30 days after V-J day. After that it depends on whether I go by boat or plane as to how long it will take. I'll take a boat if I can because I want to be

sure of getting there. Besides I'd like to make a boat trip. It probably won't take over thirty to fifty days & I guess it won't matter much, just so I know I'm going. As I said before it might be a lot easier to get away from here than any other theater. Being in a tactical command also helps & besides having a few points should put me up on the list . . .

Dad didn't mention either of the atomic bombs that had been dropped over Japan in the previous three days as a possible reason for the war ending. He had probably never heard of the bomb since the Manhattan Project was top secret, and he probably had no concept of the implications of the dawn of the atomic age.

Dad seemed to think Russian involvement would bring about the end of the war. He believed that, in typical Russian fashion, the Soviets viewed it as an opportunity to be at the negotiating table and gain more territory before the war ended. In reality, in the wake of a series of Russian defeats at the hands of the Japanese before World War II, they had signed a non-aggression pact with Japan. This freed up Russian troops who had been defending against the Japanese in the east and allowed them to transfer troops from Eastern Russia to deal with Hitler's invasion of Russia in June 1941. Also, at the Teheran conference in 1943, Stalin had agreed to declare war on Japan within three months of the end of the war in Europe.

Meanwhile, Dad was looking for any way to get home. He grew hopeful again despite his disappointment over the point system.

Aug 10, 1945

My Dearest Gloria

Am I excited tonight. It looks like this is it. It's still not for sure but the rumors & semi-official broadcasts are coming in every time you turn around. The people of Chungking are celebrating already but maybe something has gone wrong. Well, just now the local station has announced that the war is over. I still don't believe it but at eleven o'clock, 10 PM now the President is to make an announcement so maybe it's not wishful thinking on someone's part after all. Baby, you had better start thinking seriously about the wedding veil. As I said I'm excited & I repeat it. I'm so excited I can hardly write. Maybe I should break out my last three quarts of Indian Gin. I'll wait until eleven & if it's really true you'll hear about a beautiful hangover.

Well, Baby, I'm going to say Good night & keep your fingers crossed & maybe we can be together in a couple of months.

All my love

Jack

Dad worried for a moment that something had gone wrong. Little did he or anyone outside of Tokyo know that some intrigue was happening between the Emperor and the Japanese military. This intrigue arose out of a tradition among Japanese junior officers to occasionally disobey orders from higher command. Indeed, members of the Imperial Guard and a faction of officers from the Ministry of War tried to initiate a coup and prevent the Japanese surrender. Emperor Hirohito had recorded a message to the Japanese people announcing the surrender, but insurgents tried to intercept it before it was broadcast. Luckily, there was a blackout due to a fortuitous bombing raid by American B-29s over Tokyo, preventing the insurgents from finding the Emperor's agents and intercepting the recording. The Emperor's message was finally broadcast to the Japanese people at 11:00 a.m. on August 15. Many of those behind the coup, which is now referred to as the Kyūjō incident, committed suicide as the surrender moved forward and was ratified on the deck of the USS *Missouri* in Tokyo Bay on September 2, 1945.

Aug 12, 1945

My Dearest Gloria

Still sweating out the end of the war. It does look like a sure *thing though. The other night the boys were just a little overanxious, I guess, when they said it was over. I wasn't too disappointed because I felt it was something like that. I did celebrate a little but not too much, not <u>that</u> night but last night a bunch of us really went to town. Need I say I'm not feeling too hot today. Couldn't eat breakfast or lunch & very little supper. I am feeling a lot better now & I guess I'll live. I'm very sleepy though because the party lasted until four, they tell me I'd better go on the wagon & stick with beer. I certainly will when I get back. I can handle that a little better. Besides, I can't be getting "lit" or you're apt to beat up on me. I promise I won't tie into it like that again at least for a while . . .*

Aug 14, 1945

My Dearest Gloria

Still the war isn't over for sure. Everything indicates that it is or will be in a matter of hours but nothing official. Actually it doesn't mean much now when the news does come. The really big news will be when I get on the plane or boat or when I collect that first kiss. Maybe it won't be so good, after all, I haven't kissed a gal for almost 580 days. That's rough calculation it might be a day or so more or less, since the 28th of Dec. '43. The Eau Claire station the place. What station will the next one be at. Hard to say because I might go to Camp McCoy, Wis . . .

. . . Speaking of Camp McCoy, you know that's where I took my basic training. I understand the camp is a lot better now but it will bring back memories. It's been a helluva long time. It really makes one think back on what has happened, the places I've been, the people I've met, the friends I've made & lost track of. Need I say who <u>she</u> is. It also sort of makes me wonder what it will be like. After five years & all the different things I've been exposed to. I suppose my attitude, likes, dislikes, etc. have changed. Still every time I got back on leave I felt I could go right back without much trouble. Lord knows, I wanted to. The only thing that I'm sure has

changed is my self-confidence. I used to be a little afraid to tackle a job even though I knew I could handle it. I seem to have found out my capabilities. Of course there are other things but they don't seem to stand out as much. It really makes one wonder what is to come.

Well, Baby, I've got to write the folks so I'd better say Good night. Don't worry about me. I still love you & hope to be back soon.

All my love—Jack

Aug 16, 1945

My Dearest Gloria

Another rainy cool day. Seems like we brought the Burma monsoons with me or rather us. I'm tired tonight so maybe that is the reason for the error in grammar.

Well, the war is over. It's for sure this time. Can't say I feel much different. It's just hard to believe after such a long time. I hope it's the last one I ever see again.

. . . Had quite a surprise yesterday. I went to Church in the afternoon & a guy kept looking at me & seemed to recognize me. Finally the guy came over to me & asked my name & told me his. It was embarrassing as hell. He happened to be from Durand & worse than that a first cousin of mine. I never saw him that often at home but I certainly should have known him. After he told me his last name I still didn't know which of the Weber families he came from & I didn't know his name. It's not too hard to see why because he did change a lot & I had no idea he was around. He lives just a couple of miles down the road, so I should see a lot of him. He's a Staff Sgt. in medical supply of the Station Hospital . . .

This was the second time in theater that Dad had run into a cousin from his own rural parish near Durand, Wisconsin. Dad's mother (my grandmother) was a Weber, as was the young staff sergeant who recognized Dad in church that Sunday. Small world, indeed!

Aug 18, 1945

My Dearest Gloria

How is my sweet little gal on her birthday. I do hope I'm right & I'd swear I'm right. This calendar has a picture of a soldier kissing his bride & I'm really missing those kisses tonight. The most wonderful thing I've ever experienced in my life. You are the only gal I've ever went for in a big way . . .

. . . Say do you know? Well, maybe you don't but the censor is out of a job. Yes we can write anything we like except for something you don't care about anyway. I mean the political situation in China. Well, Baby, I'm in Kunming, China. My last place was Bhamo, Burma. I lived in Bhamo for about 6 months, before that it was Myitkyina, the place where Merrill's Marauders got beat up. When I got there it looked like heaven because it was just after I've got away from the British 36th Div.

Stopped for a little while to eat. At the 36th Division I was Artillery Communication Officer & had to get right up to the front lines. Sometimes forward of the main Infantry. There were many instances where I was ahead of Japs getting a line out to an artillery person who was way out front to see what the guns were shooting at. I guess you wouldn't be interested, though I left the outfit at PinWee [Pinwe] the 29 of Nov. just four months after I had joined the Chindits.

Well, Baby I'm in Kunming now. I don't have a job because the job I was supposed to take is out. I was supposed to go out the Sixth Chinese Army towards Hong Kong or Canton. I had the orders but they reached me the day the Japs were about to give up so everything being stopped I didn't go. The reason I was being sent is because the repair & supply section is needed in our setup. So I'm without a job except for wiring the area here, but I've got the boys about to finish that. There is a good chance of us going to Shanghai shortly but I still don't see where there would be a job that calls for my qualifications. Guess I'll work on that angle for getting home.

Maybe if I put up a good story I might get out of setting up the port at Shanghai . . . going into a part of the country where manpower is short & no job for me. It wouldn't help mentioning you but I guess that's the real reason for me wanting to get back.

Whoa, just was called into the Bn. HQ & I've got a job. Probably temporary, at least I hope. I'm supposed to go by plane to Chungking, about 100 miles north of Canton to set up a radio station for C.C.C. (Chinese Combat Command). I know very few of the details but it looks like C.C.C. is moving towards the coast & they want communications. That's one reason I hate the Army. You never can get set & say, well, I'm here & I'll stay. This job will keep me busy & time will pass fast. I imagine I'll be my own boss at least I hope so. Another thing is that I'll be getting closer to the coast & to a port.

Well, Baby, I'd better get ready to move so I'll say Good night. I do love you so. It's almost unbearable to be away from you.

All my love
Jack.

The phrase "military necessity" had reared its ugly head in reference to my dad. He was a communications specialist with extensive knowledge of radio and radio repair. He'd worried about this—he understood he might not be able to escape assignments that called for his expertise, and this one caught him. Little did he know the importance of this new assignment or the role it would play in history. He was also unaware that his time abroad would extend beyond Chongqing, nor did he know the things he was yet to see and do.

Aug 22, 1945

My Dearest Gloria

A long time no letter. Well, you know about the trip I expected to make the morning after my last letter. I left the old place (by the way censorship has been brought back again so I can't mention places, etc.) & got here without too much trouble. It's a lot warmer here but not as bad as Burma. Need I say I've been busy? I guess not but I have been. A couple of days I was up until 0200, two o'clock to you. Very interesting, though. Time passes much faster in addition to that things look a little more promising as far as getting home goes. I'm pretty sure of making it by Christmas, maybe before.

The place here is swell. We have a new building (not completed yet) almost like "Stateside" White plastered walls, wood floors, lights & all in all very comfortable. Showers a hundred yards away. Mess halls that compare with any in the regular camp at home, etc. It's by far the best place I've been in since I left Delhi. In fact I believe I prefer it to Delhi. There is no city of anything worthwhile but Chinese cities don't have much to offer anyway. Most of them are Off Limits & I guess it's a good idea to keep them that way.

The Chinese people here seem to be better than those I've seen in Western China. One thing is worse & that's the mosquitoes. The biggest & best I've ever seen including those in Burma. They don't give me too much trouble but they look like they would drain you if they got a chance. All in all I'm much better satisfied here & wouldn't care to go back. A job of "me" own with not to many people bothering me.

Well baby, I've got to write my folks & get some sleep so I'd better say Good night. I love you & miss you lots.

All my love - Jack

Aug 23, 1945

My Dearest Gloria

Another report coming up from Lt. Forster in China.

Not an awful lot to write about. With censorship back in effect. Don't even hear the news these days. All sorts of radio equipment but no spares. I left my National back at the Outfit & the sets we have here are all in use. I sent a radio tonight asking for a spare set so we should be able to catch up on a little current history.

We're getting settled a little better now & we do have a little more time for ourselves. I slept quite a little this afternoon but I'm still sleepy. I guess I don't sleep too well at night. I stay right where we're set up & of course don't get to bed until late & besides there always is quite a little noise all night long.

Still no letters & I'm afraid it might take a little time before we get any. Too many places for the mail to be forwarded from. I imagine some of it is still coming thru 218 . . .

Aug 24, 1945

My Dearest Gloria

On the ball these days. A letter every day. Are you happy? Why you're interested in these dry letters is more than I can understand. Same old stuff every day. Now if I were there we could get into a fight or something but maybe that wouldn't do. I remember O.K.

We got a spare receiver tonight so we can catch up on the news now. We're right here where news in being made but we know less than if it were miles away from us. The World knows before we do.

By the looks of things we're going to lose our happy home. Apparently the building is being put up to house the Base HQ & when it's finished we'll be moved out. I hope they give us a break for a new location. They seem to go in for a lot of comfort for themselves so maybe they won't be too hard on us.

Aug 25, 1945

. . . Just found out that I'll be moving again in a couple of days. It's getting me closer to home all the time but the trouble is I make stops & never know how long those stops will turn out to be. It does look though like we'll be going out by water. Of course we'll have to wait until they open China Ports. If they ever get this Peace signed it shouldn't be long. With the points I have I shouldn't be one of the last ones to leave. Naturally I won't be the first. I

don't have luck like that. I'd like to be on the "Queen Mary" right now. It will probably be a Liberty ship loaded to overflowing & as uncomfortable as hell. All in all things do look brighter than they did several weeks ago. I'm still as anxious though . . .

Although I have most of the letters my dad wrote while he was in theater, I only have a few of Mom's. The one I've included was written on August 31, 1945 and was returned to her from China as undeliverable, so it must have been sent just as Dad was about to begin making his way home. By the time she wrote that letter, Mom knew Dad's family in Wisconsin because she had visited them several times. I've included this letter to give a small sampling of Mom's life in Iowa before she married Dad.

August 31, 1945

My Dearest Jack:

Made it back from Des Moines okay, along with a kinky head of hair—result of the permanent. But it'll calm down when I go to work on it with a good brush (Trouble is, you can't find a good brush these days—waiting for the nylon ones to re-appear on the market.

I was disappointed to find I didn't have any mail from you waiting for me—but I did get one this morning. The mail is terribly slow—this one was dated Aug 14 & on Monday (this is Friday) I got 2 dated 10th & 16th—all mixed up aren't we? So, that's all we can do about it—just grin & bear it? So I'll just bide my time. Maybe it won't be so long till we can say "to heck with the postman—don't want to write any letters."

Ain't I funny today? Very amusing, don't you think? I'm all tired out. A day down in Des Moines is bad enough, but when it's so hot that (well, heck it's hotter in China, I suppose). And my feet hurt—those darned high heels again! I'm never going to buy another pair of high heels. Got home on the 7 o'clock bus, had a sandwich & Very & Betty [Mom's roommates] wanted to go to the

Show, but sat around deciding yes or no several times until it had to wait till the second show. I wanted to go to bed, but Betty thinks I have to go along, so off we went. Anyway, it was nice & cool by the time we got home & we slept good.

I did get a letter from my brother Joe, too. I saw May [Joe's wife] when I was in Des Moines & she hadn't heard from Joe since a letter written the 9th & this one I received was written the 16th. She had thought he might be on his way home, but I guess his letters might have been held up. He sent me a beautiful hanky made by a Philipino girl out of parachute silk. The hand work was wonderful. I have to write to him, Lord, it's almost two weeks since I've written him.

I also had a letter from Marcella telling me that Ralph Anderson finally turned up. She was a little bit upset because he & his girl friend were in [unintelligible] on wash day, I guess. But I hear tell that you are quite a fellow. Such praise for a little man. But I always knew that. Don't think that I can't pick 'em? It's nice to hear that you got along so well with your men, cause heaven knows one of us has to be easy to get along with & I'm not claiming to be it. I only hope I will be for you. I'll try. Could because I love you—much, very much.

Hit bottom—bye for now.

Always

Gloria

Sept 1, 1945

My Dearest Gloria

Another month gone by. Over twenty gone by & its not sure as to how many more before we can take up again where we left off then. Things are looking like we might expect an early return once the peace is signed. I have a feeling things will happen fast once we get started. Everyone will be pulling the right way anyway. It certainly won't be hard to get the men to do anything that will get us home a day earlier. Right now we can't do any more than guess but we should have a pretty good idea in a couple of weeks. Right now I don't believe it will be over two months before we start leaving, I hope.

Still no letters, getting sort of hopeless. It will take me a day to get them all read once they catch up. I do hope that I get it before I get home.

More dope coming out every day on points, etc. I'll get home one way or other yet . . .

I also have Mom's letter to Dad from September 1, 1945. It must have been hard for them to carry on a romance solely by letter for almost two years. Many long-distance relationships failed because of such long deployments.

I can relate to what my parents went through—I had a small dose of it before marrying the love of my life. She and I both lived in Honduras, but many miles apart. People always used to tell us, "Amor de lejos es amor de pendejos." Roughly translated, this means, "Love from a distance is love for fools." However, both my marriage and my parents' marriage lasted more than fifty years. I guess absence does make the heart grow fonder!

September 1, 1945

My Dearest Jack:

The first of September & for the first time in a long time we start out a month in peacetime. It already seems like it has been over a month since peace was declared. I wonder how long it will be till you get home?

If I hurry and get this written, I'll have it ready so the mail man can take it. I usually wait till after he's gone to write so that I'll have something to write about if I get any mail from you. I haven't had any of the most recent ones from you since Monday—& that was written the 16th, so they are awfully slow coming through.

But with all those troops & ships, etc. gathering in Japan, I guess we can't expect much else.

Excuse me, I think I'm going to get some dictation any minute now. I can't even seem to write longhand today. My hand just doesn't want to move, so I don't know how I'm going to do with shorthand.

I had a heck of a time sleeping last night. I went to bed at about 10:30 for a change & I was just dead tired. But Betty had to go to the train to meet her sister & she had to yell out & tell us she was leaving—just as I was dozing off. She said she hoped that they didn't wake us up when they came in, but they really came in with a lot of banging & giggles so–I heard her! Then I vaguely heard 'em talking & giggling in their room, but went off to sleep & then woke up again when Betty came to bed. She slept with me because there was her sister & girlfriend in her bed. But, after that I finally got to sleep, but after so many interruptions I didn't get rested enough—or maybe I got too much, anyway, I'm tired today!

Had that dictation, and it came out perfect, so in spite of the slow hand work (more dictation, back again) I still can't seem to make my hands work as fast as my head today. I think it's about time to get those finger nails filed down again.

The mail man has been here & left a letter from you—still no new ones, just filling in those I haven't got between the 10th & 16th—10, 12, 14 & 16, so far. So you think maybe after you land at Camp McCoy you might look me up. Well, I hate to break it to you so bluntly, kid, but if you wait even a couple of weeks, you might as well forget all about me. I'm mighty touchy about being first on your list, but after all you're going to be the first, last & always on my list. I realize you were only kidding, so I'd better not get into that "let's argue" mood.

This is all the stationery I brought today, so I'd better tell you I love you & miss you very, very much.

Always

Gloria

P.S. I always cut my letters short, but if I didn't I'd bore you even worse. Understand?

As of yet, Dad was unable to tell Mom exactly where he was or what he was doing in China due to military censorship being back in force. I don't know exactly when Dad flew to Nanking, but he arrived in advance of the formal surrender of Japanese troops in China. Nanking was still occupied by the Japanese military at that time, and there were still thousands of armed Japanese troops there. When Dad landed at the airfield in Nanking, he took pictures of Japanese warplanes on the field. He also walked the streets, which were still patrolled by armed Japanese troops. He was one of only a few Americans in Nanking at that time, and there were even fewer British. The Chinese troops were just arriving, still in small numbers. Dad's job was to set up a radio station to handle press traffic for the event, so he had to be there several days in advance. Japan had signed the surrender on the US battleship *Missouri* on September 2, 1945, but large areas of occupied China were still being administered by Japanese personnel. The formal surrender of those troops in China took place in Nanking on September 9. Dad was there—in the room.

British Major General Eric Hayes was also there and had flown in to Nanking's airport, as did some of the Allies. General Hayes was also in the room when the Japanese signed the surrender. He said, "We found that we were only the sixth Allied plane to land at Nanking airfield, which was still entirely under Japanese protection, if not control. At that time in Nanking there were only some fifty Americans and 200-300 Chinese Commando troops, against 70,000 Japanese quartered in the city."[20]

20 Rupert Wingfield Hayes, "Witnessing Japan's Surrender to China," BBC News, September 2, 2015, https://www.bbc.com/news/magazine-34126445.

Japanese warplanes on Nanking Airfield

Surrender of Japanese Troops in China

Sept 10, 1945

My Dearest Gloria

I'm getting bad with my letter writing again. Missed last night & the night before. I have a good excuse for last night. I got sick & really felt terrible. My stomach is still not so hot & the bathroom is getting a workout. (No, I didn't have a drink). The night before I was busy until late. That was the day before the surrender of the Japs in China & things were in an uproar.

Well, I'm still in Nanking & I suppose if you listened to the radio or saw a newspaper you'll know this is the place where the surrender document was signed. I got in on the signing, that is I watched them sign. It didn't take long, about twenty minutes. We were in the auditorium of the Military Academy when the Japs came in, of course the Chinese Generals were already seated & waiting. Anyway, Seven Japs, all with their heads shaved, came in, bowed & sat down facing the Chinese. The whole thing was very impressive with all the flags of the United Nations, inside & outside the building, Chinese Generals by the dozens, about twenty photographers besides the amateurs (all countries represented, English Australians, Indian, Chinese & our own war correspondents). Really a historic occasion.

Got downtown a couple of times in the last couple of days. It's quite a city. Almost everyone is buying cameras including myself. I got myself a "Zeiss Ikon" for 35 bucks. It's very cheap for this type camera but some of the fellows did even better than that. I'm satisfied though at the 1/2 price of the things. It's a German made camera that just isn't available in the States any more. Even during normal times the same camera would sell for 60 bucks. It uses 120 film & takes a 2 1/2 x 2 1/2 picture. By the way I got a Zeiss filter & four rolls of Jap film with it & of course a good case. All this came about because I believe I've lost my other camera. I thought I had it when I left Kunming but I didn't. It might still be back there but I'm afraid not. I did lend it to a guy who may still have it.

Am I slipping. I started this letter yesterday but something happened & of course I didn't get back to it.

I don't feel like writing an awful lot tonight. As I said before I was sick & still am, not serious but it does make me feel awful tired & a little "light" in the stomach. Everybody had a session of it so I guess maybe the mess (kitchen) had something to do with it.

Here's something that might interest you. It looks now like the 988th Sig. will be leaving China sometime in October. We'll probably leave from Shanghai. If that's the case I'll probably be home sometime before Dec. 1. That might make it necessary for us to wait until Jan before we can be married. Not if I can help it but usually people don't get married during Advent around home so I guess we could wait another couple of weeks after two years. I'm not stalling if that's what you're thinking? In fact I'll just let you set the date even if it's the day I get back.

By the way I'm now living in a beautiful hotel, the "Metropolitan." I never expected to see something so "Stateside" like in the Orient. It must have been built just before the Japs took over because the designs are of late years.

Well, I wasn't going to write much so here it ends.

Good night Baby. I love you so much & miss you.

All my love

Jack

Nanking, China
Sept 12, 1945

My Dearest Gloria.

Maybe I'm getting back in the groove again. Just twenty-four hours since my last letter.

I'm still not feeling too hot. That pain in my middle comes & goes all day long. I'm not really sick but still I'm not normal.

Nanking had a bad day today. It rained most of the day & wind blew quite a little too. Quite a little cooler, too. The wind still sounds like we were having a blizzard & the weather generally feels like October in Wisconsin (or Iowa). Actually the weather here is beautiful. Cool enough to be comfortable but not cold.

Not much news around here today. The Japs still walk around with their guns but I believe those who do are guards or patrols to keep order. Naturally we don't speak to them but they do seem docile & we're getting used to each other. I was afraid there might be some incidents but so far they go their way & we go ours & everybody seems to be happy to let it go at that. Of course we are moving them out of some of the buildings to make room for the Chinese & Americans & I don't suppose they like it but they have little choice in the matter. The German ambassador had to give up one of his places & he put up a howl but he should be glad to keep a whole skin. I guess that even had him worried. They're not treating these people roughly but very firmly & if we need something they furnish it. I've met a few of the people who were interned & the stories vary a little. A priest that was here said they themselves weren't bothered too much but he also mentioned one priest who was in solitary confinement for seven months because he had kept a diary. All of them have lost weight & don't look quite right & I suppose we see the best of them. Need I say that they're all very happy to see us come.

I'm in hopes of taking over a Jap radio site in a few days & am further hoping we'll get some of the equipment they have, especially the antenna systems. From what I've seen they have a pretty fair setup but I suppose like everything else it will be filthy. They seem to thrive on living like pigs.

Well, Baby I'm living more comfortably than I have since I came into the Army, have everything I need & lots more but I still am not satisfied. It's still not the U.S.A. I guess I'll never get over being homesick & most of all missing you while I'm away. It looks like I might see you within the next couple of months but it still seems like a helluva long time to wait. Will I be happy to get back.

That about all for tonight so Good night Baby & remember I love you.

All my love

Jack

Nanking, China
Sept 12, 1945

Dear Folks.

Yeah, censorship is off again and can say most anything now. I don't believe I wrote you about my China travels before so here goes.

Well, when I first came over the Burma Road, I landed at Kunming & stayed there for about a month. Then one night I was called to take a Radio station to Chik Chiang [misspelled] to furnish communications for the Jap surrender deal. Well, the Japs came & went and finally we followed them to Nanking. Here where we completed the surrender & also found ourselves mixed in with thousands of them. Nothing to worry about though because they seem docile enough. Speaking of the surrender, I was present the day of the final signing. We had quite a ceremony. The Japs came in, bowed & got the thing settled in short order. They were a pretty sad looking lot & not especially happy. They all had their heads shaved & their clothes looked baggy. Not a very sharp looking bunch. The Chinese, on the other hand, were really dressed up & looked sharper than I've ever seen them before. There were more Chinese generals than you could shake a stick at. In fact they were all Generals except a few civilians, the guards & a few aides. Naturally the Americans were in the minority. Around seventy-five I'd say about all that were here at the time. We all came in by air so you can see why not many were around.

I'm glad I've had the opportunity to see Eastern China or at least Nanking. It's the first city I've seen in the Orient that is halfway clean. It's very modern & has most everything any U.S. City has as far as utilities goes. I'm living in the Metropolitan

Hotel & it really compares with some of our better hotels. It's run down but you can see where it was really something a few years back. The style is as "State Side" as can be. Most of the fixtures came from the States. Kohler of Kohler, etc. The same goes for a lot of the stores downtown, the Post Office & banks could be planted in any U.S. city & look very natural there. Quite a city. Still I'm ready to leave & get on my way home & speaking of that little item, it looks like it might not be too long now. We were supposed to be relieved by the first of Oct & I suppose we'll be going out through Shanghai & the Shanghai Port to be opened Saturday. So maybe sometime in October will find me sailing across the Pacific. At any rate I should be home for Christmas.

I guess that's all for now.

As always

Jack

P.S. I got the letter about Ralph Anderson & it looks like he spread it on a little thick. Guess I'll have to take care of him when I get back.

Dad's report that the Japanese army in China seemed to be "a pretty sad looking lot & not especially happy" is notable because they had not suffered the same setbacks as their countrymen had in other areas of the Pacific and Asia. In fact, they had been gaining ground in China almost to the end. This could be attributable to Generalissimo Chiang Kai-shek's reticent efforts to oppose Japan in his own country. It's also probable that General Stilwell's suspicions about Kai-shek warehousing Lend-Lease supplies for his forthcoming fight against the Communist insurgency were, in fact, real. In any case, the Japanese army in China may have thought that they were winning. While officers were known to disobey orders from their superiors, as evidenced by the attempted coup to stop the surrender and a junior officer's earlier refusal to evacuate Manila in the Philippines (which led to that city's devastation),

Emperor Hirohito's surrender order would have been absolute. The new threat of Soviet invasion from the north would have also put a damper on any ideas of insubordination.

Sept 14, 1945

My Dearest Gloria

Again I missed a day but I do have a fair excuse. I was O.D. [Officer of the Day] yesterday & really had my share of troubles. If it had been a normal day I'd have had plenty of time to write but as luck would have it I had Chinese trouble all afternoon & evening. First a Chinese guard had a shooting accident & ended up with a .45 slug in his back door. Early in the evening a Chinese came in with a big long story about some G.I. beating him out of 1000 Chinese dollars. I finally got him satisfied after a couple of hours & in [unintelligible] another with a similar story. Another couple of hours of getting names and descriptions, etc. I did finish a letter to my folks & started to go to bed at midnight. I made the mistake of checking the Signal Center before going to bed & found traffic piled up & the Radio circuits not working so hot. That took until 3 o'clock before I finally decided I could take off. Which gave me about 4 hours sleep. Need I say I'm pretty tired after all that & taking into consideration that I climbed the four stories of stairs dozens of times both yesterday & today . . .

. . . Well, Baby, it looks like we are about to be relieved here. It looks like it will be at a slow rate, though, a couple of men at a time. Still, it shouldn't take too long to get myself & sixty men I have with me replaced. I will be surprised, though, if it comes before a couple of weeks. In the meantime, I guess I'll be busy. I've got to move all the equipment to a new site & set it up. Between 10 & 15 tons of radio equipment is nothing to toy around with. Some of it is pretty complex. We have a radio teletype that has a lot of special equipment including a two ton power unit & it calls for a lot of special antennas. So I'll probably be so busy I'll forget to come home. "Like Hell I Will!" . . .

Sept 15, 1945

My Dearest Gloria

. . . Still nothing definite as to "when" but rumors are hopeful but they might be just wishful thinking on someone's part. Still I can't see why not we have no business in China any more. In any event I guess everyone is trying to get us out because the sooner the troops get out the sooner the big shots can go home, I'm in favor of it.

By the way this boy Ralph Anderson came home & showed up at my home some time ago. I guess he spread it on thick by the letter I got from my mother. Must have been the drinks I gave him just before he left. He was pretty high.

Say, "Little One," if you have any questions now you can fire away because I can tell all. Just a few items we are held up on & you wouldn't ask questions on them anyway . . .

Sept 17, 1945

My Dearest Gloria

. . . Last but not least a notion that I was on my way home. Don't get any idea but it might happen one of these days but I don't expect it before a month & maybe not then. The Army works slow.

Had quite an experience yesterday. Went out with a Chinese civilian & here's what went on. First we went to a lake with lily pads all over it & went rowing (got picture of same). Came back & took a short ride on a Chinese train. Being mixed up with Japs, Chinese, etc., on a train was really something. Actually it was more like & street car ride & the train compared with most of the street cars in the States. Built like them too. Later we went to a Chinese home for lunch. Never again. How they do it I can't understand but I don't like to look a fish in the eye while I'm eating him & I don't like to eat all of him & I mean <u>all</u> of him. He was fixed just the way he came out of the water. I'm not afraid but I don't like a fish with all kinds of "guts" facing me. Of course I had to try & that's about all I did. Some of the stuff was good but my appetite was dulled a bit.

I really enjoyed the tea. We bought a camera from them and took off. They got a rickshaw, paid the guy and sent us on our way. Were nice people & comparatively clean. All the day through we were treated like something holy & nobody treated us with anything but the greatest respect, even the Japs. Later in the day I took a couple of pictures of a couple of Japs putting in a telephone line for us. Seemed like capable boys & also showed us great respect. We don't get friendly, however . . .

Sept 24, 1945

My Dearest Gloria

. . . Things are looking up now. Actually the Col. Has sent in a request for me to be returned to Kunming to be returned to the zone of the Interior. The orders are to read on or about 5 Oct. That doesn't mean I'll be shipped home immediately though. Just being sent back to Kunming to be shipped home. Something can still slip. I don't know if I'll be going with the outfit or not. If I don't I'll probably fly home. Anyway, we've got it down to a matter of weeks as to the great day. By that I mean the day I get there. By the way I'm going on points, which means I'll be able to stay home. "92 points" with a possibility of another campaign star & five more as a result. That's the way it looks now. I hope it doesn't change . . .

27 Sept 1945

My Dearest Gloria

. . . I'm still at Nanking & keeping busy at the Signal Center. I am cutting down on my hours. No use in taking things too seriously, now that the war is over. I believe I'll only have about another week & then the long & tedious trip to the U.S.A. Don't get excited because there are still a lot of places where I can be held up for a matter of days or even weeks. The middle of Nov should see me pretty close to home. I hope. I still haven't heard about the third Campaign Star that was rumored we were getting. In any case I've got enough points now so

I'm not worried about it. 92 as of Sept 2 and 94 as of now so why should I worry about five more. Actually I don't feel I earned one for China but if they are passing them out, I'll hold out my hand for one. They won't mean anything except possibly in the VFW or American Legion celebrations. I wonder if I'll ever join one of these gadgets. I suppose so but I'm not anxious about that now, it will keep. I am anxious & more so every day about getting home. The last leg will be the longest one. It definitely will be a one-way trip though. Come to think of it, this is probably the last job I'll hold in the Army . . .

Sept 30, 1945

My Dearest Gloria

Doing better tonight but I don't know whether I'll be able to write much. I'm tired as hell tonight. No particular reason for it either. Just tired. I have a nice job too, I'm O.D. again, which turns out to be an all day & all night affair now. Last time I had nothing to do with the guard but tonight I've got that too. So I stay in that office all night & catch a few winks on a cot while I could sleep on a nice soft bed. I had three jobs that I was doing at one time today. First of all I was duty Officer at the Signal Center, then I had to pay the 988th men I have & in addition to that I was O.D. Maybe that's why I'm tired.

I'm working on a deal by which I might be able to leave from Shanghai after all. I would hate to go back the other way & I rather doubt whether I'd get there any faster if as fast. Even if I took a plane it might take some time. I understand that ships leaving Shanghai expect to make it in something like twelve days. I'd have to sweat out a couple of weeks here or even a month. Anyway I hope to be home by the end of Nov. Two months is a helluva long time but things don't happen fast when you want them to. I'd much rather spend a little more time here than get into some hole & have to sweat it out there. I know how the trip over here was, it's no fun. By going out on a ship from Shanghai it would be simple as hell. I'll know in a couple of days & I hope I'll get a break. Still I guess I shouldn't be choosey. I'll be homeward bound & anything in connection with that is O.K.

I've just been thinking of what a difference there is between the place I'm in now & the place I was in a year ago. I was sitting in Hopin, Burma sweating out the end of the monsoons. Doesn't seem possible how things can change. I never did quite relax during those four months. It seemed like an entirely different world. Dead & wounded were so common that unless it was someone you knew you never paid any attention to them. We sort of added scores, they got so many of us & we that many of them. Naturally we were worried when our casualties went up & we didn't kill a like number of Japs. Usually we kill twice to three times the number we had hit. I'd better stop it.

By the way I got another campaign star. I guess this one is a gift because I don't feel like I earned it, but it does give me 99 points to date.

I've got to check the guard so I'd better say Good night, I love you & miss you.

All my love
Jack

Dad's description of what he went through in Burma is heartbreaking. Reflection is often a good thing—it adds perspective that imparts wisdom. But it can also bring pain since distressing thoughts of past events can ambush you. This is the mechanism that destroys the peace in one's soul. Many soldiers fall victim to this phenomenon—remembering the terror of combat, losing friends, even having survivor's guilt. Such things are powerful and can emerge suddenly, with frightening effect. It was like that for my dad, and it was like that for others.

When I was a young child, my dad spent a month at Fort Snelling in Minnesota to deal with the emotional fallout of the war, among other things. I've also had friends who found it even more difficult to deal with these issues later in life. The elevated suicide rate among veterans is a testament to this. September 30, 1944, must have been one of those days. That day's letter, or of those days immediately before or after, didn't mention casualties or the stress of combat. He couldn't mention those things at the time. But the memories were there and probably would be for some time to come—of sweating out the end of the monsoons in the bombed-out village of Hopin, deep in the jungles of Burma.

Oct 3, 1945

My Dearest Gloria.

Well, My work in Nanking is done. I'm leaving for Kunming in the morning, maybe. Sometimes the weather has notions. To Kunming & then who knows. I thought I could work a deal to leave by Shanghai but no soap. I'll probably fly back to Calcutta & take a boat from there. It is possible that I'll fly all the way but I'll turn it down unless they put on the pressure. Don't get me wrong, I'm not, repeat not on my way home yet, but prospects look good. Twenty-Five thousand men are to be in Calcutta by the first to fill up ships supposedly already there. I hope one pulls out the day after I get there, with me on it. Simply a matter of weeks now, then what. First of all I'll have to go to a Separation Center to get my leave time. I'll probably be on leave for something like three months before I actually get out of the Army. At the end of my leave, I go back for a few days, at the most, to get my release from the Army. Three months to get married, etc. to find a job & to see if I want out for sure. Things would really have to be rough to make me go back, I might keep a reserve commission, just in case another war followed shortly or maybe I'd keep it just to sort of stay connected with the Army. I'll cross those bridges when I get to them.

As far as getting married I guess we'll decide that when I get home. I'll leave that up to you. I want to get married shortly after I get back but I don't want it look like we're in too much of a hurry.

We might as well be set so we can live by ourselves shortly after & I'd like to have some indication that I'll be able to support a wife. I should be able to get a pretty good idea in a couple of weeks. I don't mean I'll have to be working, in fact I don't want to be working but I don't want to be living with anyone more than absolutely necessary. What do you think of the ideas. If you don't agree, I guess I can be talked into most anything so don't let it worry you.

Well, Baby I think I'll get to bed. I didn't get much sleep last night. No more night duty for me anymore, I hope.

Good night Baby. I still love you very much & getting more anxious every day about my return.

All my love
Jack

Sept 6, 1945 [October 6]

My Dearest Gloria

Well, Baby you can stop writing to me. By the time this letter reaches you I should be out of China & well on my way. I came back to Kunming yesterday & got my orders to report to the Replacement Center today. I'll go over tomorrow & probably be there for a couple of days & then over the hump for Calcutta where I expect to catch a boat. Still some steps there where there can be delays, but I'm certain to be on the water by the 1st of Nov. Home for Thanksgiving & fairly sure of that. Boy am I happy. Most of the fellows in the outfit are on the same orders but we are not going home as 988 Sig. Just so many people but we should be on the same boat. It makes it easier that way because it relieves us of all responsibilities & still have the men we worked with around. Good bunch of boys, too . . .

. . . I came here from NANKING expecting to monkey around here for a week or so at the outfit but find myself in & out. Suits me fine. At the Repl. Depot it will depend entirely upon transportation because they process you within a day. I hope they get dozens of

C-54s in there right quick like. By the way, that C-54 is about the best cargo plane & I feel pretty comfortable in one. Those four engines keep those babies up in good shape. So that's the story. Do you like it? I don't believe I'll get an answer to that one until you can hand it to me directly . . .

Oct 9, 1945

My Dearest Gloria

. . . I'm still in Kunming but I've got my orders sending me home. Sweating out a plane ride now. Still over 35 plane loads to leave before I go but I should be out within a week. After that there still is the camp at Calcutta to sweat out the boat ride, a port of debarkation & train ride from the port. Quite a few places to be held up. I might make it by Thanksgiving. You'd better have a good dinner ready. At least you can help get it ready whenever we have it. After all this good Army Chow, I'll be hard to please. I'll probably have to eat out quite a little to keep alive. But then what can you expect from a "soda jerk." At least you'll be there to keep the house clean & wash my clothes. During the winter you'll also be useful to keep me warm during the long cold nights. No twin beds. Of course I'll have to put several pair of work socks on you to keep your cold feet from bothering me. Speaking of keeping me warm in bed reminds me that I could use you now. This place turned very cold & I've been shivering for a couple of days. Not quite so bad tonight but I was beginning to wonder whether I hadn't better stay in the tropics until spring. This should help me get used to those cold winters again. We've got quite a stove in our tent. Just a tin can with holes in it & it works pretty good. Once in a while it smokes a little but this charcoal can be burned right in the room without a chimney . . .

Whoa, Dad! That's a good way to die! In the 1990s my job was to oversee a program helping migrant farmworkers. One year some of the workers were still around at the end of the season. The farmer who provided seasonal housing for them turned off the heat in the trailer where three farmworkers were still staying in early November, so they brought a charcoal grill inside to keep the place warm. We had to send their bodies back to their families in Texas. Please don't try this at home!

Oct 21, 1945

Dear Folks.

Maybe a last letter. I'm not sure yet but I might leave here in a couple of days. I got my name on the list to go out next. The ship is due in a couple of days & then out again in a day or two after that. I hardly expect it to be in soon but who knows. Anyway we might have quite a little monkeying around to do & I might not get another chance to write. I hope not. The sooner the better, tonight if possible. Even though it's raining & pretty dreary out . . .

Oct. 25, 1945

My Dearest Gloria

Well, I guess "this is it." I mean the last letter. I'm just going to quit & write no mo. I will probably go aboard the "General Stewart" tomorrow & after that no more chances to write. I'm afraid this is going to be an uncomfortable trip. We are going troop class & no doubt that means in the hold of the ship. One month of that should make a Christian out of me or kill me . . .

. . . Anyway, I'll be in Sheridan around the 1st of Dec & I'll call home from there to see what cooks. If you're there, O.K. & if not, I'll call you or at least try. I don't know what your number is but you can let me know that through my family in case you don't go to Durand. Do you get that? A lot of good that question does . . .

. . . So long & be good. I love you as much as I did when I left.

All my love

Jack

P.S. I still have all my hair.

25 Oct 1945

Dear Folks

Just one more note & then no more. I expect to board the "General Stewart" tomorrow sometime & sail a day or two later. For about thirty days I'll be on the water & then dock at New York. From there to Ft. Sheridan. First they told me I was to go to McCoy but today I got orders & definitely states that I go to Ft. Sheridan. So I'll have to stop off & I'll probably be a civilian by the time you see me. I might still be a Reserve Officer, but on an inactive status. I have a choice but I figure it might be ace in the hole in case things get tough. I'll explain it all later . . .

Dad's letter to his folks was the last one he sent from the CBI. He would never see that part of the world again. As Dad would say, he was glad to have done it but didn't want to have to do it again. He boarded the *General M. B. Stewart* and set sail from Calcutta. The *Stewart* was a fairly new troop ship that was launched in October 1944. It had sixteen 20mm gun mounts, four 4-inch mounts, and four 5-inch mounts. The ship sailed from Calcutta, made a stop in Ceylon (now Sri Lanka), and then went by way of the Suez Canal after sailing west and crossing the Indian Ocean. Dad was able to send one letter from the *Stewart* because there was a stop in Egypt at Port Said. It was written on the *Stewart*'s "stationery."

Nov 6, 1945

Dearest Gloria.

I thought I was all through writing letters, but they tell me we can mail letters at Port Said, so—

Need I say that I'm "floating" these days not a bad trip so far we are in the Red Sea at the moment. We expect to be in Port Said around the 8th. By the way we left Calcutta 0700 on the 27th of Oct. and stayed at Columbo, Ceylon for 24 hours. Another thing we expect to be in New York around the 23rd. How's that?

Nope, I haven't been seasick and as far as that goes neither has anyone else. So far a [smooth] trip. We have nothing to kick about except perhaps the fact that we sleep in the "hold" & it's hot as hell and another thing is that we have a bunch of "Chink" & Indian civilians aboard. Why in hell these people are allowed to take up space when we have hundreds or thousands of G.I.s still in the [CBI] . . . The trouble is we got so fed up with them & their methods & thought we were rid of them & then this happens. I assure you they are not having a pleasant trip, everyone delights in pushing them around. More about that when I see you.

As you probably noticed I'm getting in a little sooner than I had expected & before I go any further I want you to inform your bosses about your leaving them if you haven't already done that. Knowing the date, or about the date as to when to expect me you should be able to make your plans O.K. I would like to see you in Wisconsin if possible. If not, well I'll make my plans to fit with yours. Lord knows. I'll be able to alter them being a civilian, I hope.

Well, Baby that's all for now. Don't worry & I'll be seeing you.

All my love

Jack

Lt. Forster on the M. B. Stewart on his way home.

11

A New Life

Almost two years after Dad left American soil, he arrived home—and just in time. As Dad and Mom both said, they didn't want to write letters anymore. Years later, Dad wrote in his summary to the *Ex-CBI Roundup* that he went home on the *Stewart* by way of the Indian Ocean, Suez Canal, Strait of Gibraltar, and the Atlantic Ocean, where the ship "hit the tail end of a storm and had a very rough ride to New York." They arrived in port on the *M. B. Stewart* with 2,983 troops aboard. As they entered the harbor in New York, they were met by a launch with a band and some singers. More than fifty years later, as we were about to leave for church to attend a celebration of Mom and Dad's fiftieth wedding anniversary, I played "Sentimental Journey" on the stereo, the same song the band and singers had played from that launch. Dad's eyes welled up and he said, simply, "I don't believe there was a dry eye on that boat." That day in November, 1945, he was again on native soil, never so thankful to be anywhere in his life.

Dad's experience as a soldier was unique in one sense, but it's also fair to say that it was similar to that of millions of other World War II soldiers. Dad was no hero, or at least he would tell you he wasn't. Yet, in another way, they were all heroes. Soldiers didn't pick their duties or their assignments. They all did their duty, whatever that duty turned out to be. Many never saw the enemy—dead or alive—but the possibility was always there. Some spent their tour of duty behind a desk or a typewriter, as a guard, as a cook, or as a member of the

Military Police. They did what they were assigned to do. Some had special skills, like my dad, and others did not. They were all trained for the duty to which they were assigned. Many men in the CBI Signal Corps never made it anywhere near the front like my dad did. My dad was happy he didn't end up as a "USO Commando" and was happy to have done his part in winning the war. But after it was over, he always said he didn't need a second helping of that.

When Dad returned to India on leave after his time in the jungle, his old buddies all wanted to know what it was like—so few of them had the experience that he did. I can relate to what Dad went through during those conversations, including the impossibility of describing the indescribable. My return from the Peace Corps was similar in that I found it hard to relate my experiences to people with no frame of reference for what I had experienced. The attempts to describe such things can be exhausting, especially doing it over and over without the ability to impart the true feeling of what it was like—and it often results in withdrawing to avoid those conversations. But for a soldier who also dealt with fear and inhumanity, there's a whole new inexpressible layer.

Dad never had to kill anyone. He carried a .45 and a .30 caliber carbine but never fired either one in combat. That wasn't his job. Some of the men under his command did, however, and at least one of them died. Dad did get shot at, although in his letters he always tried to tell Mom he was perfectly safe. So many lives were on hold during that war, not only the soldiers who endured physical hardships and danger in combat, but those who loved them back home. They endured angst, fear and even sorrow as the boys they loved suffered and died in faraway lands.

Wedding at Holy Rosary Parish, Lima

The happy couple

My parents were part of what has been called the Greatest Generation, and I absolutely believe their generation lived up to the name. They were born during the turmoil of World War I and its horrendous aftermath, and they were steeled by the Great Depression. Their entire generation's sacrifices and productivity during history's greatest conflict, World War II, have become legendary. They also took us safely through the Cold War, all while producing the greatest prosperity this earth has ever experienced. It doesn't get any better than that. Their generation had integrity and strength of character that I believe is unmatched throughout history.

My mom and dad were products of those times, and I believe they were among the best of them. I am extremely proud of them both.

My parents never wrote letters describing their lives after the war, but I was there to witness most of their postwar years. As I matured, I was also able to speak with them about the war years. As a result, I've gained some additional insight into their lives, both during and after the war.

Our Former Home

Dad was relieved from active duty on February 26, 1946, and my parents were married on March 4, 1946, at Holy Rosary Parish church at Lima, just east of Durand. It was the same parish Dad had grown up in, and it was right next to Sacred Heart School, where

Dad had attended both grade school and high school. The church was also within eyesight of the Forster farm where Dad grew up just across the field. In some ways, the wedding was the opposite of what was traditional at that time. For instance, it didn't take place at Mom's parish but Dad's. The maid of honor was Dad's niece, Blanche, whom Mom had befriended during her trips to Durand while visiting Dad's family. Additionally, Mom's older brother, Joe, was the best man. I don't know why they bucked tradition, but it doesn't matter—they were happy. Getting married was what they had awaited for so long, and it was apparent from their smiles in the wedding pictures that they were elated to be living their new life at last.

Dad had a good understanding of electricity, so he began working as an electrician with a local contractor named Hubert Fox. Later, he tried his hand at being a businessman when he opened a radio shop in Durand. Finally, on May 9, 1949, he went to work as a rural mail carrier out of the post office in Durand, Wisconsin and did that until his retirement in 1979. His rural route took him through the Lima area and northward, including a stop at the farm where he grew up and where three of his siblings lived. When I was little, I often rode along with my dad over the rural roads. I would occasionally fall asleep in the back seat, or I would talk to Dad, identifying the make, model, and year of all the cars we passed along the way. Eventually, we'd stop at our favorite "pissin' bridge" on a secluded sandy road near Red Cedar.

Things were idyllic for a while after my dad came home, but life often intervenes. Soon after my parents built their forever home on the outskirts of Durand, war memories and the financial pressures of being a new homeowner began to haunt my dad. When I was only five years old, I woke up one night to a house full of strangers, all of whom spoke in subdued tones. My mom came into my room and told me to go back to sleep, and in the morning, my dad was gone. I was told that he had "bad nerves" and had to go to the VA hospital at Fort Snelling in the Twin Cities. He was gone for about a month, and I began to miss him. When we picked him up at Fort Snelling, near St. Paul, he emerged with a big smile on his face and his arms wide to give both my mom and me a hug. I had missed him so much that I somehow appreciated him more when he came home, and I felt closer to him from then on. I was conscious of the change even at my tender age.

I was born in late November 1947, about a year and a half after my parents married. Since my parents both came from large families, I believe they both wanted a large family as well. But early in their marriage, it became clear that it was not to be—in the biological sense. Soon after I was born, my mother required surgery and was no longer able to have children. However, my parents believed a house was not a home unless it was properly filled, so they adopted my sister Diane when I was six years old. A few years later came my brother, Steve, and then my sister Mary Sue.

I remember kneeling down with my mom when I was little and asking Jesus for our family to be granted a baby sister. I didn't know the normal procedures for requisitioning a sibling, but praying seemed like a good first step. When we started receiving visits from a social worker for the Catholic Welfare Services, I was none the wiser, although I knew the visits were somehow connected with our requisition. I had some sense that I was auditioning as a big brother, so I was fairly well-behaved—or maybe I should say I was a little less unruly than normal. I also was aware that my sister was five months old when the "blessed bundle" was delivered. At my tender age, I was unaware that this was not the normal way to become a big brother, so it became normal to me.

Although I knew my sister was adopted, I didn't know what that meant. I didn't have an attitude that she was different from me—other than that she was a girl and she was little. I saw us both as being our parents' children. Later, I developed the same attitude toward Steve and Mary Sue. My brother and I got along well despite a twelve-year age difference. We were buddies, wrasslin' and throwing the football around. My sisters were into other things. Thinking back on this, I marvel at the wisdom my parents had in preparing us all psychologically for the many transitions that life would bring us. I'm proud of them for that.

Both Mom and Dad were involved in the community. Dad was a member of the American Legion Post 181 in Pepin County, and they were both active in St. Mary's Catholic Parish in Durand—the parish that my great-great grandpa had helped to found almost one hundred years before. They were involved in all sorts of church and civic activities in the Durand area.

A homemade automobile is used by Louis Forster to carry mail on route-, 1, Durand. He purchased the chassis of a foreign built economy car and then constructed an aluminum body to suit the needs of postal service.

Louie VW Remake

The Forster Family

Dad was a MacGyver-type genius, and no project seemed to be too big for him. In his letter to Mom on August 14, 1945, he had said about his experience in the Signal Corps, "The only thing that I'm sure has changed is my self-confidence. I used to be a little afraid to tackle a job even though I knew I could handle it. I seem to have found out my capabilities . . . There are other things, but they don't seem to stand out as much. It really makes one wonder what is to come." This was indeed true in his civilian life. Dad was never afraid to tackle any project. One day, he saw a vehicle drive by with no body on it. It had a boat rack on top, and the driver was out in the open with no windshield. It turned out to be a Volkswagen chassis that belonged to a local car dealer who soon sold it to my dad. Dad built a body out of thin wall tubing and aluminum sheet and adapted it for carrying mail. It worked perfectly. He used Volkswagens for his mail route from then on since they were economical to drive, were good in the snow, and could carry all his mail once he removed everything but the driver's seat. Volkswagens were also narrow, which helped Dad since mail carriers have to reach across the passenger side to open mailboxes when they deliver the mail. (He was short, and his arms weren't that long.)

As we grew up, my parents and us kids enjoyed camping at various parks in Wisconsin, Minnesota, and Upper Michigan. We first started out with a canvas tent and then acquired an old Manorette travel trailer. For a while, Dad drove a school bus part-time, and it occurred to him that such a bus could be converted into a motor home. His first project was a forty-eight-passenger school bus into which he installed a small stove and refrigerator, a little "porta-potty," and foam bench seats that converted to beds. He later sold that bus and converted a fifty-four-passenger model, which he painted green and dubbed *El Viajero Verde* (the Green Traveler).

He took the family to the East Coast through Canada one summer. When I joined the Peace Corps in 1971, I received news shortly after arriving in-country that he intended to drive the family down through Mexico and Guatemala to visit me in Honduras. I thought he was nuts. He would be if he tried that today, but even then, I worried plenty. Nonetheless, he, Mom, and my siblings left on a nine-day voyage that took them about 4,000 road miles from Wisconsin through Mexico and Guatemala. A few days before Christmas, I met them in Esquipulas, Guatemala. We spent a few days in San Pedro Sula, Honduras, replacing a wheel bearing and doing a brake job, and then we camped on the north coast of

Honduras at Playa Travesía near Puerto Cortés. A Garífuna family invited us over for a party on Christmas Eve. Dad chipped in with a bottle of whisky and it was all good. In fact, it was one of the coolest Christmases ever. Then, when we headed back toward Guatemala, we visited the Mayan ruins at Copán in western Honduras, Guatemala City, and Antigua Guatemala before traveling all the way to Mexico City, visiting several places in between. Throughout Guatemala and Honduras, we stopped and visited friends my dad had made through his ham radio activity—he had prepared the way by making friends all along the route. To this day, I marvel at the adventure he created.

When I was thirteen, I pestered my dad to get involved in ham radio—it was one of my transient interests as a teenager. We both got our ham radio licenses in 1962; I was novice class, and my dad was general class. I stuck with it for a while, but as I entered high school, I grew interested in basketball, band, and chorus—and getting my driver's license. However, my dad stuck with it for the rest of his life, getting involved with the Army Military Auxiliary Radio System (MARS) and other ham radio activities. We had a backyard filled with numerous antennas, a few transmitters and receivers in the basement, and a big old surplus generator for emergencies. He even acquired a couple of surplus teletype machines and fiddled with them for a while. When I went to Honduras to serve in the Peace Corps, Dad found an American missionary priest near the small village where I lived. I used the priest's radio to communicate with Dad and Mom back home. Telephone calls were way too expensive at that time, and there were no telephones in my area anyway. Later, during earthquake disasters in Nicaragua and Guatemala, Dad was able to communicate with operators in those countries to help people communicate with family members in the United States.

Mom wasn't the MacGyver genius that my dad was, but she was competent in her own right. Early on, she was a stay-at-home mom, but she was also a trained legal secretary and eventually used those talents. She handled the family finances and later worked with a local attorney, Ryan Laue, for a few years. When people started to request assistance with their taxes, she and other secretaries in the office became tax consultants, a career that lasted until Mom's retirement. She worked out of Ryan's office for several years and then arranged an office at our home where she worked until late at night preparing tax returns during late winter and early springtime, quite often for farmers who would come to her with shoeboxes full of receipts that she used to complete their returns. In addition, she was a skilled pianist and organist—instruments she played for the rest of her life.

My brother Steve summed up Mom's role to all of us by citing the following professions: teacher, favorite chef, baker, short order cook, nurse/medic and comforter, travel guide, historian, enforcer, biggest fan, and provider of unconditional love—although the latter is not a profession, it's a gift. Being Italian, she made the best spaghetti and lasagna, and as a travel guide/historian, she would make sure we all understood the significance of the places we went to as we traveled. Before we had any idea how hard it was to fill all those roles, it was easy for us kids to take it for granted because she did it so effortlessly. My daughter, Jenni, described her as "always present." My son, Tony, said Mom's avocation was to enjoy life. Both of my kids talked about her ability to make life enjoyable—to make life fun, and always age-appropriate, from sitting at the organ playing "Little White Duck" to taking long walks and talking about life. Maybe the fun part was how she made it look so easy.

While I was a Peace Corps Volunteer, I met my wife, who is Honduran. When she came to the United States with me, she didn't know English and had to learn so many things about living in a new country. It was a daunting task, but Mom took on a mentorship role, teaching her how to cook American food, among many other things. My wife always mentions the time when she and Mom went berry picking in the Wisconsin woods shortly after she first arrived in the United States. When a collie dog suddenly popped out of the bushes, my wife thought it was a lion. Having never seen that breed before, it scared the hell out of her—until Mom began to laugh. Soon, they were laughing together.

Jack & Goria's 50th Anniversary

My kids would spend weeks with Mom and Dad during the summer, having fun fishing and swimming at the O'Neil Creek campground where my folks enjoyed living in the summer. Our son would even fly down to Florida to join my parents at the campgrounds where they stayed in the winter. Dad was our son's buddy, and they did a lot together. Mom and Dad were wonderful grandparents.

Growing up under their roof wasn't always easy, which is exactly the way it should be. I have yet to see the child who is always perfectly behaved and who always lives up to expectations, so there were frequently little episodes of drama where we learned the lessons that needed to be taught. Mom and Dad weren't perfect, but they were great parents who demanded we work, hold up our end of the bargain, and prepare ourselves for the lives ahead of us. They made demands of us, but they were always supportive and told us not only where we needed improvement but also when they were proud.

Dad passed away in January 1999. He was eighty-one years old, and I feel he died way too soon. He had diabetes and didn't always take care of himself, which saddened me. He got cranky in his old age and even fought with Mom at times—old age can bring out our worst angels. The day after my father died, I went down to his ham shack. The radio was still on. I keyed the mic and began, "This is WA9CCB, Willie Able Niner, Charlie Charlie Baker." I bade the amateur radio world "73s" on behalf of my dad and shut it down. We buried Dad in his army uniform, the flag draped over his coffin. The American Legion Post 181 Honor Guard delivered the folded flag to our mom "on behalf of a grateful nation."

In his later years, Dad had always "threatened" to sing a corny old song, "Old Hogan's Goat," as we'd roll our eyes. Needless to say, we'd give almost anything to hear him sing that song again. Mom passed away in December 2018, at the age of ninety-seven, almost exactly twenty years after Dad. For a few years, I had the pleasure of driving her to Arizona so she could spend the winter months in Mesa, living in the trailer she and Dad owned while being active with friends rather than being alone and inactive in the cold Wisconsin winter. We spent time together and took side trips during the few days I remained in Arizona with her.

We never know when we will pass, so it's hard to find the right time to say goodbye. I only hope that, in some way, I showed Mom and Dad enough love before they were gone. They were extraordinary parents.

Old Hogan's Goat

Was feeling fine
He ate three shirts
Right off the Line

They tied him to
A railroad track
They almost broke
That poor goat's back

A great freight train
Came rumbling by
And that poor goat
Was doomed to die

He gave an awful
Cry of pain
Coughed up those shirts
And flagged the train.

The authors

Acknowledgments

Several years ago, while working as an advocate for migrant farmworkers, I remember occasionally "telling tales" of my life as a Peace Corps volunteer in Honduras. Sometimes it would be on long rides I would take traveling with colleagues, sometimes it was over a couple beers at conferences, or when someone would remind me of my past through similar experiences of theirs. Finally, my friend and colleague, Steve Borders, came-up with the inevitable, "Man, you ought to write a book!" It dawned on me that indeed, maybe I should write a book. I had already written a couple of chapters of things I remembered from my experiences, and I wanted to pass these things on to my kids and grandkids. My father had passed away in 1999, and inevitably I missed talking with him and hearing not only about his past as a soldier in the Far East, but about his life as well as the lives of my other ancestors and their journeys through life. This became more important to me as I grew older, and I wished that I had learned more from my mom and dad before they passed. I only had old pictures, a few clues and artifacts, a box of old letters and remembrances of conversations with my parents. It then occurred to me that maybe my kids and grandkids may someday appreciate knowing more about their ancestors—including me and my wife, Mariantonia. From time to time, I would remember things, dig through my own old letters and artifacts and write another chapter, until it finally became the manuscript for my first book, *Mariantonia: The Lifetime Journey of a Peace Corps Volunteer.*

Then in 2017, as my parents had reached the end of their lives, my siblings and I cleaned out the house our parents lived in and a found “the shoebox.” My parents were engaged before Dad left for the far east in late 1943, and he had written to Mom during his long deployment in India, Burma, and China in 1944 and 1945—twenty-three months in all—and that shoebox contained almost all of those letters. It was truly a treasure trove for me. It became this book.

Especially helpful to me, for his encouragement, advice, and mentorship, is my friend and fellow author, Dr. Kerry A. Trask. Kerry is an American historian, professor emeritus in the University of Wisconsin system, and taught history in the town where I now reside, Manitowoc, Wisconsin. He has written several books, notably, *Fire Within: A Civil War Narrative from Wisconsin, Black Hawk: Battle for the Heart of America,* and *In the Pursuit of Shadows: Massachusetts Millenialism and the Seven Years' War.* He provided the first edit for my first book and gave me valuable advice for my second, which was extremely helpful. He introduced me to my editor, Signe Jorgenson, whose professionalism not only helped me make my Peace Corps memoir better but helped me organize the story of my dad's service in the Far East. I thank Kerry for his kind and generous nature, and Signe for her professionalism.

I would be remiss if I didn't also mention my wife and life partner, Mariantonia. Many of her stories are part of my Peace Corps memoir. In a very real way, it was *our* memoir. Some of the stories she shared were not easy for her to recount. But it wasn't just the stories she gave to me, but those that she lived with me that made our lives special. I couldn't have made a better choice for my wife.

Finally I thank my mom and dad for being my parents. They helped me to be the best version of myself, but also for leaving me their written record for this story. When I finally got around to reading Dad's story, it was not only captivating, but it was a whole new level of learning about them and their lives. I didn't just write this for me and my descendants; I wrote it for them, members of our greatest generation.

References

Allen, Louis. *Burma: The Longest War, 1941–45.* London: Phoenix Press, 2000.

Special Service Division, "A Pocket Guide to India" – Service of Supply, United States Army. Washington, D. C., War and Navy Departments, August 12, 1942.

Bauer, Eddy. "The Allies in Burma" In *Illustrated World War II Encyclopaedia* 19, 2579.Westport, CT: H.S. Stuttman, 1978.

Center of Military History. *India-Burma: The U.S. Army Campaigns of World War II.* Washington, D.C.: Center of Military History, 1992. https://archive.org/details/IndiaBurma/page/.

Hersey, John. "Joe is Home Now." *Life* 17, no. 1 (July 3, 1944): 68–80.

History.com Editors. "FDR Dies." *HISTORY* (April 8, 2021). https://www.history.com/this-day-in-history/fdr-dies.

Huizenga, Tom, and Ashalen Sims, "Sing Out Mr. President: Harry Truman Takes the Lead," National Public Radio, February 17, 2011, https://www.npr.org/sections/deceptivecadence/2011/02/20/133755317/sing-out-mr-president-harry-truman-takes-the-lead.

Martin, Jonathan, director. *Secrets of World War II.* Season 1, episode 22, "Merrill's Marauders." Aired May 28, 1998, BBC Worldwide.

Masters, John. *The Road Past Mandalay.* New York: Bantam Books, 1979.

McAvoy, Tom. "To India and Back in 10 Days." *Life* 16, no. 23 (June 5, 1944): 91-100.

Rayburn, M.P. *I'll Never Forget: The Forgotten Theater of World War II, China, Burma, India.* 3rd ed. Columbus, OH: Self-Published with assistance from Charles Fuller, Editor and Publisher of the Connecticut Beacon, 1996: 124-143.

Truman Library Institute. "The President is Dead: April 12, 1945." *Marching to Victory* (April 12, 2020). https://www.trumanlibraryinstitute.org/wwii-75-marching-victory-7/.

Wingfield Hayes, Rupert. "Witnessing Japan's Surrender to China," BBC News, September 2, 2015, https://www.bbc.com/news/magazine-34126445.

Zimmerman, Dwight Jon. "Stilwell in China: The Worst Command in the War." Defense Media Network (March 6, 2012). https://www.defensemedianetwork.com/stories/stilwell-in-china-the-worst-command-in-the-war/.

Printed in the USA
CPSIA information can be obtained
at www.ICGtesting.com
LVHW091107190924
791240LV00004B/16

9 798888 244661